SHAPED BY A SECRET

SHAPED BY A SECRET

JILL BIROS

MILL CITY PRESS

MINNEAPOLIS, MN

Mill City Press, Inc.
212 3rd Avenue North, Suite 290
Minneapolis, MN 55401
612.455.2294
www.millcitypublishing.com

ISBN-13: 978-1-937600-73-0
LCCN: 2011946262

Cover Design by Al Feuerstein
Typeset by Sophie Chi

Printed in the United States of America

Table of Contents

Acknowledgements

Thank you for your time, skills, encouragement and friendship: Adriana Rosman-Askot, Bonnie Bawel, Paul Bawel, Margaret Biros, Mark Biros, Karen Cantor, Amy Conte, Mary Ellen Cook, Roger Crook, Sue Crook, Judi Curto, Ann Fallon, Al Feuerstein, Naila Francis, Gail Galazan, Jennifer Garfield, Ron Glick, Agnieszka Godlewska, Amy Grossman, Patti Hankins, Charlotte Levitan, Fran Leyenberger, Chris Marrazzo, Glenn Marrazzo, Candis Mirande, Keith Mountford, Jean Ryersbach, Barbara Santone, Ashley Schumann, Janice Schumann, Justin Solonynka, Molly Stephenson, Laura Jo Trojan, Marcie Venella, Chelsea ViaCava, Judy ViaCava, Allen Weintraub, Bob Weintraub, Linda Weintraub, Sally Weintraub, Anthony Wellington.

A special thank you to…

Andrew and Benjamin Biros – for making me proud to be your mom. Your creative spirit, as well as your passion for making the world a better place, has been inspirational.

Greg Biros – for the love and support that has let me live a life filled with creative pursuits and meaning.

Courtney Gable – for your amazing ability to tweak, fix, see an opportunity, and simply make this a much better book. You are a wonderful editor and dear friend.

Preface

Ann is confused and hurt by her husband's anger toward their family – then learns of his affair with another man. Emily is repeatedly abused by her college boyfriend and is unable to tell anyone until his last brutal act. Sheila, a minister's daughter, strives for social acceptance and gets caught in a dangerous drug ring. Sixteen-year-old Margaret watches her beloved uncle sent to a mental institution, and seventy years later still wonders if there was anything she could have done to help him. All are true events from the lives of wholly unique women, united through a common bond: they are the keepers of secrets that have shaped their lives.

Secrets have power. What we keep hidden from the outside world is born of a potent blend of personal and cultural influences. Secrets can snake through our psyche for years, gnawing at our self-worth and happiness – or they can give us the strength to persevere. When something happens that makes us feel different from others, the stage is set. Add to that sense of alienation enough shame, confusion or guilt and you have the makings of a tenacious drama. Whatever the origins, a truth emerges when what was hidden is revealed: secrets can greatly influence our lives and shape the people we become.

For all its shrouded energy, a secret brought to light can be a force of healing. Even when disclosed in anonymity, giving voice to what has occupied space in one's private emotional vault is often a liberating event. When the honest, raw stuff of a secret is shared, healing can transcend personal boundaries and impact others facing similar challenges. I've witnessed this in my counseling practice and experienced it with the women who were brave enough to share their stories for this book.

My fascination with people's stories took root a while back. When I was about fourteen years old, I read a nonfiction bestseller that may have been the impetus for becoming a psychotherapist and writing this book. Studs Terkel's *Working* was the first time I experienced honest, first-person accounts of the way people really felt about their lives. I listened to voices that, as a sheltered white girl in suburban Pennsylvania, I would have never heard if not for Terkel's efforts. Mine was a family that did not often muck around in feelings, and suddenly I was privy to the raucous emotional world of waitresses and truck drivers, farmers and hairstylists. These were expressive, shoot-from-the-hip people who painted a vivid picture of their everyday lives and what it meant to be immersed in their occupations. I loved this book – it opened my eyes to the idea that the world was filled with unique souls living with passion and integrity, disguised as regular folk.

Early in my practice I ran a series of workshops for women striving to make positive changes in their lives. One of the recurring observations made by participants was a sense that many women wear masks that say, "Everything is great with me," and don't usually let others see behind the façade. Group members were frustrated by this social charade, and felt if we could be more honest, we would feel less alone in our struggles and more compassionate toward each other. After just a few weeks of facilitating the workshops, it became apparent that people are truly interested in the things we endure, celebrate, survive, and sometimes keep very hidden.

Over the years, I've become intimately engaged with people's deeper-layer stories. In a professional capacity, I've listened to clients' struggles and successes, and on a personal level, shared stories with dear friends on our frequent walks. Whenever a trying situation loomed ahead we reminded each other, "No matter how ugly things get, it'll make a great story for our next walk!" The tales that showed up in both realms of my fairly small world were often astounding. This collection of stories reinforces my belief that everyday people are the keepers of surprising secrets.

Just before my fiftieth birthday, amidst the ambivalence of nearing that milestone, I became motivated to start on this story-gathering journey, and a plan was hatched: Ask women for a story from their lives that had profoundly influenced who they had become, and that they had kept secret. Those were the only two parameters; the story could be a joy or a sorrow, and each woman had the latitude to determine what qualified as a secret. In return for her story, the teller was promised anonymity, with only her approximate age revealed.

I gathered stories first by listening and recording, then transcribing, and did my best to stay true to each person's unique voice. As the women shared their tales, two threads began to emerge. The first was the prominence of relationship challenges; we are fundamentally social beings, and the things that most deeply affect us involve the people we love (and sometimes hate). The other was a theme of inner strength. Many of the women had come to a greater awareness of who they were and the personal power they had achieved. Some explored this with subtlety, while others recounted pivotal moments when their true grit emerged.

The collection had turned into a colorful tapestry of female cultural wisdom, and I knew there was fertile ground for digging into every facet of life. The exploration questions following each story provide a frame to process and delve into the most relevant issues.

The women who shared in this endeavor opened their hearts and spoke with more candor than I'd ever imagined. A request letter e-mailed to about ten friends grew cyber-legs and began roaming the country. I recorded stories in person and over the phone with women of all ages and backgrounds. Allowed to share without recrimination, these women reached into their lives and handed over their pain and triumph. They remembered, laughed and cried, and I was overwhelmed by their generosity of spirit. Collecting significant moments of emotional history was a humbling and beautiful experience, and I am deeply thankful to every woman who gave me the gift of her story.

Guide to Exploration

The exploration questions after each story are a starting point for reflection and discussion. This gets at the meaty stuff of human experience – the challenges that make us wonder how we would handle tough situations, the dilemmas lacking simple solutions, the meaning we attach to the milestones in our lives.

I believe that a group (book club, friends, psychology or women's studies class) is the best forum for discussing these questions. There is a palpable energy generated when people explore at this depth, and I personally feel a group investigation is a richer, fuller experience than a solo endeavor. It may take time for a new group to gel, but once members trust each other, a strong bond can be formed from sharing thoughts and feelings.

Here are some suggestions for creating a safe space for exploration: What is shared with the group stays with the group. Understand that none of the questions has a "right" or "wrong" answer. Members should share of their own volition. Although you may vehemently disagree with another's opinion, please respect that she is entitled to it. And if you're touched by something you've read that's not included in the questions, I encourage you to put it on the table.

Depending on your personal history, some of the questions may generate intense feelings, and some may touch on areas you would rather not explore. Remember that however you choose to engage with these questions, *you* are the person who decides the extent to which you participate. You may even prefer to first read the stories and return to the explorations at a later time.

If you don't have access to a group, or you're more comfortable processing alone, I recommend journaling your responses, especially those that provoke a strong initial reaction. Although you may simply want to think about the questions in your mind's eye, writing can sometimes be cathartic and enlightening. If you're working with a counselor, you may consider talking about some of the discoveries gleaned from your writing.

Whatever avenue you pursue, I hope you find the process beneficial. As with any introspective journey, there will probably be tears and laughter along the way. If you approach the exploration with openness to whatever may unfold, I believe you will finish the book with a deeper self-awareness and a more compassionate heart.

"The personal life deeply lived always expands into truths beyond itself."

Anaïs Nin

Heather, 23

I've only told maybe three people this story. Growing up with my father – he was kind of terrifying. He was never physically abusive, but he was an intense, very weird guy. Just scary. My sister and I kind of lived in fear of him, and my mom did a little bit, too.

He would get *very* upset over small things, to the point where you would cry yourself to sleep and he would say, "Good, you need to be thinking about this." I was always very good in school and I worked my ass off because he put *so* much emphasis on that. My sister was not that way at all. One time she failed a quiz and he sat her down at the kitchen table and wrote a big "F" on every page of a legal pad, ripped it off and threw it at her. Crazy stuff. He's a good person; I think he's just got some strange issues. I remember playing with clay and I got some on the carpet. I locked myself in the bathroom because I was terrified hearing him come up the stairs; I knew he was going to be so upset. And he was. I remember him pounding on the door and yelling at me.

He used to check my homework when I got home from school. I had specific instructions from him to be at my desk with my homework, a legal pad and two sharpened pencils, all aligned. So OCD. I would sit there and have to wait for him to come home. He was just scary. He used to highlight our report cards every quarter. Grades that went down were highlighted in pink, grades that stayed the same were highlighted in

1

yellow, grades that went up were in green. And we would have conferences about how we were tracking. I was perceptive, and I think I aged beyond my years having to deal with someone who was so difficult to please. I learned how to read a situation and be very cautious. Something was weird about him and we just weren't close to him.

I was very close to my mom; I still am. I *love* my mom. She's more like a best friend to me than a mom. When my mom ran for state office, we moved to another city. I was in sixth grade and my mom told me, "I think I'm going to leave your father." And I said, "Please, do. Please get a divorce." Some people might think that's a bizarre reaction, but I was so excited; I knew she was miserable. I was too, and so was my sister.

They separated and he really couldn't handle it. He didn't want to get divorced. For a year he would tell me things to tell her because he wanted her to change her mind. After they divorced, he did a complete one-eighty with us. When we were younger kids, he wasn't at all concerned with being *nice*, or a friend, or even there. I think it was more like he had an idea of who we should become and he just did what he had to do to mold us. Maybe after the divorce he thought, "Shit, now I have to compete for their time and affection." He's honestly a joy to be around now.

I had always wondered what happened between my mom and him. I kind of had the idea that he cheated on her. I would beg my mom to explain things to me. I knew he had some skeletons in his closet; I just never knew what they were.

My senior year of high school, before I went away to college, my mom decided to tell me. First of all, she said she and my dad never had sex. He didn't want her sexually. Then, when my sister was four and I was six, she said we were on a vacation and my dad had to leave for a day or two. He's carried the same briefcase for twenty-five years; the handle has duct tape on it. My mom had to go into the briefcase for something, and she pulled out a notebook. The entire notebook was filled with drawings of him having sex with her mother – my grandmother. I was thinking, "Holy shit. If I ever pulled that out of my husband's briefcase, I would just..." She said, "Heather, it was just pages and pages of writing and drawings of such bizarre, weird stuff." She called him and said, "Ken, I just opened your briefcase and saw this. What *is* this?" He got really quiet on the phone and I don't think he wanted to address it. She had no idea what was going on and wanted to start seeing a counselor.

My grandmother told my mom that my dad had been calling her and leaving very strange messages, like, "Estelle, I miss you and I'd really love to see you." Disturbing messages that my grandmother said were creeping her out. My mom was obviously completely freaked out. My parents started seeing a counselor separately and together. My mom began to hear from other women how my dad would cheat on her all the time. Not with random other women; it was always prostitutes. (*Pause.*) Talking about this is so weird. My mom said that she found photos in his coat pockets and hidden in his closet of him having sex with these bizarre looking women. It was almost like a Freudian Madonna complex type of thing. He was leading this double life.

Our housekeeper, who's really been part of our family forever, found a duffel bag that he always carried to his car in the mornings. She opened it once and it was filled with high heels and wigs. All of this stuff, you can just imagine, is like,

3

absolutely crazy for my mom to hear. I always knew he was an odd guy, but I never imagined *this*. So my mom said she found out all these things and shared them with her counselor. The counselor said that perhaps my dad's mother had abused him as a child. It wouldn't surprise me; she's a rotten woman and he doesn't like her. I asked my mom, "When did you know you were going to leave?" Because obviously, someone could've heard all that and thought, "I am getting out of here. What the hell is this? I can't even believe this is who I'm married to." She said she was just so in shock. We were four and six, and they got divorced when I was twelve. That's a long time.

My mom's father is a serious alcoholic and addicted to painkillers, and just a nutty guy. I love him. He's like one of those guys who has wanderlust and a zest for life, and he's a little crazy. I think when my Mom was younger he was drunk all the time and abusive to her mother. She said when she and my dad were dating, one of the things that impressed her so much about my dad was how he dealt with her father. One time they were having dinner and her dad got so drunk he fell out of the chair, and my dad went and picked him back up and was totally cool about it. She said she was so impressed by that. My dad was always obsessed with becoming a successful lawyer, and so he seemed very stable. She said, "I think I saw how stable he was compared to my dad and thought that was great." She was very attracted to that.

The minute she knew she was leaving my dad was when the counselor said to her, "Well, you are accustomed to being abused. Your father did this to you, and now Ken's doing it to you. This is who you are." She thought, "That's *not* who I am." It was a "whoa" moment. Literally, that week she said, "Ken, we're getting divorced."

So my mom told me all this when I was a high school senior. I was so *glad* she told me because it helped to explain some things. He and my mother never kissed affectionately. If they ever did, he was like, "Kids, I am *so* in love with your mother. I am *so* in love with this woman." It was a big show. He's all about appearances and is a huge narcissist. He weaves this web of what he wants his life to look like: "I'm a successful lawyer and I have this, this and this." I think he believes it.

He used to take me to restaurants when I was in high school. We'd be sitting there and he'd say, "Heather, you see all these people in here? You wouldn't believe, but half the men in here are cheating on their wives. Everyone here has skeletons in their closets." I mean, totally unsolicited. At the time, I'm thinking, "Why are you telling your *daughter* this? What are you doing to me? This is the strangest thing, ever." Now I can see that he was just trying to validate himself in some twisted way – trying to convince himself that what he was doing was normal. Before I knew any of this, he would just kind of monologue about things he thought were important, things similar to that cheating commentary. As I look back on it, I can see how they're all related. It's almost like he was talking to himself to rationalize the behavior *he* knew about, but didn't think anybody else did.

He doesn't have a lot of friends. He's been engaged to a woman for five years; she's twenty-four years younger. She worked in his office. I wonder all the time if she knows about any of that. I think she must. They never live in the house at the same time, and our housekeeper told me that his fiancée is having an affair. I think the reason he's with her is, again, for appearances.

He really is terrifying. He just has a presence and firmness about him. I don't like conflict. Some people ask, "Why don't you confront your father about that?" I'm like, "No." As deep as that runs with him, I think it would just *shatter* him if he knew I knew. I'm not taking the easy way out, but I don't see anything that can be gained from it. It's not like he's gonna up and say, "I'm gonna change now." He can't; I mean this is who he is. I think it would just absolutely break his heart if he ever knew that my mom told me everything. She probably shouldn't have. Sometimes I do wonder, what if I ever sat down to talk with him about this. I mean, where to even start? I have absolutely no idea. What would he say? I just have no clue. And what would my goal be?

When they got divorced, he really, totally changed as a father; he's pleasant, giving, nice. I can still sense all the weird eccentricities. He'll never lose those, but he's not an angry person to be around anymore. The way I deal with it is I just say I so appreciate how much he's changed in those ways, that I'm just going to act like that other man is another person, because as a father to me, that's not who he is anymore. I just don't think about all the weird things. I think about the father he is to me now. If you think about it like that, and I mean this, I really mean this: I am so lucky, because he really is a *great* father. I really can talk to him about almost anything. If I want to talk to him, he'll sit down and listen. I think he's probably still doing weird shit, but the divorce changed him. He said he saw a therapist after they got divorced, to deal with anger management issues. I guess it helped because he's a lot better about that.

I'm very trusting of people but I do look at things cynically. I worry about my future husband cheating on me. I think the way my father was when my parents were married affects me a lot more than all of the strange stuff. When I found out about everything, I just felt sorry for him. I was detached because of the relationship we had growing up. I could kind of look at him from faraway, knowing all these things. I didn't like what he had done to my mom, but I could finally understand him better. I didn't understand him before. I guess I feel compassion, and my mom does too.

Maybe it affects me in ways I haven't yet understood in terms of relationship. My mom is so blissfully happy with her current husband, I cannot even tell you. I was in ninth or tenth grade when they got married. My mom always says, "I hope you and your sister know that *this* is a normal relationship, and not what I had with your father." And I do know that. Seeing my mom go and find what she deserves and what's healthy, and my dad going off and continuing his bizarre relationship – sometimes I wonder, "Is he gay?" I do; I wonder that. He's a very successful lawyer. Does he think, "All the things are in place so when people look at me they'll think I'm straight"?

He went to Princeton; his father went to Princeton. And he used to take me there all the time to visit. It was no secret that he wanted me to go there. He tells the same stories over and over again about Princeton. He used to take me to the dorms and point out where he lived his freshman year. He tells me the name of his roommates, the parties he went to, the things he used to do, names of his friends, his professors. One Christmas, my mom is talking to his sister, who is gay. She's not out of the closet, but we all know. And my Aunt Abby says, "You know he didn't get into Princeton right away.

He went to State for two years and transferred to Princeton his junior year." My mom had *no* idea. He'd been regaling us with made-up stories about college for all those years. Why would he do this? It mattered so much to him; I think he truly believes it.

My dad is also a closet chain smoker. My mom said he used to smoke two packs a day and hide it from her – whatever. He still smokes and I know this because he reeks of cough drops and he keeps perfume with him everywhere, and I find cigarettes hidden. I remember one time, three years ago, he demanded that I go to a doctor's appointment with him. I have no idea why. He wants me to come in the room with him. The doctor asks him, "Do you smoke?" I don't know what kind of doctor would ask like that. If he's your longtime doctor, he knows if you're a smoker. So I'm sitting on a little stool in the corner, and my dad just turns to me in the most intense, bizarre way and says, "No. I'm not a smoker." When I think about that, he must have thought I found out and was maybe trying to prove to me he wasn't. He's a weird person, I just can't tell you. He's crazy. He really is like two different people.

I worry a lot about if I have any of my dad in me. I do have some of his great qualities, but I worry sometimes, "Do I have any of *that* in me?" I don't even know what to call it; any of that narcissism, any of that sexual proclivity, any of that social stuff. I just wonder if I have any of the odd qualities that he has. The only one I can see is that I care a *lot* about what people think about me. Not in a way that I would lie, but I care a lot about that; more than I should.

I think the way it's affected me the most, is it's made me scared to have children. Not really scared, but it's about what your children know and what they don't. When I think about the fact that he probably thinks, "I have these two great girls, and didn't I raise them well." And here I sit knowing all this stuff. The fact that your children can know that about you and you can have no idea freaks me out. (*Crying.*) I can't think about anything for myself I'd want to hide, but that thought is so disturbing to me.

I worry about telling a serious boyfriend or fiancée. You never want to hear that the person you're marrying has something like that in their life. I worry about telling him what's in the family. It's so much to handle. It's such a kicker, kind of a stop-you-in-your-tracks story. It's a lot of crazy information. I worry about my dad getting lung cancer from smoking. What would he say to us then? I worry about him just getting old. Will anyone be with him? It might become my job; I worry about that a lot. Provided he doesn't die of lung cancer, I think he will live a long life. He knows how to persevere.

My grandfather has been a nightmare for my mom, as he's grown older. She hates dealing with him. When he finally moved into a home, we cleaned out his house and found all of this gay pornography. In high school I remember finding letters between my grandfather and my father, back and forth. Not at all sexual in nature, but they have some sort of relationship and they still write to each other. When I told my mom she was really surprised; she had *no* clue. Her father used to say to her, "You shouldn't have left Ken. Ken's such a great guy." What do they know about each other? They must know something because they have this weird bond and they must somehow be alike. It's just a *web* of weirdness. (*Laughing.*) Honestly.

I think I have an ability to understand a situation and what people are thinking because of years of trying to read my father and figure out how best to please him. And I think I have compassion for people who are weird or struggle. It's also taught me to not feel sorry for myself. People my age are always whining about how awful it is when their parents are divorcing. This is going to make me sound like a bitch, but I don't have a lot of patience listening to stories about how miserable everyone is because of a divorce; in the scheme of weird family shit someone can have, I think my situation pretty much takes the cake. It has made me realize that life is not a bed of roses. People are weird, and all you can do is try to find the best in them and surround yourself with people who are healthier. I don't feel sorry for myself at all, and I'm happy I have that quality.

Exploration – Heather

1. In speaking of her childhood, Heather said, "I think I aged beyond my years having to deal with someone who was so difficult to please. I learned how to read a situation and be very cautious." Were there people in your childhood who forced you to grow up faster than your peers? What did you learn from that experience?

2. After recalling her father's sexual obsession with her grandmother, Heather commented, "Talking about this is so weird." Is there a situation from your family history you've never shared with an outsider? What are the potential risks and benefits of discussing it?

3. Heather first said she was glad her mom told her everything because it "helped to explain some things." Later in the story, Heather thought her mom "probably shouldn't have" told her, and believed that confronting her dad "would just shatter him." Can you empathize with Heather's conflicted feelings? If you were her mother, what would you have shared?

4. Post-divorce, Heather's dad was "great," and she appreciated the ways he had grown into the role of a giving father. She dealt with the knowledge of his issues by "acting like that other man is another person." Have you known things about someone that forced you to compartmentalize like this? Were you able to sustain the relationship?

5. Heather said, "I worry a lot about if I have any of my dad in me." Are there mental health issues with your own parents you worry about inheriting? What tendencies in

yourself give you cause for concern? What do you know about yourself that gives you comfort?

6. Her struggle with authenticity resurfaced when Heather talked about being scared to have children: "The fact that your children can know that about you and you can have no idea, freaks me out." Do you think she would be served by letting her father know she is aware of his personal issues? How would you help her come to terms with the relationship she has with him?

7. Heather also worried about sharing her family history with a serious boyfriend: "You never want to hear that the person you're marrying has something like that in their life." What counsel would you give her concerning this kind of disclosure? Have you been afraid of judgment when sharing family secrets with significant others?

8. There were complex issues in Heather's extended family. Because of this, she feared for the health of her future relationships. Are there patterns in your family you've seen repeated? Who has been able to break that cycle? How did they do it?

9. Heather's mom was attracted to her first husband because of "how stable he was" compared to her father. Have you been attracted to someone because they exhibited qualities you thought were lacking in other close relationships?

10. Heather disclosed a lack of patience for peers whose parents are divorcing, and stated that she doesn't feel sorry for herself. Why do you think this was important for her to share?

Carol, 49

I have a big secret that nobody knows about, except maybe two other people. For fifteen years I had an affair, with the same person, while I was married. My kids were young when it started. I went to a christening for my friend's daughter. I'd been married about seven years, and Stan didn't want to go to the christening 'cause he never wanted to go anywhere with me. So I went with my friend. We walked into the restaurant and this Hank was seated at our table and he just... Now, I was never one to chase men. Really, I wasn't. A guy with long hair would turn my head, but I looked at this guy and thought "Oh, my God." I was so hot for him. Very strange. And much to my surprise, I really pursued him. He really didn't want to get involved with me 'cause I was married, but I was persistent about it. I would call him. He had his own business in the next town, so at lunchtime I would go to the food market where he got his lunch, and buy my lunchmeat so I could run into him. (*Laughing.*) I would do stupid stuff like that. One thing led to another and we started to see each other.

I knew the day I got married I made a mistake. At the time I got married I was twenty-three and Stan was twenty-eight. I had never really dated anybody. I had one long-term boyfriend from the time I was in high school until the time I started working. After we broke up I started to go out with Stan. Stan always was the way he was. He was no different when I dated him than when I married him. I didn't think anybody else would want me, honestly. Nobody ever told me

I was pretty. I never thought I was pretty; I always wanted to be 5'7" and have blonde hair and blue eyes. Those were the people I thought were pretty. When I went to high school those were the popular people. I never heard it from my parents. I really didn't have a lot of self-confidence. I know I didn't have a lot of self-esteem. I just thought this is probably it for me. I also was the kind of person who didn't like to be alone, so I'm sure that played into it. I thought Stan was safe. He didn't do drugs, didn't drink. He was very responsible. Had some money. I knew we would get a house. I thought I could probably have a nice, safe life with him.

There were things that I was not happy with when I dated him, but I thought I could change him; I thought things would get better. Not really knowing who I was, or the kind of person that I was, played into it a lot. I didn't place any value or give any consideration to the things I felt were important in a person. I just kind of brushed everything aside and thought things would change, would get better. But what I learned is that for the most part, what you see is what you're going to get. So I walked down the aisle and got married, and was sorry right afterwards, which was not good.

I didn't feel guilty about the affair at all, didn't feel bad. As the years went by in the marriage, deep down I knew that I probably was not going to spend my life with this person. I never had a vision of us at sixty-five. That just never even entered my head. Stan was always much nicer to people on the outside than he was to the people who lived in his house. He had issues with his temper.

He could scream and yell and shout and be frustrated with things very easily, but no one else in the house could be frustrated with anything. There was pushing, shoving. I've had his hands around my neck. If I brought it up and said, "You threw me on the bed and put your hands around my neck," he would say, "But I didn't squeeze." He was a son-of-a-bitch. He's miserable, he screams all the time. He scares people.

Over time, I just learned to be quiet and did what I had to do. I had two kids. I wasn't happy when they were younger, but I didn't have the option to go back to my parents' house. There was more than one time when things got physical, and there was one particular time, that if I had somewhere to go, would probably have left. We were having an argument in the basement and Stan was complaining about something and said, "You know what? We should've never gotten married. Maybe we should just get a divorce." And I said, "No problem. I don't have a problem with that. Let's do it." I walked past him to go up the steps and he got behind me and put his fingers in my belt loops and pushed me up the steps. He pushed me into the refrigerator at the top of the steps, and I was on the floor against the refrigerator and he was facing me on the top step. Beside him on the wall was a row of pots and pans and a rolling pin. He grabbed the rolling pin and held it over his head. I remember looking at his face. It was all red and the veins were bulging out of the side of his neck. I remember screaming, "Don't you dare! Don't you dare!" I thought, "Jesus Christ, if he hits me with this rolling pin I am fucking dead." I don't know where my head was 'cause all I had to do was take my foot, and push him down the steps or scoot to the opening near the door. But I could only focus on the rolling pin and being terrified it would bash in my skull. He brought it down hard and bashed it into the top step. It shattered into a million pieces. That's when I told him, I said, "You know what, I've had enough. I'm leaving here in two years."

I picked two years 'cause I'm always the practical one and I had to get a job. I didn't have a job. I had no job, no college degree. The last time I had worked was seventeen years ago. I had part-time customer service jobs but nothing that meant anything. Where was I going to go? I was going to go *nowhere*. At that point, my mother had passed away, and my father had moved into an apartment. My father was one to say, "You make your bed, you lay in it." Bottom line: I had nowhere to go. I had plenty of friends who said I could go to their house, but I had two young kids. When people talk about shelters, what are you supposed to do when you have two kids? And you have somebody who really didn't hit you, who really didn't choke you, who really didn't do anything. I mean, you're not hurt. Your psyche is hurt, but where are you supposed to go? Literally, the next day, I called a friend and said, "I need a job." I started working a few months later.

Hank had bought a duplex two years before I left, with the thought in mind that I could move in there someday. It's really, really nice. It's the kind of place I always wanted. I never lived in a really nice place because Stan never did or bought anything for the house. He controlled all the money. It just got to the point where, honestly, Hank started to put a little pressure on me: "This place is done now, your kids are grown, and you said we were going to be together someday." Not together like being married, but me being on my own and available to see him. He does his own wash. He takes care of himself. If I decide to help him, that's fine. If I want to cook dinner for the two of us, that's fine, I do it. If I don't, I don't. It was about having some kind of a life together, not having to lie and scheme all the time. And quite honestly, I couldn't do it anymore; I was just exhausted. I had become very unhappy at home; whereas before I was able to balance out the lives, it got to the point where I started to get older. All of a sudden, I was in my mid-forties thinking, "Jesus Christ, I'm almost fifty, how much longer am I going to be doing this?" Am I going to wait 'til I'm sixty-five and Stan's dead, and then have a life with this man? He's a good man, a kind man, always concerned about me. It became an overwhelming burden.

But I was scared shitless to do it. Some of my friends who knew said, "What are you going to do? Are you going to shit or get off the pot here?!" I was scared to tell Stan, thinking he was going to kill me. I really was afraid I was going to get killed. I had to pick the time when I was going to do it. I didn't tell him at night because I didn't want to have to run out the front door into the dark. And I didn't want to do it in a closed-in space. I decided to do it during the day in my living room with the front door open 'cause it was summertime. I said, "I think I want to move." And he said, "You want to move? Ok, where do you want to move?" He thought I meant with him. But I didn't phrase it right. I said, "No, I want to move. By myself." He knew I wasn't happy and he knew from the rolling pin incident, when I said I was leaving in two years, that we were at the two-year mark. He said, "Oh. Well if you're not happy, and that's what you have to do, then that's what you have to do."

That was in September. Even after I said that, I was still dragging my feet. I was afraid to do it. I was still afraid I was going to get killed, that I was really going to get hurt. Finally, about two months later, I woke up and said to myself, "I can't do this another day – this has to be done." I drove to his work and called him and said, "Can you come out here for a minute?" He came out to the car and I said, "I want you to know I'm leaving." I don't know what day that was. I said, "I want you to know I'm moving out on Monday. I want you to know I'm leaving." He said, "Okay." I said, "Are you going to kill me? 'Cause if you are, you know what? Don't." I felt really stupid. I probably did everything you're not supposed to do.

'Are you going to kill me?!' What asshole is going to say yes? He said, "I'm not going to kill you, Carol." I said, "Good. I hope not. You know what? I want you to be happy, and I want me to be happy, and we're just not."

I was emotionally done with Stan way before the rolling pin incident. I don't think I could've carried on an affair with someone if I was not emotionally done. The affair started before the rolling pin. The thing that's so interesting about it is that I never really felt bad about it. I feel much worse about Stan now than I did when I was having an affair. Back then, I still took care of him. I took care of the house, I washed, I cooked, I cleaned, I paid the bills; I kept things functioning there. And now that I've picked up and left, he has no life. Well, he didn't really have a life anyway, even when I was there, but I was taking care of things. Now nobody takes care of anything there. There are some days I feel really bad about that.

Here's the thing: I don't hate him or anything, and actually we talk and get along fine. I don't hate him and I wish that he would find somebody or wish he could find some happiness. He was never a happy person, never. I kind of thought in the beginning I could make him happy, but I've realized you don't make other people happy. You can't make somebody else happy. So I feel worse for him now because he's living this lonely life. For Father's Day I took Stan and my father out to breakfast with the kids. Like I said, I don't hate him for anything. I sometimes don't like the kind of person he is, the way he handles himself, but that's the way he is, and that's the way he was when I dated and married him. Shame on me for not knowing myself better. "Shame" isn't really the word I want to use – I just didn't know any better.

Hank and I enjoyed each other's company, we were both close in age, went to high school around the same time. Hank's a fun person. We would always go out and do things. I used to lie through my teeth to get out of my house. I was always doing something with someone else. I could've been caught very easily, but I guess Stan never thought about it. Hank and I would hang out and have a good time. All the time this is going on, we're sleeping together. I loved him, literally from the first time I saw him. And then as I got to know him, I liked the person he was.

He has never been married and comes from a very troubled background. His parents were alcoholics who fought all the time. He himself was an alcoholic. When I met him he had been sober for six years. He never really wanted a family; didn't want the pressures of kids or a wife because his own parents had such a disastrous relationship. His older brother was a heroin addict.

Things kind of worked out because I didn't look at him like my ticket out. I didn't have any intention of doing anything when the kids were younger because I thought it would be too much of a mess. I didn't make enough money, there would be child support issues, custody issues. It was just going to be easier for me to stay put. It just got to the point where I would go through the motions with Stan and the kids – do what I had to do, then go out and have my good time – and then come home. Maybe that's a screwed up thing to be able to do. I don't know. I've heard this word "compartmentalize" in reference to what Bill Clinton used to do. Maybe that's what I was able to do somehow. I was able to have this part of my life where I was very responsible. I lived up to all the expectations of me as a wife and a mother. But then there was this other thing I was doing. Somehow I was able to separate it enough so that it didn't spill into my life, make me miserable and cause me to make decisions that were stupid. I was always very practical like that. I wouldn't think, "Oh my God, I love this man, I have to be with him at all costs." There were costs to be paid, like, "What about money and what about these kids?" I never looked at him like I wanted to marry him.

We're together now. He owns two duplexes and I moved into the duplex next-door to him. He completely refurbished the whole thing for me; it's a beautiful place, I'm very happy there, and my father lives upstairs. We pay Hank rent. Here's the thing: At this point in my life, I don't really have any desire to live with anybody. I love him dearly and he's right next-door. So he comes over or I go over there. But I like my space. I don't need to be with him all the time. When I know my kids aren't going to come over, he'll stay the night. But he usually beats it out of there by eight in the morning. He was the one who said, "Why don't you ask your dad to live here?" My dad is eighty-six. He's in good health, but if something happens to him, I need to be right there to take care of him. There's nobody else. I don't have any brothers or sisters; there's no other family. It's going to be me. The three of us have dinner together sometimes. Hank and I go away together. We have a life. It's not a typical married life, but it's a nice, happy life. I love him to death and he would do anything in the world for me.

Exploration – Carol

1. When Carol first saw Hank, she was immediately infatuated, and surprised herself by pursuing him. Do you believe in love at first sight? Have you ever been completely surprised by the way you've behaved?

2. One of the reasons Carol married Stan was because she didn't think anybody else would want her. What do you think a girl has to experience in order to feel attractive and desirable as a woman? How critical are those qualities to confidence? Did you leave your home feeling that way?

3. Stan was a "safe" choice for Carol. She said, "He didn't do drugs. He didn't drink," and she knew they would own a home. Looking back, what were the primary motivations for you to get married (or involved in a long-term relationship)? Would you be driven by the same motivations today?

4. After the rolling pin incident, Carol considered her options for leaving and said, "Where was I going to go? I was going to go *nowhere*." What role do you think her father's "you make your bed, you lay in it" attitude played in Carol's decision?

5. Although she feared Stan would kill her when she left, Carol sometimes felt badly for no longer taking care of him: "I kept things functioning there...now nobody takes care of anything." Can you identify with her ambivalent feelings of abandoning her caregiver role?

6. Carol had newfound awareness and compassion for Stan when she said, "You can't make somebody else happy. So I feel worse for him now because he's living this lonely life." Have you ever felt you could make someone happy? Could you feel compassion toward an abuser?

7. Reflecting back on her marriage, Carol used the word "compartmentalize" when thinking about how she coped with being both a dutiful wife/mother and mistress. Have you ever used this strategy in coping with your own challenges? Was it effective?

8. When Carol married Stan she believed she could change him. Has anyone ever tried to change something about you? What was the outcome?

9. Carol said, "... you have somebody who really didn't hit you, who really didn't choke you, who really didn't do anything..." What behavior warrants the label "abuse"? If you knew someone in a situation like Carol's, what would you say to her?

10. Carol felt she didn't really know herself when she got married. At what point in your life do you know yourself? How do you come to that awareness?

Connie, 47

Dana was my firstborn, my first girl. I was eighteen years old. I was in my last year of high school and my mother did not take it too well. She was tough love. I did finish high school, but was out on my own by the time I turned eighteen, so I basically started raising my daughter on my own.

Dana was a very responsible child; never gave me problems. Even as an infant she was an extremely good baby. She slept through the night; only cried when she was totally wet. Very agreeable, which is sort of unusual. It was four years later before I had my son, and Dana was very motherly. As the other children came along – I have four – she actually took on a mother role. She would say, "The baby needs a change. I got it." Or if I would come in and say, "I'm not up to fixin' dinner. Let's get takeout," she'd say, "Oh, no. I can fix us dinner." Actually, in my situation at the time, I was married, but I might as well not have been. It was a horrible marriage; I ended up working two jobs to support the family. There was very little down time, or me time. But I never had a problem because she was always there. I felt guilty about it, but it couldn't be helped.

Dana inspired and motivated me a lot in things I wanted to do. If I had made it to college I would have gone for literature. I wanted to be a writer, reporter, whatever I could be. But with the family, children and work that all went away. At certain times I would write something in a notebook and put it away. Dana would find it and say, "This is really good! You need to really work on this!" She encouraged me. She was basically my best friend as well as my daughter.

When my youngest was four, I found myself pregnant again. I had been sick prior to that and my body was stressed and fatigued; it was a strain. I was about twenty weeks, coming home on the train one evening and my water broke. I was rushed to the hospital. The doctor told me there was nothing they could do – they had to induce. It was just devastating. Prior to them taking me down to surgery, Dana was there, holding my hand and talking to me. I blacked out for a minute, and she shook me awake and said, "Oh no, you can't go anywhere. There's still a lot that you have to do." She was just so solid. She was only nineteen, but saying things like, "Stay strong. I'll be right here when you come out." And she was. She was there. After the fact, she kept me positive and didn't let me fall into the kind of depression I could feel coming on.

During that time I had decided to let one of the jobs go, because it was just too overwhelming. I knew it would be even more of a struggle, but I just couldn't do the two jobs. One thing led to another with finances and we ended up at a place in the worst part of the city you can imagine. A man and wife with four kids in a one-bedroom apartment. I've always had a wonderful relationship with my kids. That's basically the thing that held us together, that kept me strong. Their laughter, and their accomplishments are the highlight of my life.

I was working the eleven p.m. to seven a.m. shift at the hospital during this time. Fortunately, the night that everything occurred I happened to be off and I was home. Dana had gone with her cousin to do some braids, the hair braiding. That was like her extra income; that was her way of helping me. According to what the girls say, it's better if two people work on one head, it takes less time. And you have someone to talk to. (*Laughing.*) By this time, Dana is twenty-two and had two children of her own, two little girls. So she goes off with her cousin and I'm there with the kids, and we all fall asleep in the living room watching television. I'm expecting her in late, maybe twelve at the latest.

I'm woken suddenly by gunshots, which is not unusual in this area, at all. It's common. It definitely wakes me up and I'm on alert, sitting there trying to adjust myself to say, "Okay, let me get up and get the kids into bed." In the process of me sitting there, I hear the door slam downstairs, someone running up the stairs, and then banging on my door and someone *screaming*, "Dana's been shot." As quick as the person came, that's how fast they went. To this day, I don't know who that person was. It was sort of like a freezing moment...in that I'm dreaming. It's sort of surreal. My youngest son, who was thirteen, snapped me out of this thing I was in. I noticed him moving and throwing his shoes on. I told my youngest daughter, "You just stay here and *do not* come out." I go barreling down the steps behind my son. People are out on the corner; they're standing there. (*Crying.*)

One of the kids comes up to me and he can't really speak, but he's pointing up to the corner. We started to run in that direction, and we just saw her with blood pooling under her. I had fallen on my knees by her, and I guess being medical, my instinct was to not touch her. I wanted to touch her, but I didn't know what to do. I couldn't comprehend things, but someone else had a hold of my son and he was hysterical; he had made it to her before I did. I don't know when or how, but my husband appeared. His hand was on my shoulder and I heard his voice, but I can't remember. I ended up with him removing me and sitting me next to a fence. I remember crawling over to her with the paramedics there, and finally found my voice to call out her name. And she heard me, because I grabbed onto her hand and she squeezed my hand. At that point she was still alive, so I felt a little hope, but it was barely there.

They got her into the ambulance. I rode in the front because they were working on her in the back. I was talking to God. I really can't remember what I was praying or asking for. I was in a daze. The driver was talking to me, but it's all a blur. It's enough to realize there is conversation happening. The hospital was the same. I remember freezing my husband out. I sat alone. I sat away from him. I could not make eye contact with him. We should have not been there. I was worried about her, but his presence was disturbing to me. I think I could have dealt better, or reflected on what was necessary had he not been there.

We waited for a couple hours, or maybe just one, I can't remember. Something happened while I was sitting there. Sort of like a – this is really hard to describe – like you're shedding something. It's dense; it just slips away and you can't grasp it back. But it's more of a sensation than anything else. (*Pause.*) They finally came out to give us a report. Knowing how a hospital operates, the moment they walked through that door I knew that she had not made it. To see the doctor walking through the door, I knew. She had slipped away while I was waiting.

I was numb. I did not break down; I did not cry. It was like the doctor delivering the news, asking if I was okay, did we want to see her, and getting up and walking out. I had no emotion. I just went right to her. Seeing her laying there, she just looked asleep. They must've cleaned her up pretty well so we wouldn't be subjected to blood all over the place. She just looked like she was sleeping. I walked over to her and just kind of put my arms around her, laid my head next to her and I started talking. (*Crying.*) I told her that I loved her and then I started to relay things about her growing up; little expressions she would make when she was mad – just talking and trying to remember everything about her – to hear myself say it so I could remember. I really didn't know what to do, how I was supposed to react. I just did what came natural. She had a habit, even at twenty, she would get into bed with me. (*Laughing.*) If I was sick, I'd say, "You can't get in here with me, I have a cold." And she'd say, "Oh, just turn your back, I'm right here." And we'd just sleep back-to-back. If we were watching TV or something, she'd just lay her head on my shoulder or my lap and we would watch a show together. (*Crying.*) Being there with her just gave me peace.

Afterwards, I went to the police station for questioning and they handed me a bag of her clothes. I opened the bag and there was her scent. I had never thought of her even having a scent. When the smell of my daughter hit my nose, my body just convulsed and instead of puking it came out the other end. It was an overwhelming realization that she's not here anymore. They had to give me a change of clothes.

Facing the children – that was the hardest thing after. My youngest son took it really bad. He was the one I was really worried about. The funeral was very hard. I was able to make arrangements. Everyone commented I was very businesslike, very direct, very detached. Later, I remember hearing that it was commented I was very cold. It all went through. During the actual funeral, I recall getting sick. I had to leave to go throw up in the bathroom.

The year following this, I was useless. I went to work, I came home, went in my room and closed the door. I worked, I slept, I ate. I wasn't able to be there for Dana's kids and I feel really bad about that. I couldn't really talk to anyone. I had these children to feed; I had these bills to pay. Three months following, I picked up the second job again. I really had no choice. All I could do was provide for them. I could not give them anything emotional. Even my own children; I had kind of frozen them out. That was so hard for them because they had never known that. I cut myself off because that was the only way I could function. I was really afraid to feel, because I thought if I started to, I would not be able to go on. I couldn't let that wall crumble yet. What I didn't realize then was that even though I was providing for them, they were still lacking what they needed from me. Dana's children needed me to show them love and I wasn't giving that to them. Thank God my children gave it to them.

That first year I was basically like a walking zombie. It was my oldest son who said to me one evening, "You need to wake up. We're doing the best we can with these children, but they need *you*." I think I remember slapping him. I argued with him and said, "Who the hell do you think you are? You're dictating to me; I'm your mother." And he said, "Well you need to act like it." It got to me. I ended up in my room and brood over that; I spent more than a week on it. His words made me reflect on everything I had not done during that year. I remember coming home one day and having that weekend off from work. My son said, "We're going to take the girls to the zoo because they're having some event." I said, "Okay, we'll all go together." That was the first step I made into becoming part of my family again.

The investigation into Dana's death moved slowly. A year later and they still didn't know who did it. The detectives kept up with me, but I would have to say it wasn't enough. We just didn't know what happened. We didn't know if it was a drive-by, if it was about her, we didn't know anything. There was an article written up in the paper with a summary of her death, like, "Young mother was killed…" giving the information that had been released. At the end of the article the writer made the comment, "Why would a mother with two children be out at that time of night?" That really fired me up. I called the paper and put in a complaint. I expressed that I was this child's mother and before that was printed maybe someone should have called me to ask me that question.

Twenty-two months after Dana was shot, I got a call saying, "We've got a suspect." By this time, I was back on track with my life and was more aware of what was going on around me. So when they called to say they had found a suspect, I pursued the detectives. "What's going on? Who is he?" They could only tell me so much information. Shortly after that, it came to trial and they suggested I bring my granddaughters, but I just couldn't do that. So I get in court and they bring out this guy in an orange jumpsuit and handcuffs. This guy shows no remorse. He stands there with his head held high and a "can we please get this over with" look on his face. And I could not take my eyes off this boy; he's probably no more than twenty years old. I'm lookin' at him saying, "This is somebody's kid." And then I look over and I'm lookin' at his family. It was strange. I had the question in my mind, "Why does he have no remorse after what he's done?" I was more confused than angry.

The whole process starts and I'm listening to the events unfolding that led to her being shot: Dana's cousin dropped her off and someone at the corner, a girl she knew, called her name. Dana walked toward her friend, who was standing with a couple of people. Just as she reached them, this guy walked up and tells one of the boys that he wants his coat and wallet. The boy refuses and says, "You gotta be kidding me. You're crazy." So the guy pulls out a gun and everyone runs. My daughter was shot in the back.

It pierced her artery, the artery to her heart. She got caught in the crossfire. All I could do is sit there, and in my mind go, "For a coat. You took a life for a coat." He wasn't allowed to speak, but I could talk to him. I said, "You've taken the life of this young mother, and am I supposed to go home and tell her girls she died because of a coat?" He just had this look like he didn't care at all. There was nothing there. He only got fifteen years.

But I had reconnected to my family and was healing. I started to notice a lot of my daughter in my granddaughters, which helped me a lot. It was sort of like I had her with me. I saw it in a smile, or a pout that showed up when I told her no, she can't have something. (*Laughing.*) But it was there. And then I started to realize a lot about what my daughter had said to me over the years, and how adult she was in the way she saw things. She'd say, "You're capable. You're a smart woman." I recalled how she would tell me to write, and I have. I always wanted to learn a different language, and now I'm studying Japanese. Whenever I want to try something, I think about what she'd say to me and I find some courage. I finally left my husband. My whole perspective about how I live my life has changed. Life is not promised to you. The next day is never promised to anyone. If I leave this world and not accomplish even a part of what I have desired to do, then what is it about?

About three months later, I woke up in the middle of night and caught her scent; the clothes were long gone, but it was *her* scent. It was a peaceful thing, like everything hard was washed away. That was the most at peace I had felt since losing her. I felt her presence as a request, and I said, "Yes, I will take care of your girls. I will love them."

Exploration – Connie

1. Connie gave up on her professional dreams when she started her family. Did you have to let go of certain aspirations when you had children? Were you able to secretly nurture them as Connie did with her notebook writing?

2. When Connie first heard the words "Dana's been shot," she called it a "freezing moment," and felt like she was dreaming. Have you had similar reactions to hearing shocking news? What brought you back to reality?

3. Dana's spirit departed as Connie sat in the waiting room; she felt as if she was "shedding something." Have you been near a dying loved one and sensed they were leaving their body? What made you aware they were departing?

4. At the funeral, Connie was "businesslike" and "very detached." She later heard that people thought she was "very cold." Does your family culture expect women to grieve in a particular way? Would you be critical if a grieving mother shed no tears?

5. Connie coped with grief by cutting herself off from the rest of her family. She said, "I was really afraid to feel, because I thought if I started to, I would not be able to go on. I couldn't let that wall crumble yet." Can you empathize with this depth of pain?

6. Connie's son finally confronted her about grieving in emotional isolation, and she slapped him. Why do you think this was Connie's first response? Do you think her

son's approach was appropriate? How would you have tried to reach her?

7. Connie found the courage to speak to Dana's killer at the trial. Would you have asked the same question of him? What else would you have said?

8. Dana's scent, which was such a brutal assault for Connie in the police station, showed up again, this time as her greatest source of comfort. Have you been comforted by the felt presence of a departed loved one? What did that mean for you?

Sheila, 45

This is kind of hard, because I realize there are things we talk about so little, we just forget; we block them. One of the big life-changing moments for me was in college. I was young and free and wanted to try and do everything. I got connected to a group of folks who were heavily into drugs, and got arrested. The whole thing about getting high and hanging out with this group of kids was the classic story of wanting to be with the cool kids – and realizing, "Okay, being with the cool kids is on the verge of getting you kicked out of college."

I have not even thought about getting high since the day I was arrested. It wasn't like I was addicted; I was just doing it because everybody around me was doing it. It wasn't bringing me anything that I was telling me it was bringing. When it happened, everybody had to separate and take care of themselves, so there wasn't this great network of friends who had become family. It wasn't helping me in school. I was growing more distant from the other I people I lived with; they weren't doing it. And it put me in some dangerous situations.

But I was in my twenties, and you think that life goes on forever and there's no consequence for anything; you just keep doing whatever it is you want to do. I also realized that because that happened to me so young, I didn't have to wait to learn those kinds of lessons later, which I saw some people doing; at thirty they were just learning this lesson I had already learned. When I got my first full-time job, and you answer the question 'Have you ever been arrested?' I realized I *could* answer 'yes' because of the way the case went. I realized I could've really ruined my entire life, set it on a really bad course in terms of building my own future.

I was, and am, an overweight person. The cool folks were a lot of very pretty and cute girls and guys. I thought, "How can I be in with this group?" This was end of freshman year, beginning of sophomore year. People would tell me, "You're a pretty girl, you're a sexy girl," but I wasn't getting a lot of boyfriends, so it just felt very surface from them, and I felt I needed to do something more to be in this crowd.

I was at a frat party, and I was with my roommate, and she said, "Sheila, you're always so intense; try this," and she handed me a joint. I'm a preacher's kid, so in my mind I'm thinking, "This is so wrong, so not what I'm supposed to be doing." College, socially more than anything else, overwhelmed me. I had been restricted from so much growing up; I just didn't know what to do with all this freedom. The marijuana gave me this feeling of not having to *think* about everything – I got out of my head.

I started using the marijuana for two reasons. One was as a connection tool. The other was that it just caused me to stop thinking the things I was thinking in my head about myself: "I'm not good enough. I'm not pretty enough. I'm not ready for my classes. I'm stupid." I'm making really stupid choices, and I'm aware of the fact that they're stupid choices, but I keep making them. Marijuana would put my brain on pause.

It escalated pretty fast 'cause once the group saw that you were okay, that I would get high, they invited me to more things. They were very insular; if you weren't getting high you weren't going to be included in certain things 'cause they didn't trust you. So this quickly became, "You can go to the party *and* the after-party now." That felt good in one sense, but it also took me away from my ability to really study. I was too busy trying to make sure I got into the party and the after-party. I was tired and stoned – what a great combo. (*Laughing.*)

The every weekend scene started creeping into the week. I tried coke once, but really didn't like it 'cause I was a voice major and didn't like the drip on the back of my throat, so I didn't mess with that again. (*Pause.*) These were just people I was getting high with; they weren't necessarily good friends. Did I spend more time around them? Yes. Was I feeling any better about myself? Truthfully – no.

There were some guys who were also dealing. There were guns around. They dealt some drugs out of my room, which is actually why I got arrested. I remember this one guy coming to pick up his drugs, and he didn't have the money and he was trying to snatch the drugs, and guns got pulled, and voices got raised. I'm like, just being still, like, "Don't move and maybe this moment will pass." I was terrified. I went through this whole thing: "How stupid could you be to put yourself in this position?" It didn't get me out of the crowd but I stopped hanging out with them as much. I'd still see them on campus and maybe we'd still have lunch together. I'd go to a party but not the after-party. It caused me to back up, but it didn't cause me to back completely out.

The bust happened right around Thanksgiving break. There was a knock at the door. I was sleeping, didn't feel like answering the door. Kept sleeping; the knock got harder and harder, louder and louder. Opened the door and there are police officers. They go through the whole thing, "You're under arrest…" I ask, "What for?" and they say, "We'll tell you that down at the police station." I get taken out of the dorm in handcuffs; it was embarrassing and humiliating. And it was very scary. This was one of the tallest dorms on campus so there were a lot of people walking around, in and out. This was part of a sweep that was happening in Maryland, as part of a response to college basketball star Len Bias's death, and the knowledge there were drugs on Maryland's campuses.

Once we got to the police station, there was a lot of questioning about people that I didn't really know. They were going after the cocaine ring, and I didn't really know those folks. The police officer interviewing me had checked my background and realized that my older brother was a prominent national musician. The officer's wife was a big fan and he started saying how I let my family down, and I might be tarnishing my brother's reputation. It was pissing me off. Okay, I am sitting here trying to deal with the fact that I am chained to a chair. They still have me restrained because there's this big drug ring on campus, there's guns involved, there's violence involved, and they don't know who knows what at this point. I was thinking, "What the hell? How did I manage to get myself here, to this place? How do I get out of here?" I'm realizing they're asking me about people I don't know. This being the Eighties, with Miami Vice on TV, I'm wondering if I could get swept up in something that's so much bigger than me that I can't get out of it. I'm young and I'm scared – I'm terrified – and I don't know what's going to happen next, and this man is now asking me about my brother, who gets on my nerves. (*Laughing.*) My brother was living a very different life from the one I was living. The officer could've picked anything else to push a button, and he might've gotten a different response, but that just caused me to lock down. "Okay, I don't really have anything to say to you, and I don't really want you to say anything else to me."

I didn't realize it at the time, but one of the people in our group on campus was an undercover police officer. She gathered all the names of who was involved in this circle of people. That kind of jarred me, because it jarred my ability to trust my judgment on who I should be around. I really liked her. I thought she was a really nice person and I felt so betrayed. She was doing her job; there were like ten people who got arrested. Even when my trial date came up, she was there, and she came up to me and said, "I'm really sorry. I didn't mean for *you* to be one of the ones that got arrested." I remember looking at her like, "Well, you just shouldn't have mentioned my name." That would've been easy.

So I get put into a cell, and basically my choices are to make a phone call or I'll just be there until trial, some time in the future. The last thing I want to do is call my parents with this. This is not what a preacher's kid wants to do. It gets to be about four or five o'clock in the morning and I was in a cell by myself, and then they started putting other people in there. They weren't related to the sweep, they were just people getting arrested. This girl came up to me, rubbed my arm, and said something like, "We could have a good, good time together here." And then I was like, "Yeah, I'm going to need to make that phone call."

So I make the call to my parents, crying. My mother answers and she drops the phone, so I have to reiterate the story to my father. They were there in a few hours. It was during finals, and I had to get back to campus to take my exams. Of course, I did not do well. As they drove me back to campus, my father asked, "I need to know, do we need to make arrangements for you to go to drug treatment now?" This is probably the deepest shame I've ever felt. Because they didn't go fire and brimstone, just, "Do we need to get you treatment? How did you get into this? *Why* did you get into this?" Basically, it was, "What can we do to rescue you at this point?"

My mother couldn't speak. She was crying. I was thinking, "How could I do this to them?" I was taking into consideration everything that my parents had given me, the opportunity given to me, the financial sacrifices they were making for me to be in college. I just felt this heavy shame from wasting all of these opportunities. That look in my mother's eyes (*crying*) like I had broken her, was just heartbreaking. I'm crying now, just thinking about it. They weren't fire and brimstone parents, they were the "you can be whatever you want to be" parents – and lived through my "I'm going to run away and sing with Prince" phase. (*Laughing.*) They had turned to our friends to help pay for college. I was able to graduate without the debt of student loans because my parents carried that burden. I didn't know all this then, but I knew I wasn't paying anything for college at that point. (*Sigh.*) It was a ten-minute car trip, but it felt like hours – hours upon hours.

The next day, trying to go to finals, where the story is all across the campus, and people are looking and pointing, I remember telling myself, "So, you want everybody to notice you? Well, here's what you got." And, "Was it worth it?" It wasn't worth it at all. I was fortunate that my parents had connections, so we got a great lawyer who basically got me probation before judgment, so that by the time I was twenty-one my record was expunged. I never have to acknowledge this.

During that period of being arrested, getting through finals, and going home, I went into the deepest depression I have ever experienced in my entire life. Even since, I have not been that low. It was the "I can't lift my head; if I lay here long enough, will I just die?" kind of depression, trying to figure out who I am and how I am going to get through this. I was able to come out of that place because of friends. Friends who called to say, "We love you. We know that this is not all of who you are."

My first boyfriend had gone through his own issues with shame and embarrassment, revolving around gender orientation. He called and had a very gentle way of saying, "You know, Sheila, shame will not kill you, but you have to work through it. You have to figure out who you are and embrace that, and get past this moment. Don't just stay in this moment; you have so much more to give and so much more to live for." It was good to speak with someone who I knew really understood.

It took a while for my parents to trust me again. But again, they never lowered this, "You're a horrible person, you're going to hell." It was never that. It was always this thing about, "What can we do?" My mother was dealing with her own shame. It was as though she had been a really bad parent. And where did she go wrong? I couldn't take the weight of her shame with my shame. I didn't address it with her until years and years later. I just couldn't, couldn't take it.

There were several positive things that came out of this, later. In the moment, not so many. I began getting very clear about who I am, and walking in that, versus trying to figure out what other people want me to be and trying to live that. Authenticity became a very key, underlying thing for me the rest of my life. I want people to know they can be authentic with me, and I want to be authentic with the people in my life. It definitely showed me who my real friends were, the people who stuck with me through that. Those people are friends with me to this day. It allowed me to see that you create family outside of your gene pool. These friends are people my blood family considers family.

There's also this thing that happened with me spiritually. What I had heard growing up was, "If you do this, God will do that." I realized the first time I got high, I didn't get struck by lightning. The sky didn't separate, nothing dramatic happened.

For me, it meant that God was not present; God was possibly not even real. And all the stuff I had been hearing was bullshit.

During those very dark days, having to be quiet, develop my own relationship with God, and define spirituality for myself, I realized it's not this big, bad, God. There is this connection universally, to this thing that's bigger than me, and that life is teaching me lessons through people, through music, through all kinds of things, and that I need to listen to that voice that tells me, "This is yes. This is no." It's not going to be thunder and lightning, and bushes burning; that's not what happens. There is a presence in the universe that is moving, and that's moving in all kinds of ways, and I need to be sensitive and aware of it. In each of these major decisions I was making in school, I knew there was something telling me, "No, don't do this." But I ignored it. I've learned how to listen to that voice.

Exploration – Sheila

1. Sheila thought back on the choices she made in her youth: "…I was in my twenties, and you think that life goes on forever, and there are no consequences for anything…" Were you as cavalier in your twenties? At what point in your life did you start thinking about danger and consequences?

2. College was a socially overwhelming experience and Sheila remembered, "I had been restricted from so much growing up; I just didn't know what to do with all this freedom." Was it hard for you to acclimate to the freedom of college or life after high school? Did you feel socially prepared?

3. Sheila began behaving like the "cool kids" because she desperately wanted to be included and accepted. What have you done that was motivated by peer pressure? What were the ramifications?

4. Negative self-talk like, "I'm not pretty enough," and "I'm stupid," was quieted when Sheila smoked marijuana. Getting high also helped her gain entree into the "cool" group. What role did recreational drugs play in your life? Do you have any regrets about using them?

5. After her arrest, Sheila wondered if she had been swept up in something much bigger than her own small involvement. Have you ever been caught up in something that you originally thought was not a big deal? How did you extricate yourself? What did you learn?

6. Sheila's ability to know who was trustworthy was "jarred" by the undercover police officer. Has someone ever totally misrepresented themselves to you? How were you affected when the truth was revealed?

7. When Sheila told her parents she had been arrested, she experienced "the deepest shame" she had ever felt. Have you done anything that resulted in a similar feeling? Were you able to find your way through and make amends?

8. Following the end of the semester, Sheila sank into a deep depression and "was able to come out of that place because of friends." Who or what has helped you climb out of depression? Have you had occasion to find out who your "real friends" were?

9. Carrying her own burden of guilt, Sheila was unable to shoulder her mother's shame as well, and it was years before they discussed the arrest. Has your family gone through something that wasn't talked about until years later? Why do you think it wasn't discussed until then?

10. It took some time after the arrest, but Sheila became "very clear" about who she was. She remembered, "Authenticity became a very key, underlying thing for me the rest of my life." Have you experienced a defining event that set a theme for the rest of your life?

11. Sheila had a profound shift in her spiritual beliefs as she started to heal from her ordeal. How has your spiritual orientation evolved over the years? What precipitated your current views?

Juracy, 42

One of my lowest points occurred in 1998. I was in my second bad marriage. I decided I was going to leave and go back up to New York where I'm originally from. My mother graciously invited me to live with my stepfather in an apartment that was in her name; she had left my stepfather to go live with another man.

Let me go back a little ways. It started off as a good year because I became baptized. I remember going to the creek, in Belhaven, North Carolina. I had been aware of the fact that I was very unhappy and needed Christ in my life. I was going to church on a regular basis and my marriage was in trouble. Based on the suffering and pain, and feeling unfulfilled, I started seeking the Lord and became baptized. I remember going to the creek and the fish were flying and it was just a wonderful baptism.

I made the decision about a month afterwards to accept my mother's invitation. So I went up to New York, and I felt spiritually strong. My stepfather and I had always had a good relationship. He was suffering with his pain from losing my mother. My stepfather and I grew close, and in the process he started going to Narcotics Anonymous, and N.A. self-help groups, and he became stronger. I was able to get a temporary job with a mortgage company. The position went from temporary to full-time, and I could see God's grace upon me.

It seemed like everything was fine until I found out that my mother had acquired HIV. It was devastating. If I had not been girded spiritually, I may not have been that strong. She had come over, and she was in the kitchen. I could tell that she was troubled, and I asked her what was the matter, what was going on. She revealed that she had HIV. It was a tremendous blow. I felt a mixture of being numb, like, "This is not really happening," and, "Oh my God, my mother's going to die." And the stigma of what she had, what she had confessed to me, and my ignorance not knowing about it – so much emotion. I remember feeling strong. (*Pause.*) It's hard to explain. But I felt like with prayer and seeking God, we could get past this, and I could live with her condition, her confession. It seemed like she was relieved that she finally shared that. It was a secret that she had been keeping and no one other than me and the man she lived with knew about it.

Her health continued to deteriorate and more family members became aware of her condition. I then moved back to North Carolina. Poverty looks different in the south than it does in New York. In New York I still wasn't able to get an apartment, and I wanted my own place. My income has never surpassed clerical wages. They were decent wages for clerical work in New York, but it wasn't quite enough to afford me a home, nor did I have the credit. Living with my stepfather was becoming uncomfortable because I was in one room with my eight-year-old daughter. My mother, when she did come over, was sometimes careless. She had diabetes, so she would prick her finger to check her sugar level; I felt that was an unsafe environment for my daughter. In addition to that, I couldn't find an apartment that would afford me the kind of lifestyle I wanted. I knew if I came back down south I could provide for me and my daughter.

During the time from 1998 'til 2009, my mother would go back and forth, in and out of the hospital. As her immune system was getting weaker, her diabetes and other ailments were coming about. Her lifestyle wasn't good. She wasn't ever a pro-active person. She was more of a reactive individual. She eventually was back in the home and my stepfather moved out; he would come and visit every once in a while. My brother came to live with my mother, and became the caregiver. The fact that I didn't have the funds to visit New York the way I should and needed to, and the fact that a lot of times there wasn't a phone that was kept on in her place. (*Pause.*) The easiest way for me to cope, to live with it, was to think that she had already made the transition to eternity.

Since then, I have always tried the best that I could to maintain a seemingly functional lifestyle for me and my daughter. I learned how to be a mother by watching bits and pieces of other people mothering and what I fantasized a mother should be. I don't want to affect her by my fears. Every decision she makes, I find myself on pins and needles, praying that her choices are wise. I can be judgmental and critical. I'm aware of that; it's a controlling issue I have to work on. I mother, at times, based on fear. I have to work on that on a daily basis. I pray and ask God to wrap His arms around her. I need to love her unconditionally without the fear.

My daughter is nineteen years old. She's made some choices I'm not in agreement with; I have these ideals in my mind. I have to remind myself that my daughter is not my mother. In a strange way, in some kind of way, I place her as my mother, and then I'm her child. And I'm fearful that *this* mother, though I know she's my young-adult child, will make poor choices. I'm thankful she's not on drugs, thankful that she's not pregnant or doesn't have any children out of wedlock. I'm thankful that she is the first generation to go on to a university. Those are things that have helped ground my fears.

I'm going to give you a way-back story: There were times that in my mother's household there wasn't tissues to even wipe yourself after using the bathroom. And there wasn't food at times. That was based on negligence induced by drug addiction. So it wasn't the best life. When I was able to get away, I literally ran, and tried to not ever look back. Nor did I want to, because it was just too much to handle, in a sober, not-saved mind. As a young-adult I was not saved; I wasn't going to church. My mother's mental illness was transferred down to me, and I didn't even know I had mental illness or would accept it as an illness because of the stigma.

I'm not absolute poverty, but I am poverty. I am working poor. Even back then, it wasn't absolute poverty, but it kind of looked and felt like it; there wasn't toilet paper, there wasn't food. In one of the richest cities in the world, it was substandard living conditions, living with her. That has affected my mental health. I can get in a depressive state. Through God's grace I have become aware of ways to cope with depression.

Each time going back to New York was traumatic. It was almost as if I had been in a war. That was another reason why I wouldn't make those trips as often as I maybe should have. In the years that all this occurred, I would make it every once in a while, like maybe every three years. And I would see her totally changed.

My mother, when she passed away Christmas Day 2009, (*pause*) my mother was fifty-seven years old. There's only a sixteen-year span between us, so there's not much of a generation gap. But I saw her missing toes and looking like she was *ninety-five*, and it was enough to send me totally to the edge. I just thank God for the awareness of what I was feeling, what I was looking at, and knowing that there were coping mechanisms. I guess it's the ability to step outside of the situation. (*Pause.*) I don't know how I learned to do that, but I learned how to do it; I stepped away from it. I pray whoever reads this will just know that we have choices – we live and die by the choices we make.

Our value as women is not what we appear to have, but what we have gained in experience. There is something to be said about suffering. Suffering is a wonderful teacher. I've put on my makeup and I dress my pain up with whatever makes me feel pretty, but deep down inside there's so much. The real beauty can be found in sharing the pain.

Even though I had resolved in my mind that my mother had already made the transition, when she truly passed away and she went to meet the Lord, she did not have any insurance; I have not ever been properly able to memorialize my mother. If you could please acknowledge her in your book – her name is Angela.

Exploration – Juracy

1. A strong spiritual foundation helped Juracy cope with the news that her mother had HIV. What role does faith or spirituality play in your ability to get through tough times?

2. After Juracy returned to North Carolina, she told herself that her mother "had already made the transition to eternity." Can you empathize with her need to alter reality?

3. Juracy "learned to be a mother by watching bits and pieces of other people mothering." Who modeled good mothering for you?

4. Because of the poverty and turmoil in which she was raised, Juracy was fearful for her daughter and "on pins and needles" about her decisions. Have you ever found yourself navigating by fear? What are some of the ways you have been able to ground those fears?

5. Juracy equated her mother's drug abuse to a legacy of mental illness. Have unhealthy habits come down the line in your family? Have you been able to break the cycle and live a healthier life than previous generations?

6. Juracy was able to cope with the shock of seeing her mother's deterioration by having awareness of her feelings and "the ability to step outside of the situation." Are these skills you have used for your emotional health?

7. Juracy believed "suffering is a wonderful teacher." Do you agree? What are the most profound lessons suffering has taught you?

8. Wanting us to leave her story with a deeper understanding, Juracy said, "We live and die by the choices we make." How does "choice" factor into your philosophy of life? Do you believe our personal choices are as influential as the environments into which we are born?

Jennifer, 46

Stacy was one of my best friends. Our families vacationed together, our kids played together. We were very, very close. Stacy came from an unstable upbringing and needs a lot of attention, especially from men. So she's naturally flirty. But we all kind of knew that about her, even if she was coming on to your husband, we always assumed it was harmless. Stacy needed to be loved by everybody because she was so insecure.

I used to make excuses and forgive her because she was *fun*. When we moved in I was a working mom and had a little tyke. And you know what? The moms were really mean to me. They don't like working mothers in suburbia, in general, and they were mean. After I had been blackballed in my first attempt to find some friends, Stacy was the first mom that included me and welcomed me in. We were a lot alike; we were the same size, we'd trade clothes, and we both loved to have fun. I was willing to forgive her and make excuses for a lot of things because she was nice to me when nobody else was. I felt very indebted to her because she *was* so nice, when other women weren't.

Our kids were close in age and over the next few years we spent a lot of social time together. I had a fourth baby, and after eighteen months my husband and I decided we needed an au pair; we hired a male au pair because my third son was eight-and-a-half and we thought it would be better for him. We were really hiring the au pair to work with my son on homework and stuff, and to help out with the little guy.

So we hired Miguel; he's twenty-three, adorable, very handsome, very sweet, everybody loves him. He started right around Christmas so I had a post-holiday cocktail party so everybody could meet him. Stacy shows up at the party, a little tipsy, without the wedding ring on, without her husband, and honestly, I don't think any one of us gave it a second thought because her husband is a physician, and he's not around a lot. That very first night, she was all over my au pair. A few people who didn't know her that well commented how inappropriate it was. I said, "Oh, you don't know her; that's just Stacy. She's harmless, don't worry about it."

The party ends and I'm in the living room around two a.m., talking with a few friends, and my cell phone rings. It's a friend of mine who says to me, "You need to send your husband outside." So he's goes outside and sees my girlfriend and the au pair leaning against the car, making out. Some of the couples saw them, which is why they called. My husband comes back in the house and says, "You're not going to believe what I just broke up."

I still, at that point, just chalked it up to Stacy having too much drink, didn't know what she was doing, whatever. And Miguel is new to my family; he doesn't know who she is. He doesn't know she's married with kids. She shows up, no wedding ring on, and a hot little bod. I don't fault him at all, and I don't want to make him uncomfortable in our house 'cause he's so new. So we decide we're just going to deal with this by talking with Miguel. So we sit him down, and say, "You didn't do anything wrong, but here's what you need to know: She has a husband and two kids, and she can be a little flirty, so you just need to know." I figured just letting him know that she was not single, had kids, and is part of the social circle, would be enough of a warning. Mistake number one.

From that point on, she conveniently was always coming to my house. *Always* coming by. And I, at that point, was working part-time. She was *very* clever. She would call me every morning, find out if I was on my way to work, and then she'd miraculously show up at my house. Besides Miguel, I had another babysitter taking care of the baby in the morning. So the babysitter used to call me all the time to tell me that Stacy was coming by, looking for Miguel. It got to the point where Miguel would ask the babysitter to lie to her and say he wasn't home. Stacy was basically stalking him. And this went on for months. He was clearly uncomfortable with her. I did nothing because I still thought, "It's Stacy. It's harmless, she's a flirt." I didn't think of it as stalking at that point. I didn't really pay attention to it.

We're this tight little circle of friends; we hang out on weekends and vacation together. One night, Stacy and our other friend Annie go into the city drinking together. I couldn't go that night. Annie also has an au pair who happens to be good friends with Miguel. My friends lose their car keys and end up calling the two guy au pairs to come get them because it's one-thirty in the morning, they don't have money, they can't get their car home, blah, blah blah. Whatever. The four of them all went back to Annie's house, and Annie ended up going to bed. She woke up at six o'clock in the morning, and Stacy was still there. Annie doesn't give me all the details, but just says what a weird night it was. Stacy says nothing.

So we go into the summer and we're all going on vacation together, to the beach. Annie and her family, Stacy and her family – there were seven families who all vacation together. The week before we go, Annie and her husband Scott call me and say, "We don't think you should bring Miguel to the beach." I was like, "Why? I have a toddler; why should

I pay my au pair to stay home so I have to work?" Scott's like, "Stacy is so flirty; she's always flirting with Miguel. I just think it would be better if you left him home." They're thinking I can read between the lines, but I'm not thinking anything except, "Why the hell should I have to watch my own toddler when I'm paying somebody?" If Stacy wants to flirt with Miguel, that's her husband's problem, not mine. I hung up the phone and didn't think twice; I'm bringing him. This is not my problem.

We drove to the beach and it was *embarrassing*. Everywhere Miguel was, Stacy was. It was really an awful vacation, because every time you turned around, she was missing. It was the joke of the vacation: Where's Stacy? Miguel was doing his job. He was always taking care of my little guy like he was supposed to. But if Miguel was at the house, Stacy was at the house. I figured Stacy was being pretty bold to be doing this in front of her husband, but I still wasn't convinced it was anything more than her typical idle flirting. That's just her M.O. It was stressful because people were so uncomfortable. A couple times her husband made comments to my husband: "Why does Miguel need so much help with the baby?" My husband would say to him, "Miguel doesn't need any help; Miguel's fine. That's Stacy's choice." She was literally ignoring her own kids to be wherever Miguel was, under the guise of helping him. It was *ridiculous*.

We stayed at the beach for two weeks and I don't keep my au pairs the second week. Miguel was scheduled to leave at the end of August, so he went home for the next week to pack and get organized. I told him, "I don't want Stacy in the house. If she shows up, whatever, I do not want her in the house." It was getting too weird.

So we come home and it's time for Miguel to leave and the new au pair, Gunther, to come in, so we do a combined party with my family and Annie's because we had both signed up for new male au pairs. A 'goodbye to the old, welcome to the new' kind of party. That whole week, Stacy kept calling me wanting to know: What were we going to do for Miguel? And was there going to be a party? Finally, I'm like, "Stacy, bring the kids over after dinner. If you want to come by and have dessert and say your goodbyes, that's fine."

She shows up that night dressed to the nines, in this skin-tight little white get-up; no kids of course. Miguel's friend, who he's going to be travelling with, is staying at my house now. She's this very beautiful Spanish girl: Tall, thin, young and *stunning*. And you could see in Stacy's behavior she was very upset. Really upset. She honestly carried on like a jealous girlfriend the night of this party. My new au pair is German and also happens to be very nice looking. So halfway through the party, she attaches herself to my new au pair, typical Stacy flirting. I had to go to bed because I was driving Miguel to the airport at three a.m. So I went to bed at midnight.

The next morning I get up, drive him to the airport, come home and try to wake my daughter up. She's fourteen. I spent forty-five minutes trying to wake this kid up. Finally, Carly picks her head up and says, "I have a headache. I'm exhausted. I was up all night, babysitting your best friend." I looked at her and was like, "Babysitting? What the hell are you talking about?" She looks at me and says, "Mom, she slept with Miguel, and everybody knows it, and I'm not letting her have Gunther." I slapped her across the face. I was like, "How dare you lie and accuse my friend of that." It was awful. She looks at me and she's like, "Mom, everybody knows it but you." I couldn't even believe it. She is mad at me at this point. I'm condemned, because if I knew about it and I let it go on, shame on me, how could I be friends with Stacy's husband? And if I didn't know about it, how could I be such a stupid mother? No matter which way the story goes, I let Carly down. Totally let her down. I leave her room and I'm shaking. I really didn't believe her; I just thought she had gotten emotional and too wound up in it.

I called Annie at work and said, "I have to come over and talk to you and Scott tonight." So I went over that night and I was like, "Carly said something that's really awful, and I don't know where she's coming from, and I need to know." They both looked at me, and they're like, "Oh my God, we are so sorry, Jen. We really thought you knew." I'm looking at them and I'm like, "Knew *what*?" At which point, they unwind the whole story. It comes down to the night of the lost key escapade, when the au pairs had to go claim Annie and Stacy. Annie went to bed but woke up later to noise, and came downstairs and literally caught them in the act on her couch. She threw Stacy out and they sat down and had a serious talk with Miguel. They basically said, "Whatever's going on needs to stop. It's not appropriate, people are going to get hurt; it needs to *stop*." I never really was upset with them for not telling me. I think I felt stupid. They were friends of mine, but they were friends of hers, too, and Stacy is really manipulative. She suckers you into her game. You're so busy feeling sorry for her that you'll do anything to protect her.

I think things died down for a while. And then summer came and Stacy started pursuing him again. He's a guy, and he'll take it if it's offered. They thought I was reading between the lines that summer, but I never got the warning. They apologized for not being more blunt with me. At this point, Scott was like, "You know what? We have to confront *her.* At the end of the day, who's she going to go after next? Obviously she's proven now it's not harmless, there's no line she won't cross. We're all going to have teenage boys soon; where does it end?"

I came home that night and asked Carly how she knew about it. She wouldn't talk to me about it; I couldn't get anything out of her. I ran into one of her close friends later that week and pulled him aside and said, "I need to know what happened at the beach, and how Carly knows." He said, "Carly came up from the beach to go to the bathroom and heard noise in your bedroom. She opened the door and saw Stacy and Miguel having sex." (*Crying.*) That's about as bad as it could get. I don't think a fourteen-year-old's first exposure to anybody having sex should be her mom's best friend and her babysitter. She opened the door, saw what was going on, and closed the door. I'm not sure that Miguel ever knew that she knew. But I'll tell you she hates him, with a vengeance. She won't talk to him when he calls. This all unfolded after he finished his job and was on the plane. So luckily for him, he wasn't here. And thank God, because my kids loved him. He was such a part of the family. Other than this major faux pas, they loved him. He was such a positive influence in their lives, I don't even want them knowing about any of this.

At the end of the day, I used it as a lesson with Carly on how boys operate. I said, "I'll be honest, teenage boys and young men – they think with their penises. They just do. And you know what? At some point, if it's thrown at them so many times, and they're not getting it anywhere else, they're going to take it." I said, "Do I think Miguel did the wrong thing? Yes, I'm extremely disappointed in him, because he should have known better. But if he wanted to have an affair with a married lady, he's twenty-three-years-old, not twelve. What am I going to do?" I said, "But there is no excuse for Stacy. It's inexcusable that she could do that to me, to my family, to her husband. It's wrong, and I don't understand her."

It took a lot of effort to get Carly to start talking to me about it. Because she was really mad at me, for being stupid. And how could I be Stacy's friend? I'm still trying to process it all in my own brain. I'm trying to not upset the apple cart. I pulled away from Stacy and tried to not have too much to do with her. We did sit our new au pair down and read him the riot act. We basically told him, "Here's the deal: If we catch her on your cell phone, catch her in this house, catch any communication between the two of you, you're back on the plane to Germany. We have zero tolerance for a friendship with that woman." So I wised up with the next one. Because Stacy was doing convenient little coy things, like, "Oh, my son just started taking German. I was thinking Gunther could come over and tutor him." Very convenient ways to be friends with a nice little German boy.

I couldn't confront her. She was one of my good friends. I don't know how to let go of a good friend. I was stunned and hurt and I honestly didn't know what to do. There was a group of us, like six couples, that had gotten to be very good friends, very close. Part of the Stacy psyche is that all the time she's, "Woe is me! I'm not happy with my marriage; my husband doesn't pay attention to me, and you don't know what it's like." She worked us all for a long time. I swear to God, I think everybody would've forgiven Stacy for almost anything, 'cause we felt so bad for her. Here's my thing: I have a daughter who says, "How can you be friends with her? Are you kidding me? And you're going to look her husband in the eye?"

I got stuck between a rock and a hard place. I was scared to death of losing my circle of friends, which was a big comfort zone to me. Or lose my daughter. But it was going to be one of them. I didn't know what to *do*. But I stalled, of course, on the confrontational front, because I didn't even know what to say to Stacy. As much as I knew what was true now, I still didn't want to believe she could do this to her family. The fact that they had sex in my room, in the beach house – it was *disgusting* to me. That she would do that, in my own room. It was the worst kind of betrayal.

I was quietly trying to figure this out in my own head, and not tell any of our friends, because I didn't want to lose them. I was trying to pull away from Stacy without losing the whole circle of friends. I still saw her in our group but I pulled back from the one-on-one stuff. I made up excuses a lot for being busy and not having time for her. I had as little contact as I could. I didn't want to deal with it because I knew it wasn't going to be good. Annie and I were trying to figure out how to sit her down and deal with this. Scott's whole point was that she couldn't come back to the beach. He got tired of waiting for us to get our act together, so he picks up the phone and calls her, and basically says, "We need to talk because I really don't think you should be coming back to the beach." The conversation didn't go well and he got very frustrated with her. He finally said, "I know you slept with Miguel. We all know you slept with Miguel." She hung up the phone on him.

This is how clever she is: She goes to her husband, and plays the "They're so mean. They don't want us there because I drink so much, blah, blah, blah" card. She then proceeds to call the circle of friends and says, "Woe is me. Jen and Scott are so horrible. I've worked so hard on fixing things with my husband, and we were just getting in a great place, and now Jen is threatening to ruin it all." So all of a sudden, I get phone calls from our friends: "What the hell is wrong with me? When am I going to apologize to Stacy? Do I have any idea how much stress I've put her under?"

I still wasn't ready to blow the whistle on her, but Scott was. He had also gotten a bunch of nasty phone calls. He had no qualms discussing everything that went down. Some people chose to believe Scott, but there are a few who still think Carly and I cooked this all up. This was why the hurt got worse. It's bad enough that I was an idiot of a parent, defending one of my best friends to my own child, but now the circle got broken, irreparably broken. All I would say to people was, "You have no idea the stress I am under with my own daughter. My family has been ripped to shreds right now. All I can focus on is fixing my family." I can't worry about Stacy and her husband. I don't care about that marriage; I care about my own marriage, and my kids.

The friends in the circle proved to be very shallow. It's as though they were mad because I upset the status quo, and now we can't all have fun and make light of the world any more. But at some point you have to be parents. The fun was going to end anyway. It would've ended when Stacy slept with someone's son or husband. Fast-forward nine months later: Stacy had another affair, with her neighbor. She busted that marriage apart and is now divorcing her husband. She imploded; it happened all over again, and she *really* hurt people this time. And it's not that there's been any mea culpas coming back my way: "Oh I'm sorry Jen, that we ever said you'd make up anything."

The social scene getting blown up was so painful to me. When you live in suburbia, it's so cliquey. Everyone has their little groups. I no longer have the Friday night happy-hour crowd. And you can't really explain to anybody why. You were always part of a group, and now a faction of that group is still together, but you're not there. We were outliers. People look at you and say, "I thought you were friends with that whole group." And what are you supposed to say? Which is why this is such a hard secret to live with. It was very painful. One couple we used to see have a Tiki bar and a pool; life was always fun. I lost my Superbowl party and my Fourth of July party and my Labor Day party. I let myself get too safe and comfortable in that little circle of people. It was a mistake on my part because I don't belong in a world that small. I've made some new friends, but we're still outliers.

When Stacy finally found out that Carly knew, she didn't care. There was never an apology from her. Stacy is only out for Stacy. After all this was blown up, I finally wrote her a letter. And I wrote a letter, not an e-mail because I didn't want anything cut and pasted, played with and forwarded. I hand-wrote a letter and gave the scenario of events, because I wanted her to know how hurt I was, and what she did to Carly. Her response was, "I'll stay away from your family." She's an extreme narcissist. I don't miss her. I don't miss the drama. I'm closer to my kids because I care more about what's going on inside this house than I do in a bigger crowd of adults.

I apologized to Carly. And I think, long term, it helped us. We *had* to talk about sex. We *had* to talk about friendships. And we *had* to talk about all these other really ugly topics. And you know what? I'm not perfect. She saw me go through a lot of pain with my friend. It absolutely brought us closer, once she got through the anger. When you're young you think your parents are infallible.

I have to be not so totally trusting. Stacy exhibited outright signs that I dismissed. You can't just assume that everybody is good. I was so caught up in making excuses for her behavior, that even when other people would say things to me, I would defend *her* and her crappy behavior. That's how she's been successful for forty-some-odd years. I call her "the black widow." She spins you in, and you get so caught in her web you'd do anything for her. I should've been smarter about that.

Exploration – Jennifer

1. When Jennifer first moved in, she felt "blackballed" in her attempts to make friends. She said, "They (other women) don't like working mothers in suburbia...and they were mean." Have you ever felt ostracized due to your employment status? Are there biases in your community regarding whether women work inside or outside the home?

2. Because Stacy was fun and openly welcomed Jennifer, she felt indebted and would "make excuses" for Stacy's behavior. Are there friends in your life to whom you've felt indebted? Did you make allowances for them that you wouldn't have normally extended to others?

3. Jennifer's friends suggested that she not bring Miguel to the beach because of Stacy's flirting. Jennifer was adamant about having his help and decided he would join them. She justified her decision by saying, "If Stacy wants to flirt with Miguel, that's her husband's problem, not mine." Do you agree with Jennifer's rationale? How would you have handled the situation?

4. When Carly told her mom that Stacy and Miguel had sex, Jennifer slapped Carly's face and said, "How dare you lie and accuse my friend of that." How do you feel about Jennifer's reaction?

5. With regard to the clandestine relationship, Jennifer was less judgmental of Miguel than Stacy. Jennifer said, "He's a guy, and he'll take it if it's offered." And later, "...young men – they think with their penises...At some point, if

it's thrown at them so many times, and they're not getting it anywhere else, they're going to take it." Do you agree with her assessment of male sexuality? Was Stacy more culpable than Miguel?

6. After she learned of the affair, Jennifer framed her dilemma as either losing her friends or losing her daughter. Do you see the problem in the same way?

7. Jennifer felt betrayed by Stacy, but could not confront her. If Jennifer were your friend, how would you suggest she handle the situation?

8. Losing her circle of friends was very painful, and Jennifer perceived herself as an "outlier" among the suburban cliques. Have you had the experience of losing an entire group of friends? How did you rebound?

9. Jennifer referred to Stacy as "the black widow," saying, "She spins you in, and you get so caught in her web you'd do anything for her." Can you empathize with Jennifer's feelings of being manipulated? Have you ever been involved in a similar kind of friendship?

Mary, 66

I'm an only child. My mom had... I think it was three misses before she had me. And in having me, her placenta broke and she had toxemia. I think she had the Last Rites two or three times. By the time she was released and just getting on her feet, I was thriving and doing well. I was about eight or nine months old, I was just beginning to stand, and she brought me into the doctor and casually mentioned, "The baby is walking on her toes on her left foot. Is that anything to worry about?" It was very offhanded. He took some x-rays and it turns out I had no hip socket. I had nothing there; I didn't have the socket, I didn't have the ball. So what they did was to put me in the hospital. Now, this is after she had just finished recovering. I think I was in for five months. I was put in a frog-like cast on both legs. They didn't do surgery, thank God, because there was no such thing as replacements at the time. But they pitted whatever was there against one another, bone on bone, and after that long a period of time, it made a little groove. Certainly not a ball and socket, but a groove. And that did last, not without pain, through thirty-one years and two natural births.

My mom was a very private, rigid person. She was a perfectionist. If she knitted, she knitted straight through for thirteen hours and then didn't understand why her hands were all cramped up. If she did needlepoint, you could frame either side, truly. My father, on the other hand, was very gregarious, very open, very outgoing, and very personable. Kind of like an emcee personality. He was so different from her. Early on, I knew there was tension with her, but not with him. My dad was not around all that much; he was working. He had a political job, a lower-level political job in the city, but there were dinners and meetings. So I spent more time with my mother, but *loved* to be with him, because it was, of course, easier.

She was going to make me perfect. In her way, she adored me – in her way. I felt that I could not live up to her expectations, and to this day I cannot hold a needle in my hand. She was a finisher on very expensive dresses as a young woman in Little Italy. I don't hold a needle in my hand. I don't knit or do any of those things she did so beautifully. I guess I just did not want to put myself in that position, to be criticized. I was always a good student, not cum laude, but a good student as a youngster. If I came home with a ninety-eight, she would scold me: "If you could get a ninety-eight you could have gotten one-hundred, with a little bit of effort!" And that was very crushing.

My mother was very quiet. She always took a back seat. Not because she was shy in the sense of shy and sweet; it was more that she really didn't have people skills. She took a back seat, but she was watching all the time. They'd go to political dinners, he would work the room, she would sit back. I don't ever remember my mother saying that her friend was so-and-so. She didn't have any friends. If she recognized that somebody did her a good deed, she was then compelled and pressured to top that so she wouldn't owe that woman anything, not even friendship. She was polite to people, but never extended herself. Now these were all things that I recognized as I was growing up.

When the grandchildren came to visit, she would always sit back, and if the grandchildren did not go up and acknowledge her, kiss her, immediately, she was put out. And then everybody knew she was annoyed. She took umbrage at things so fast, so quickly, so unnecessarily. Recognizing that, I consciously have gone out of my way as a grandmother and mother-in-law, not to put pressure on people. "If you'd like to come to dinner, that would be great. If not, I understand you're tired." Sunday was always Sunday dinner. I walk into my grandkids' homes and shout, "Where's my babies?" She would never do that; she *couldn't* do it.

The only thing my mother really enjoyed, believe it or not, was the casino. I would take her there on day trips. One Mother's Day, when my son was about fourteen, he went out of his way to buy gifts for the two grandparents. For my mother-in-law, he bought a little plaque that said "Grandma," and for my mother, he bought a very cute ceramic piggy bank to put her quarters in, so when she went to Atlantic City she'd have them all there. She was outraged. She says, "How dare he! The other one gets a plaque, and me, he's telling me to go save money?" She twisted everything.

I was in a private high school, and in sophomore year I was put in an honors program. I had made friends with a gal freshman year and she signed my book after sophomore year. She had written something like, "I hope you're not in the honors program next year," meaning, "then we can be together," because she wasn't in that program. My mom was *furious* that I did not see this girl was putting the evil eye on me. (*Pause.*) It was hard as a child – especially since I was alone. If I had had a sibling it wouldn't have been so isolating. It was an intense environment.

I started to gain some insight into her when I was in college and taking some psychology courses, and even more so when I was teaching. I taught kids who had real problems at home with alcoholism and parents who leave. My principal was taken aback one time when I talked to a girl whose mom was an alcoholic and dad had left. I said, "Janie, your mom loves you. She loves you in her way. She's got her own demons she's dealing with. She does love you as best she can." (*Crying.*)

I was fortunate I was able to come out of it. Maybe because of my background, I can see the other person's situation, that side of the story. I had to find contentment to survive. I remember one time telling my mother, with one of these tests that was a ninety-eight, and she was angry that I didn't see it her way; I remember so well, where we were, and telling her, almost in a joke – I wasn't challenging her, "Mom, I'm normal. I'm not perfect like cousin Betty. She's a nut. She's crazy." My mother kind of laughed because she knew I was right. "I get a ninety-eight, but I'm happy. I'm happy! Aunt Margaret's got a crazy daughter, you got a happy daughter." I remember trying to explain it.

She had judgment about everything. And very much the glass is half empty. She was the first child of five children that my grandmother had. There were three other sisters and one boy in the middle, who was the Second Coming. I've heard my grandmother was a taskmaster but openhearted. My mother's memories of her childhood were colored by her visions of everything being negative: She was the oldest; she had to do everything; everything was expected of her. But I think the strongest influence was her own negativity.

My mother was very bright in school at a time when people weren't really valuing education for girls. One year, she had a male teacher who she just didn't like. She shut down and would do no work whatsoever. She dropped out of school. I think it was her mental health issues. Her sister is ninety-six now, goes to Bingo three times a week; she laughs at everything. I tell her she's my hero. Yet in school, she was supposed to be the dummy. I think by the grace of God I was able to understand

and have the ability to see my mother as she was, and work around that. I don't know where that came from but it was a survival technique for me.

I hated the holidays as a young adult. There was such measuring; you were five minutes *here*, but you were seven minutes *there*. I hated, hated the holidays. When she passed, I consciously said, "I'm never gonna do this to my kids." I make an effort not to put pressure on my kids. I could have gone either way, but I was fortunate, for some reason, to be able to see... I see now what I was doing was recognizing that it was *her* problem. I recognized as a youngster she never had a friend, never cared to have a friend. She was judging all the time.

She died in '96. She had dementia. I had remained very close with her. My father died in 1985 of Alzheimer's. He was seventy-six and she was seventy-three. She lived in the area, and every day after school I would go over and spend a couple hours with her, made sure she ate. She came to my house on the weekends, but I had to make sure she ate during the week. You know it's funny; once we finally moved her in with us after she had some mini-strokes, she lost her anxiety. She was easier to be with during the early stages of dementia. She had lost that anxiety, the hardness. You weren't standing on tippy-toes with her.

Through friends, I met a psychic last winter. We were at my friend's home and after a while the psychic said to me, "When you walked in, your father came through to me very strong." I looked at her. She asked if I wanted her to continue and I said yes. "He's up front, he's got a big smile... But I don't see your mom. Your mom passed? There's a woman sitting in the back, but she's just sitting there and not talking, not approaching." I said, "That would be my mother; sitting, not coming forward." The psychic asked if I had recently had big medical problems, and I told her I was recovering from having my spine fused. She said, "Your dad wants you to know he was there with you." (*Crying.*) My mother was just in the background. Then again, that's her. She can't help it. She is who she is.

Exploration – Mary

1. After her mother had three miscarriages and a round with toxemia that required Last Rites, Mary was born, and soon showed signs of a serious hip problem. Why do you think she opened her story in this way?

2. Her dad was "very, very different" from her mom, and Mary remembered that she "loved to be with him, because it was, of course, easier." Are your parents very different from each other? Is it easier for you to be with one more than the other?

3. Mary was scolded for her almost perfect test scores and remembered feeling crushed. Is there a perfectionist in your life? How has knowing that person affected you?

4. Mary's mother had no real friends, and even had trouble accepting a "good deed" from someone. What did you learn about friendship from your parents? Are your friendships similar?

5. Her mom often "took umbrage at things so fast" that Mary made a conscious decision to interact with her family in a completely different way. Have you made similar decisions based on the way you were raised?

6. A student's problem helped Mary identify with her own mother and find some compassion. Mary counseled Janie, "She's got her own demons she's dealing with. She does love you as best she can." Has another person's challenge helped you come to terms with your own struggle?

7. From a young age, Mary had an awareness that it was her mom's issues more than her own that were causing unhappiness. Can you empathize with this early emotional maturity? What other gifts do you think could spring from a childhood like Mary's?

8. Mary had a complex relationship with her mother that moved between anger and compassion. What is the most complex relationship in your life? Which emotions best define it?

9. Mary described her mother's biggest challenge as "her own negativity." Do you believe negativity is innate? Are there any members of your family who seem hard-wired toward a glass-half-empty outlook?

10. Looking back, Mary felt that if she had not been an only child, her situation would have been easier. Have your siblings made challenges with your parents easier or more complicated?

Karen, 49

W hen I was born, I was to be the son for my father. And
that was taken literally, because the nurse accidentally
told my father that I was a boy. She was almost fired over that
one. When they found out the nurse's mistake, my mom would
tell me that he was *totally* disappointed and made it his point
that I was going to be the son and that he would raise me as
the son. I'm the second born; I have two sisters. That's basically
how that all started. Ever since then I was the son of the family.

I can remember living on the military bases all through
my childhood. We covered a lot of places: Maine, Wisconsin,
Michigan, Bermuda, New Jersey and Pennsylvania. I think we
moved about every year. My father was an alcoholic. I believe
the drinking started in the military, and my mother drank, too.
There would be times, on several occasions, that they would get
into altercations.

My first memory is that on the bases, there was always
some kind of gathering going on after he would get home from
work. Card games, dancing, anything with drinking, in the
home. It was not a fun time because some of the times were
school nights. Most of the times, because he loved his *daughters,*
we were brought out of bed to perform, to sing and dance for
the friends. Mom was drinking and part of that, too. He would
showcase us. "Come look at my girls, my girls are this, my girls
are that. *This* is my boy. Nurse told me I had a boy." My mom
would be like, "Stop that, she's a girl." At that time, it didn't

really bother me because I was getting the special attention – I was the boy.

My father worked a lot. He was a cook and baker. My mother stayed home, but she did some work in the canning factory, or she worked odds and ends, but most of the time she was home with us. I don't remember her drinking during the day; I just remember it at night. It was a nightly occurrence. He would come home from work, and that would be his thing – he would drink. Or he would be drinking on the job. There would be many a time where the MPs would call her and she'd have to go get him, or he'd get reprimanded for being drunk at work.

I became aware of the drinking when the abuse started – when the arguing and the fighting started. Because with the drinking, we'd be, "Oh, Dad's drunk. Everybody get in bed, keep quiet. Don't make a ruckus, get him stirred up." But then they would get into it over something simple, they would actually start physically fighting, and that's when it's no longer "Dad's drinking." It's, "This is serious, he's hurting mom," that kind of thing. I would go in my room and cover my head with a pillow so I wouldn't have to hear it. It was very upsetting, very upsetting. Because I thought he was going to hurt her. I don't remember her being in the hospital or anything, but I can *vividly* remember blood on the walls, I can vividly remember her face being swollen, I can vividly remember her patching up her face before she went out, police being called all the time. Shoving and pushing in front of us. Lots of verbal abuse: "You don't know anything; you'll never know anything; you can't do this, you can't do that…" That kind of stuff. There were many times when she would cook dinner and he would throw the food on the floor and make her get down and pick it up.

Sometimes at night he would come home in a drunken stupor and pull everything out of the cabinets in the kitchen, and wake us up on a school night and make us clean the kitchen. Or make us clean the living room. Or make us clean something. That was his thing. He had a little OCD going on there. If we protested, he wouldn't hit us, but he would whack us in the head. So he would pull that kind of stuff. Mom would say, "You need to leave those girls alone. They got to go to school in the morning." And he would tell her to shut up, and we would say, "Mom, don't." You don't want to get it started. You would do what you had to do to keep the peace.

When the fighting was bad, I had my own little record player and I liked gospel music, so I would play my record player, loudly. Or turn up the TV, loudly. As I got older, I started going out the windows to the neighbor's when they would fight. I have gone out many a window to the neighbor next door, looking for refuge. The people in the neighborhood knew, the people at the bases knew, when we got out of the military people knew that they were always at it. When I was in high school, I ended up going to church a lot with this one family. Did a lot of prayin', a lot of prayin'. Just prayin' to try to understand what was going on.

My dad was a totally different person when he was sober. He was really nice. Being the boy, he bought me my first softball mitt. He got me into sports, would throw the ball with me. We did a lot of fishing; fishing was his thing. If he had neighborhood friends come over when he was sober, I would be the one who could stay in the room with his friends, because I was the son. He was very stern, all about school, all about your chores, and there was no talk about his drinking, not at all. And there was no talking with her about the drinking. It was really about marching to his orders.

As I got a little older, I became a tomboy. I started hanging out with the boys and didn't want to dress up for church. No heels, no pantyhose, no girly stuff. My mom would always get on me: "You need to put a dress on, you need to stop hangin' with those boys." I was getting conflicting messages from them. I was a softball player from grade school all the way up through college, and outside of college. I don't remember my dad or my mom attending any of the games. You kind of become numb to it.

I'm starting to get a little attention in high school from the boys but not really wanting that attention because I'm not interested in them. There was no talk about sex with my mom, no sitting down and having questions answered. The whole reproductive stuff came from school. But the whole dating and boys and all that stuff, I don't remember that talk ever happening with my mom. I remember she always used to think that that's what was going on because I was always hanging out with the guys, but that's not what was happening. She threatened me: "I'm going to put you in a girls' home because you don't never come home." But sex just wasn't on my radar; it didn't cross my mind. I was still Dad's son.

My mom slowed down her drinking when I was in high school. She was getting older, and we were getting older and really realizing what's going on. And he was still going out drinking and falling down. He was out of the military by then, trying to find work. He found a job in a little café. Sometimes we would see him, sometimes we wouldn't see him. Sometimes he would come home, sometimes he wouldn't come home. We never knew. Most of the times when he came home, he was drunk. Even when he wasn't drinking, they would still argue and get into big fights. Nobody's discussing anything. My older sister was already out, so it was just me and the youngest. Sometimes we're home together, sometimes we're not. I'd be at a neighbor's and she'd be at a cousin's house.

As all that was going on, one thing I remember that really bothered me comes to mind. I remember them having sex one night, and she called out somebody's name, and he beat her for that. And I was so angry, so mad. I remember him slapping her around, saying, "What are you doing? Who the hell is that?" And then the next day, he was sober, never remembered what he did or anything.

Without a doubt, he always provided for us. We never wanted for anything. School clothes, school books, whatever. Sometimes he read to us at night, but mostly it was her. So we had that solid unit; with all that other chaos, we were taken care of. I think mostly I did feel loved. Mostly from her – not from him because I never knew what mindset he was in. There was not much physical affection. I knew my mom loved me by her actions, her wanting the best for us.

My father died when I was seventeen, and he was only forty-two years old. He died in his sleep right next to her after a drunken stupor the night before. But no beating; just the drunken stupor the night before. That week was the first and only altercation I had with him drinking. I remember pushing him down the stairs. I do remember that. I don't know what was going on, I don't remember what was said, but I remember getting into some kind of altercation and he was drunk, and I remember pushing him, and I remember him going down the stairs head first. I think he was trying to do something to her. At that point, I had had enough. I was angry, I had had enough, and I was older, and I was like, "We're not going to allow you to do this anymore. It's enough of this, *enough*." And I remember her tending to him, getting him back up. At that point, I said to my mom, "Why do you continue to let this happen?" She didn't have an answer. He got up, she got him together, and I think I went to the neighbor's. He died the next day of a pulmonary edema.

I was home when he died. She got up in the morning and said, "Your dad's not moving," and we're like, "What's wrong with him?" 'Cause you know, hey, we're just like, enough of this. And there were times when we would say we wish he would die, wish he would go away and not come back. She said, "He won't wake up; I can't move him." And, he was cold, I remember that. And then we called the ambulance and they came and got him. I don't even remember her being upset. It was kind of like a calm kind of thing, but it was sad. It was like we knew that was coming eventually. He used to have seizures, but he never went to the hospital to find out what was causing them. But all of it was tied to the alcoholism.

After the funeral, there was some relief because I left for college. I thought, "I am so done with this." I was older and didn't have to deal with it anymore. There was a lot of frustration with my mom. I think she meant well, but there's alcoholism in her family, and I think a lot comes from there. She was young when she married my dad, and she didn't have an education; he had the education. She wanted to get out of her situation at home. And she had these kids, and I think she just got bogged down, and I think she just let him *rule* the roost.

When I was getting ready to go to college, I basically opened the book, picked out a school and went. I had a mentor, a friend, who was my freshman year high school teacher, who was my guidance at the time. She carried me all the way through, and we're still friends today. She took me under her wing. My sisters stayed in the area; I'm the only one who left. (*Pause.*) Too many bad memories.

It wasn't until I started taking psychology and sociology courses that I really started to understand what was going on in my life back then. I actually took a class and had to write a paper, and decided to write about alcoholism. I chose to interview my mother and asked, "Mom, why, why would you let this happen all these many years?" That's when I learned about what she grew up with.

I think, growing up in that chaos, I learned resilience, because the one thing he instilled in us was not to depend on anybody else. It was like a double standard with him: I'm doing this, but I'm telling you that. I remember when he got out of the military and we drove from Maine back to New Jersey, he made us map out the whole trip. We drove the exact route we mapped out. He made us recite his Social Security number; a lot of little things like that. I learned how to depend on myself.

Even when I started college I was not interested in having a relationship. With my parents, absolutely, I see that's where that comes from: not trusting people, not liking being around people who drink, not liking any kind of altercations, not liking arguments. That was in college, but it still goes for today. Relationships are still a challenge for me.

I would say that the whole trust in relationships has been difficult. I found myself mimicking his OCD behaviors in my second marriage. "Don't touch that, that's mine. This has to be a certain way, that has to be a certain way." Things had to be in order, and I was driving him crazy. We went to counseling and I realized I was doing what my dad was doing around the house – trying to control. Both marriages ended in infidelity on their part, but I own a part of them failing. I've spent a good amount of time in counseling so I can learn about my piece, and take responsibility for it. I learned a lot about me. I'm at the point where I don't tolerate too much from anybody. I know what I want in a relationship, I know what I don't want, I know when something's not good for me. I know how to set my boundaries and I'm a very straightforward type person, which is sometimes hard for people to take because they're not used to you saying what's on your mind. I've learned from counseling to do more filtering. I've gotten myself in trouble not taking into consideration people's feelings. That's a thing that's constantly in my mind – courtesy for other people. I'm working on the sensitivity.

Coming out of the tomboyish thing and into the feminine thing – I wouldn't say it was tough, but it was challenging, because I wanted the affection and attention, wanted the sex, and wanted somebody to take care of me, but I don't want to tell you that, don't want to show you that. And being raised as a boy, you're not supposed to cry, you're not supposed to show feelings. So when I'm in a relationship with a man, you're hiding that. You have your guard up all the time; it's exhausting. I can talk about my feelings now, but there are still some times I revert back – it's a protection thing. I am definitely a product of my past, and what I've gone through is now my weakness and my strength.

Exploration – Karen

1. Karen knew that her dad "was totally disappointed" she had been born a girl. Taking into account her heightened status as "the son," how do you feel about her dad's decision to raise Karen as a boy? Were you welcomed into your family for who you were?

2. When their parents drank and entertained at home, the girls would sometimes be "brought out of bed" to perform for guests. Were you ever put on display in your family? How did that make you feel?

3. Karen had some effective coping techniques when she heard her parents fighting: covering her head with a pillow, blasting her record player, sneaking out her window, and praying. Did you grow up with domestic violence? How did you cope? (If not, were you aware of friends or neighbors who dealt with this issue?)

4. Karen said, "My dad was a totally different person when he was sober. He was really nice." What role did alcohol play in your family? Were you aware of personality changes when your parents would drink?

5. Softball was an important part of Karen's life from grade school beyond college. She recalled, "I don't remember my dad or my mom attending any of the games. You kind of become numb to it." Why do you think she used the word "numb"? Was your family supportive of your interests and talents?

6. Even in the chaos of her home, Karen felt the family was "a solid unit" and that she was "taken care of." She said, "I knew my mom loved me by her actions, her wanting the best for us." How was love expressed in your family? Is the way you now show love different from the way you were raised?

7. Karen stepped into the "son" role when she intervened in a physical altercation between her parents and pushed her father down the stairs. She remembered thinking, "We're not going to allow you to do this anymore. It's enough of this, *enough*." How did you feel reading about that event? If you had been in her shoes, would you have responded in a similar way?

8. In reflecting on her father's death the following day, Karen said, "There were times when we would say we wish he would die, wish he would go away and not come back." No one in the family seemed upset that he would not wake up. Can you empathize with their feelings of relief? Have you ever wished that someone in your life "would go away and not come back"?

9. Later in her life, Karen explored her mother's role in their family chaos, and learned about her unhealthy childhood. Do you empathize with Karen's mother in the same way you feel for the daughters?

10. Karen felt she learned independence and resilience from growing up in her family. She credited some of her dad's more involved moments (such as letting the girls map the driving route), in teaching her independence. What else

do you think influenced her sense of being strong and capable?

11. Issues of control, trust and emotional vulnerability remain big challenges for Karen. She said, "I am definitely a product of my past, and what I've gone through is now my weakness and my strength." Do you hold your painful childhood experiences as both a burden and a gift? Does one view hold more sway than the other?

Jasmine, 22

It was junior year of college, so I was just twenty-one. I lived in a house with five other girls. The last girl to come into the house was April. I didn't know her, but another roommate did, through sorority stuff, and said she was a really cool person. So six of us were posted up in this big house, and we each had our own room, which was nice because we had a lot of space.

In the beginning of the year, April was talking about getting a dog, and we had discussed it before she was even in the plans, and decided that it would be a lot of responsibility and didn't want to do it. But when she brought it up and was like, "Okay, I'll get it, no problem," we were like, "All right, cool. Let's get a dog." So she went out and bought a five-hundred-dollar dog from somewhere on the internet, and brought it back, and it was the cutest thing *ever*, and we were all really excited. Because April bought it, she was like, "Yeah, it'll totally be my responsibility. I'll pay for everything and take care of it." That lasted about five minutes until she went out shopping right after she dropped it off at home.

So all semester, pretty much, it was me taking care of the dog ninety-five percent of the time, my best friend Leah probably three percent of the time, and random others the rest. Not only did April have classes all day, but she was also in a sorority and decided that was more important than the dog. Oh, and she had a job. She was never around for this puppy she had just bought, and it was not house-trained. I was like, "Okay, we need to train this thing. I don't want it pissing all over the house." So I went to the public library and got training books and videos.

In that house, we had to hold meetings, because clearly, women cannot communicate with each other, successfully, in any way. I was getting pretty fed up and said, "Everyone needs to be here at nine o'clock." I handed out the training videos and manuals and said, "Get crackin'! This dog is not going to train itself and it's peeing all over our floor." It was sitting in its crate, literally pooping and rolling in it all day. I don't think anyone besides me even looked at the house-training material.

April would leave every morning at six. She'd feed the dog, and that was it. I'd get up and have to take it out for walks. It's a puppy, so it clearly can't handle being inside for more than an hour without peeing itself. My schedule was different from my roommates because my first class wasn't until eleven. So I'd wake up at nine, and that was the time I tried to get my work done, before class. When you have a dog chewing on your toes and peeing all over the house it's really hard to get anything done.

We weren't supposed to have a dog in the house; that would've cost us an extra five-hundred-dollars, so the pet was a secret. Our neighbors weren't allowed to see it either, so I couldn't flaunt around in our yard with the dog. I'd have to take it up the hill and run around with it. When I was home, pretty much my whole day revolved around the dog. Eventually, we got this indoor fence thing for her, so instead of being in her crate and rolling in her mess, she could go in multiple places and not have to sit in her own pee. It was disgusting; the dog smelled like pee all the time. In this fenced-in area there would clearly be poop and puddles of pee, and no one would clean it up. People would just walk by it. I would come home and there'd be multiple piles. This animal was cooped up all day; I *couldn't* just sit there at home and not take care of it. It ended up being up my problem. I was really stressed. Besides my schoolwork, I was the president of club soccer and had a life. But apparently April's life was more important.

By the end of the semester, I knew I would be going abroad in the spring, and Leah was going to have a long internship. Leah and I talked about things all the time because we felt like April was being completely irresponsible; it was out of control. We decided, "Yeah, we need to sit down and talk to her." April had agreed when she bought the dog, if it didn't work, she would give it to her mom. She agreed to this. So Leah and I were like, "OK, this is what needs to happen," since we were the only two people doing anything with this dog.

Leah and I let her know how upset we were that we got the burden of being responsible for the dog the whole time. Right away April starts making excuses, saying, "That was not your job. The dog was fine." I'm like, "You're right, it's fine to have your dog sitting in its own crap all day. Very responsible." I had asked her to help before, but this was me saying, "This is over; I'm sorry, no one's going to take care of your dog." It was stupid of me to do it the whole time, because I suffered for that, and she was like, "Whatever, I'm going to my sorority." I mean, I love the dog but it was just out of control.

During the house meeting, one of the girls refused to come out of her room because she felt like we were ganging up on April. I was like, "You know what? This is her responsibility. I'm sorry if it looks that way to you. I'm sorry – but I'm *pissed* and I'm done being friendly about it. I'm leaving the country, and I'm the only one taking care of the dog, so she really needs to give it to her mom." April starts having the biggest hissy fit I've ever seen. She was stomping on the floor and crying hysterically. And she was getting super defensive and denying everything that had happened over the past four months. Because the dog's *alive*, she thinks she's been responsible!

April runs off to her room, sobbing, and spends like twenty minutes bawling to her mom on the phone. Then she comes back upstairs with her blanket wrapped around her, and takes a seat on the floor. She tries to explain to us that she can handle this, she can do it, she knows she's been pretty bad about it, but she's going to turn everything around. Leah and I are pretty good judges of character, so we're sitting there like, "This is bullshit." The whole time I'm worried for the dog. The poor dog is going to die. I'm like, "I'm sorry, I don't believe you. We've talked to you about changing your ways and taking care of your own dog, and you've done nothing. April, it's a living thing. I'm sorry you feel like you've been doing a good job, but you haven't. Clearly, this isn't working out."

After that huge blowup, it was really awkward to live with her. I had liked her as a person, but after this, I hated her for what she was doing to the dog, so I just didn't want to be around her.

A short time later, I go abroad, and maybe two or three weeks after that, I get an e-mail from Leah telling me the dog went to April's mom, because April could not take care of it, and finally realized it for herself. Yup. I had to laugh. How much could I see *that* coming? Winnie got to be outside and have interaction with their other dog. Winnie's really skittish; I'm sure it's because she was so neglected.

This is kind of sad, but I learned that I shouldn't rely on most people, and maybe not have much faith in people. It was kind of naïve of us to say, "Yeah, let's let this girl, who we don't really know, bring a living thing into our house." I mistakenly trusted she would be true to her word and take care of it – that this wouldn't be a burden on me; that it would work out.

Something else I learned is that I'm somewhat passive-aggressive and that kind of screws me sometimes. The whole time I was taking care of that dog, yeah, I'd say things once in a while, but every day I'd be angry about it. Every day I'd be upset that this ended up being my job. But then again, I'd just go do it. When it came down to it, I sucked it up and did it, and didn't confront her 'til the end of the semester. I've realized, in a lot of aspects, not just in this situation, I do that quite often. For some reason, confrontation is hard for me.

I feel like I have gotten better at confronting, but it still takes me a while to get worked up enough to do it. When something happens, I need to address it the first time, talk to somebody about it way earlier. I think a lot of times when I confront people, it's because I'm pissed off. When I'm pissed off it's not good. I think my mom does the same thing too. She'll keep it in, and then all of a sudden blow up. So I think if I could kind of deal with it in the moment, it would work better.

Exploration – Jasmine

1. While in her communal living situation, Jasmine came to the conclusion that "women cannot communicate with each other, successfully, in any way." What are your beliefs about the ways women communicate? What experiences shaped your opinion?

2. Jasmine opined, "When you have a dog chewing on your toes and peeing all over the house it's really hard to get anything done...When I was home, pretty much my whole day revolved around the dog." When did you first realize the enormity of caring for another life? What were the biggest challenges?

3. Because the dog was being neglected, Jasmine took responsibility for its well-being. She spoke of her outside obligations and said, "But apparently April's life was more important." Can you empathize with Jasmine's decision to take care of the dog? How would you have handled anger about it?

4. After confronting April in a direct manner, Jasmine said, "It was stupid of me to care for the dog the whole time, because I suffered for that." Do you feel Jasmine's decision to care for the dog was "stupid"? If she were your friend, what would you say in response to this comment?

5. The final roommate confrontation resulted in further stress within the house, creating divisiveness and making it "awkward" for Jasmine to live with April. How important was it for Jasmine to speak up about the dog? Do you think the household stress could have been mitigated?

6. Learning that she "shouldn't rely on most people" was Jasmine's first lesson from this experience. What would you have taken away if you had been in Jasmine's shoes?

7. At the end of her story, Jasmine reflected on how being passive-aggressive "kind of screws (her) sometimes," and how hard it was to confront without anger. Have you resorted to passive-aggressive behavior in favor of confrontation? What role does anger play in your ability to communicate your needs?

8. Jasmine observed that her mom's style of confrontation was also volatile. Do you handle prickly interpersonal situations in a similar manner to your mother? Are you conscious of modeling your approach for your children?

Laura, 50

I have a sister – Elaine. She was an exceptionally beautiful girl in the Seventies. Just quintessential Seventies: long straight blond hair, blue eyes, very athletic, very fun, very witty, always dressed great. Men loved her and she just oozed confidence. She's my older sister. I have three sisters and she's the second from the oldest. She's five years older than I am. She and my oldest sister had a different mother who died when they were little. My mom is their stepmom, and the girls came to her when they were four and six.

I always just kind of worshiped at the altar of Elaine; I thought she was just the cat's pajamas, and I was not – I was a queerball little girl; I loved old movies and I loved singing. She was just everything to me. One Christmas she gave me a pair of her old workman's boots, which was a big style back then, and I just thought that was the greatest thing. I thought if I put on those boots I would be Elaine. I truly did. Even to this day, and she doesn't remember much of anything, she would remember that, how happy those boots made me.

When my mom married my father, the older girls were immediately sent away to camp, and they were very young. I was born when they were gone and they came home to a new baby. There's this myth in the family that when I was born, I brought the family together. So there was allegedly all this *love* for me. *Allegedly*. (*Laughing*.)

I was the jokester; I was the entertainer. At dinner, if things got ugly, I could play *Do You Know the Way to San Jose* on the piano and make them all laugh. I wanted to distract them from their fighting, but sometimes I would just get upset and have an asthma attack. I would just totally cry. I might have made myself sick because that would stop the fighting. I definitely would be upset, but I could make myself get more upset to stop what was going on. It was just loud and horrible and mean. And the two older girls could be vicious to me. They called me "the bucked-tooth fairy," and made fun of my singing. They were either very, very loving or very, very mean. There was no happy medium, so you never knew quite what you were getting. I was sick a lot and wouldn't go to school for quite a while, and they just tortured the heck out of me. My parents made them babysit my younger sister and me every Saturday night, and they were so resentful about that; they put vodka in our Hawaiian Punch so we would pass out and they could have their parties.

Growing up, it was a very turbulent household. It was the beginning, I guess, of the age of drugs. Elaine was always kind of a bad kid. She stole as a child, she lied, there was deceitfulness, the phone would always ring in the middle of night when she was out, and there would be some kind of trouble. There were huge, loud screaming arguments between her and my mother, and my older sister and Elaine. The two older girls would get in these horrible physical fights. I was very scared. Sometimes I would try to break them up and make them laugh or distract them. Sometimes my younger sister and I would just hide. If my father was called home from work, which my mom often did, then we'd just totally disappear. It would just be horrendous – the screaming, the yelling, and definitely the violence was just horrible.

All that bullshit drama growing up, that was all the girls and my mother. And then Daddy would come in and have to put an end to it. All he wanted was peace. Maybe at the end there was yelling and hitting, but those girls always started it. Those people always started it, and this poor man was pulled away from *work* to go deal with a bunch of nuts.

Elaine was married at an early age. We were actually happy to have her get married because she was leaving. She was sixteen. Predictably enough, the marriage did not work. She and her husband were in and out of our lives, living with us, whatever. And yet, still, through all of this, I still thought she was just the greatest thing. She could be fun; she could be irreverent. She would give me clothes to wear. She could pay nice attention to me and throw that sunshine on me, that light that made everybody love her – she could throw that my way. And when I was with her, I felt included in that sunshine. If her friends came over, they would be nice to me. It was just a feeling of belonging and kind of being as cool as I thought she was.

She went on and had a son, and left her marriage, and went through a couple different men. Even through this kind of sordid life she led, she still retained an aura of beauty and innocence, with people wanting to help her. She had not become dried up or bagged out. She still had the ability to get a lot of people to do a lot of things for her. And I was definitely one of those people. I would do anything. I've gone to pick her up in the most horrendous situations in the world. And she knew that. When I was fifteen, I started hanging out with her full-time. My mom allowed me to go over to her apartment; we'd smoke pot, I'd babysit her kid, I was kind of friends with her friends. And for me that was enough, because I was part of Elaine's world and she professed to need me. I lied for her; I'd do anything for her.

As time went on, we had this relationship, but drugs started playing a bigger part of it. I was smoking pot with her at fourteen, she gave me diet pills when I was sixteen, she gave me coke; she started me on every drug I ever did. And then doing it together was also part of our relationship – that's what we did. It was a bond, and it also felt good. I think when alcoholics take their first drink, they say, "Ahhh, this is how I want to feel." That is how I felt; I felt good, I felt relaxed. I didn't feel weird or nerdy or nervous anymore. I felt good, and I felt good with her. And she was protective in a strange way. She took care of me in the way that she knew how.

The years went on. Her drug use progressed, and mine probably did, too, but Elaine did indeed become a heroin addict. She fell in with a very shady group of people. I was actually working by that time, and had a semblance of my own life, but Elaine was definitely still part of my social circle. I was about twenty-one or twenty-two. She was living a few miles away and I was starting to see the beginning of things that weren't quite right with her. I saw some of the fractures in her personality. I saw maybe a little bit the way she used people; I saw maybe a little bit of her rationalization of her life.

She gave up custody of her son, which was actually one of the better things she's ever done for this boy. But she tells this story how her ex's family sent five big men to her house, held her down and made her sign the paper giving up full custody, and the child was wrenched from her arms, and they were crying for each other, and then the guys drove away. Back then I believed it, and then it seemed a little funny because Elaine would never visit the child who was actually just three miles away. She was in a party scene, and would sit at the bar and cry that she never saw her son, and tell people this sad tale of how he was wrenched away, with only me having the knowledge that she actually had access to him. It wasn't until years later, knowing the whole scope of her stories, that I realized the five guys tearing him away probably never happened. (*Laughing*.)

By this time, Elaine had been through perhaps her second husband, and was moving home with my parents again. I hadn't left home yet. I was working; I had my little social life. Elaine came home in a big flurry and told my father that she was a heroin addict, and she needed to stay a heroin addict because she would be forced to testify against this guy who was in the mob, and if she was a heroin addict she couldn't be forced to testify because they wouldn't believe her testimony. So therefore she needed to get out of the country, or stay and be a heroin addict. Those were the choices she gave my dad. I kind of believed it because I hadn't wrapped my whole head around the fact that everything she did was addict behavior, which I now know because I've gained some knowledge about that. My father was panicked and fearful because he had no knowledge of this kind of life, whatsoever. And this was his daughter, and he loved us all very, very much, and he would have done anything, as he had shown many times before with saving Elaine.

So she stayed with us for about a week. During that time, Elaine called the police because she believed cars filled with people who wanted to kill her were driving by the window. She was sequestered in the guest room, but let someone come in who drew her horoscope, which was all about her imminent death. I mean, it was all so weird and dramatic, and you're thinking, "Well, this isn't right," but you're scared. I was scared for my sister. And I felt scared that my dad was frightened; he was generally a no-nonsense, cut-through-the-bullshit kind of guy, but he was in over his head with this one.

Now during all this, I was having an inappropriate relationship. He was a married black man, and I thought myself very much in love with him. We both worked at the same store and I really liked him. He was my confidante and we had been close friends before getting physically involved. My father had inadvertently learned that I was seeing this guy and was not happy about it at all. The fact that he was black was a huge deal for my dad, not to mention the married thing. He said, "No matter what, don't ever bring him into my house." Well, apparently because I was kind of an asshole, I did. But it was when my dad wasn't there. Oh, I guess that was nice of me. (*Laughing*.) My dad would go down the shore for a couple days each week to see my mom, so I brought this guy back to my house a number of times. Elaine was aware of this, because I had confided in her. At this point in our lives, we told each other everything. I perceived her to be my closest friend, somebody who I loved dearly, and still had on that little bit of a pedestal.

So it was finally decided that Elaine would get on an airplane and go visit Uncle John in Hawaii. And she would live there and get clean, and the mob would never find her. The day my dad took her to the airport was not a good day for him. This whole decision was a hard one for him because he thought these threats were real, and not that his daughter was just a junkie. At some point on the way to the airport, Elaine told my dad that I had been having sex with my married black boyfriend in the house. He dropped her at the airport, and off she went to Hawaii.

Daddy came home to me and he looked like a broken man. He looked horrible. He vocalized to me that he did not think he'd ever see Elaine alive again. He felt like he was saying goodbye to her forever. I don't remember exactly what he said to me, but it was something to the effect of, "I know that man has been in this house. I'll kill you or I'll kill him if he ever comes to this house again." And then he went into his bedroom and started crying. I'd *never* heard him cry. I was horrified, sick, sick, sick to my stomach, sick. The pain of Elaine, and then *this* on top of it – how disappointing to a man who's lived his life right, his whole life, and did nothing but love us. How could I do that to him? I was just such an asshole. And then how could *she* do that to *me*? I had protected her, I have picked her up, I have given her money, I've lied for her, I stole food for her. I was so stabbed in the back it was not even funny. It was not even funny.

Hours later she called to say she got to Hawaii. My dad answered the phone, and then he made me get on the phone with her, and he said, "Tell her you love her." Elaine was hysterical: "I'm so sorry, I'm so sorry I did that to you." And I was just like, "I love you. I'll talk to you later." The only reason I said those words was because it was what my dad wanted. It was like a piece of stone growing in my heart; that was the beginning. How could she do that to my dad? How could she do that to me?

She was knocked down from that pedestal I had her on, and I saw a horrific glimpse that maybe I didn't matter so much to her. Maybe this thing we had was one way. And it was a small glimpse because it took me years to buy out of the whole thing. Because I couldn't believe that this girl, who had been given so much, physical beauty and a charming personality, and the capacity to have hundreds of people love and take care of her, could actually, intentionally hurt someone in her own family, and do it for her own gain and satisfaction. I know now that she did, and I think I even knew then why she did, because it was looking pretty bad for her. She decided she wasn't going to be the only one who was looking bad in this family. I was going to look bad, too. But I blame myself, because I let her bring me down. And I did drugs with her. Years later, when Elaine finally got clean, she tried to apologize, but she said, "You did drugs with me." And I said, "But I was fourteen." I finally took the onus on myself and said, "You're right, I did them with you." And that seemed to wipe the slate clean – for her.

I did not read one letter she ever sent from Hawaii. And she wrote *pages* to me, to my mother, to my father. This was the beginning of not trusting her. I just didn't want to deal with her; she was dead to me. I couldn't deal with the horror of those moments facing my dad. (*Crying.*) I couldn't deal with it. If I opened those letters, she would just go on and on and on about how sorry she was. She wasn't there to see him; she went away. And I had to stay. I had to stay.

Four months later she came back and immediately started getting high again. And when I saw that, I was just like, "I can't believe it. I just can't believe you completely lied." All that money it took Daddy to get her to Hawaii, all that heartache is just forgotten. She was acting like, "Now I'm back, now I'm fine. And now I'm gonna get high again."

Unfortunately, I think this experience made me not believe people as much as I would like to. It's hard, because I don't believe anybody. I'm so suspect of people's stories. And I still have been kind and giving in many ways, but man, when I start to hear a rambling tale, I think, "There's something wrong with them; they're junkies or alcoholics." My heart is hardened.

I also wait for the betrayal. If it's a new friend, or a new person, or even with some of my old friends, I wait for them to say, "No more. (*Crying.*) I'm not going to be your friend anymore." It's taken a long time to figure this out. I think when you grow up with that drama and that nonsense, you tend to gravitate toward friends with the same stuff. It felt familiar. It took a while to dissect that and see, "This is baloney." Slowly, slowly I've learned not buy into that. When that feeling comes up that somebody's going to hurt me, or drop me, or tell me I'm horrible, or that something's my fault, I can mostly recognize it and push it away. And I can even go through the list: I haven't hurt them, I haven't called them names, I haven't acted inappropriately, I feel like I've been a good friend; it's ridiculous to think this person is going to drop me. But I do have to talk myself through some steps and look at the big picture. I believe I now look for positive, accepting and kind people – people who don't pick on you for sport.

The reality now is that we have this family, and, believe it or not, I still love those people. I love them very much. And when we are together, and it's just us four girls, and there's not too much alcohol involved, and we're just laughing and having a good time, the bond is unbelievable, and you forget about all the other hurts for a few minutes. And then you think, "Okay, well, they're my sisters. I do love them."

Exploration – Laura

1. As a little girl, Laura worshipped her older sister, putting her on a pedestal that would stand for years to come. Did you grow up idolizing someone in your family? What about them captivated you?

2. Elaine's old work boots delighted Laura, letting her believe she would "be Elaine" when she wore them. Were you ever the recipient of a gift that mesmerized you like this?

3. Laura was the family "jokester" and could sometimes distract family members from fighting. What role did you play in your family? How did it serve you?

4. When the fighting was intense, Laura would cry and have an asthma attack. She recalled: "I might have made myself sick because that would stop the fighting." Did illness play a part in your family dynamics? How did things change when someone was sick?

5. While babysitting, the older sisters ensured a night of partying by spiking the younger girls' drinks with vodka. Did things go on in your family about which your parents were clueless?

6. When Laura's mom couldn't handle the children, she called her husband home from work in order to regain control. Did you grow up with a similar gender dynamic? How does that compare to the way you are raising your children?

7. Laura defended her dad "yelling and hitting" his way to "peace." How was conflict handled in your family? Was physical aggression condoned? Do you resolve problems in a similar manner to your parents?

8. Drugs became a bond for the sisters and helped Laura relax and feel good. She said of Elaine: "She took care of me in the way that she knew how." Did recreational drugs play a role in your family? Do you feel differently about the experience as an adult?

9. In her early twenties, Laura's awareness of Elaine was expanding: "I saw some fractures in her personality. I saw maybe a little bit the way she used people, I saw maybe a little bit of her rationalization of her life." At what age did you start seeing your heroes as human beings? How did it feel to become aware their flaws?

10. After Elaine's betrayal, Laura remembered, "...I saw a horrific glimpse that maybe I didn't matter so much to her. Maybe this thing we had was one way." Has one incident ever caused you to reexamine the entire nature of a relationship?

Tina, 48

I'm not sure exactly when I started taking notice of my mother stabbing at me about my weight. She would throw my obese cousin's weight in my face, saying I would end up looking like her. It was always happening, from the time I can remember. My mother was paranoid about my cousin because she was so obese; I think she ended up weighing close to three hundred pounds.

I was stocky in my mother's eyes. My sisters were all very skinny and scrawny, and I was always very athletic with a different shape. I tended, in her mind, to be more like my father's side, where the women were a little stocky. She saw that resemblance because I had big shoulders, I guess; I was bigger-boned than my sisters so she thought I would turn out just like my cousin. Basically, she said, "If you keep eating all that starch you're gonna look like your Cousin Anita." At the time I didn't *like* hearing it, but I don't recall it ever really impacting me until I got older. At the time, I just felt like she was picking on me. Always picking on me. My three older sisters never got any of that and don't even remember the comments that were said to me. I've never talked with my mom about it; she couldn't comprehend it – it just wouldn't compute.

I grew up in a small house; there were three bedrooms and eight children. There was no communication in the family. We weren't allowed to talk at the dinner table. My father would come home from work, be tired and not want to talk. He'd eat his dinner in peace and quiet, and watch TV. I'm sure we said *something*, but if it carried on too much my father would yell.

My mom still has Sunday dinners and I won't eat with them. I'll go for a run while they're eating. They all make fun of that. Once in a while, I'll eat something after they're done. If she sees me, she still makes a smart comment. I can't hate her for it; she doesn't know any better and was raised by a horrible person. I honestly got to the point where I was concerned if I had a daughter, I would be even harder on her, and want her to be the perfect person I could never be. I used to want to have ten children, when I was eighteen. I always thought I would be nicer to my children than my mother was to me, but I don't know that I could have. I would want my daughter to be happier than I was, and feel better about herself – but I'd be afraid that I would make her unhappy.

I always felt fat. When I looked in the mirror, I always saw a fat girl. I guess it was when I was thirteen that I started comparing myself to my friends; I felt like I was fatter than them. I was just never happy with my body. I never felt good about what I was wearing, and remember just beating myself up about it. I don't know exactly when it began, but I started starving myself. When I was young, we used to have to eat whatever was on our plates at the dinner table. If I wanted an extra portion or rice or pasta or whatever the bad thing was, that's when I would hear the comments. When I got to the age where my meals weren't monitored so much, about sixteen, and I could skip a meal, if I was working or whatever, I would skip dinner and binge on something else. I worked at a fast-food restaurant and had access to food and ice cream. I would eat a *huge* bowl of ice cream. And I would just pick on the food my whole shift. Then I got into this pattern where I would not eat for three days, not eat at all, and then when I finally did eat, I would ruin what I did for three days. I would hate myself for eating.

Going three days without food never really affected me. (*Pause.*) It would probably make me tired. I started noticing that when I began working in an office, when I was about nineteen. If I broke down and ate lunch, I just felt like, "I'm never going to have the body I want if I keep eating." I never wanted to be skinny; I just wanted to be thin. When I look back at photos now, I actually was pretty thin.

When I didn't eat, I felt good about myself. And then when I would eat, I would beat myself up for eating. I'm much better about it now, but the first thing in my mind when I would wake up in the morning would be, "What did I eat last night?" And then be mad about myself if I ate. I always felt like I was just bigger than everyone else – that my bones were bigger no matter how much weight I lost.

I never really cared that much about *food*. To this day I don't care that much about it. I eat because I have to. But ice cream, I could live on. I never crave a particular food, but ice cream is always hard for me. And I remember bingeing with my friends on candy; I would eat one of the big bags of M&Ms and a big chocolate bar; I wouldn't stop eating until I felt sick.

The three-day-starving pattern went on for a long time. It's amazing how your body gets used to it. To this day, I can still go a day without eating. And I don't do it on purpose. But my system just got used to it.

The one thing I've learned about myself is that the thing that frustrates me that I can't control, that I've tried to control, is my body. The best thing that ever happened to me was starting to run. I worked out like a maniac; would run six miles, go right to aerobics, and then three hours of weights. Obsessive. It enabled me to eat things I would not normally eat – running would just burn it off. But it was also the obsessive side of me; working out made me feel good, and it was challenging and rewarding. So, if I ate something, it was, "Oh my God, I have to make sure to work out." I've beat up my body a lot over the years – between the starvation and the miles I've run.

I think it affected relationships because I never felt good about myself and was always very self-conscious. Unless I was skinny, I'd have to have relations in the dark. The only time I ever felt pretty decent about myself was when I was running crazily and dropped a lot of weight.

I hated my legs, my hips. I never really had too much trouble with my waist except for thinking it was bigger than it should be. To this day, I think to myself, "Why can't I just lose and stay there?" I don't feel good in clothes so I never want to go anywhere. So I wear sweats and big clothes. I do feel better when I'm thinner, and if I'm not, I walk around the house in the dark because I can't stand looking at myself.

This past year I was working two jobs and lost a ton of weight. I just never appreciate it or see it until the weight is back on and then I realize how thin I was. When I dropped all the weight, I noticed I was enjoying getting dressed because I somewhat realized I had lost weight. But I wait too long to appreciate it. A lot of times I wonder, "Why do I care about being thin?" Because that's just *boring* and then I want to just go and eat.

Now, I don't care as much, and I feel so much more content with myself. I think a big thing was that in relationship I always felt like I had to be skinny and was very self-conscious. Once I stopped dating I didn't have to worry about that. I made the choice to stop dating fifteen years ago. I had three back-to-back relationships and felt like I never stood on my own. I got to the point where I felt like it's just not meant for me, and I threw myself into work. Between work and working out, I found contentment.

I went out on a couple different dates; I think because I'm off on my own so much, and kind of set in my ways, and surrounded by so many people in failed relationships, I just kind of feel like it isn't meant to be for me. I don't have to worry about all that physical stuff I put myself through. It's much easier for me this way. I don't feel like I'm missing anything; I don't ever crave it. I'm happy with my dog and two cats.

I'm very hard on myself, in general. At least I don't care as much. I'd love to look good wearing something without sleeves, but now I'm at the point where I can't do anything about it because of my age. But I don't care as much. I know I look good for my age. I get a lot of compliments and that helps me a lot.

No one knows this, but I did have liposuction in my late twenties. I worked out so hard, and all I wanted to do was see my muscle tone, but no matter how much I worked out, I could never get tight buns; could never get the washboard abs. My legs always rubbed together. They were the areas I wanted to get done. The doctor said I had to be at my lowest weight in order for it to work. So I had to lose weight, which was hard because I had fractured my foot and couldn't work out. I got it done and regretted it instantly. He screwed up. I had to go back three times. The fat comes back in different places, so where I used to have a waist, I don't have a waist. I totally regret getting it done. It never gave me the tone I wanted. I wanted it to get rid of cellulite and it gave me *more* cellulite. My butt looks horrible; it made me look worse.

I know at my age I'm not gonna win any contests, but I just want to feel good about myself. I have a neck and back injury from running, and if I can't work out, I can't eat right either; If I'm not working out, I don't have the health attitude to go with it. I *hate* the thought of putting on a bathing suit right now. Because of my bingeing, during the summer I would always lose more. But since the liposuction, I have all this fat around my belly. I'm thinking about going on a strict diet; a good eating diet, and see how I look, and see how it affects me mentally.

I know I'm a control and neat freak. I don't know that anyone could ever live with me because of the way I am in the house; that's something I can control. I couldn't control my body and kind of reached out in other ways – work and my home. I'm a perfectionist in everything that I do. That's why I think I'm never happy; it's never good enough. I just could never control my body. I look at people like my niece; she looks like a model. She's *never* had to struggle with weight. And it comes so naturally I just want to choke her. I wonder what that feels like, to never be obsessed about your body. It just must be such a feeling.

Exploration – Tina

1. Her mother often compared Tina to her obese cousin, saying that Tina would "end up looking like her" if she didn't curtail her eating. As a child, were you compared to relatives? What effect did that have on you?

2. Tina had a more athletic body shape than her "skinny and scrawny" sisters. Her mom told Tina she was more like her father's side, "where the women were a little stocky." Were your unique physical characteristics criticized or celebrated in your family?

3. Talking was generally not permitted at the family dinner table. How do you think this dynamic influenced Tina's relationship with food? What was the emotional tenor of your family meals?

4. Reflecting on the children she once thought she'd have, Tina said, "I would want my daughter to be happier than I was, and feel better about herself – but I'd be afraid that I would make her unhappy." Have you been afraid of passing on a legacy of unhappiness? Has it impacted your decision about becoming a parent?

5. Tina remembered, "I always felt fat. When I looked in the mirror I saw a fat girl." When did you first notice your physical self in relation to other girls? What would you see when you looked in the mirror at that time of your life?

6. As an adolescent, Tina would go three days without food, binge, and then hate herself for it. Have you entered into unhealthy patterns in order to change your appearance? How did your emotional state play into that?

7. Although she tried in many ways, Tina felt she could not control her body. Can you empathize with her frustration? What would it mean to you if you were to "control" your body?

8. When Tina didn't feel thin, she would wear big clothes and "walk around the house in the dark" because she couldn't stand looking at herself. What thoughts and feelings arise when you look at yourself? Does your perception influence your behavior?

9. Tina stopped dating fifteen years ago and remembered, "...I always felt like I had to be skinny and was very self-conscious...I don't have to worry about all that physical stuff I put myself through. It's much easier for me this way." What are your thoughts about her decision to not be in relationship?

10. In her twenties, Tina went through multiple liposuction procedures, which she later regretted. What is your opinion about women surgically altering their bodies?

11. Tina revealed how she continued to struggle with family dinners: "My mom still has Sunday dinners and I won't eat with them. I'll go for a run while they're eating. They all make fun of that." If you were Tina's friend, how would you support her through this weekly ordeal?

12. Tina said, "I look at people like my niece; she looks like a model. She's *never* had to struggle with weight. And it comes so naturally I just want to choke her." Have you experienced this level of jealousy? How do you normally manage intense feelings of envy?

Karina, 24

I think my story starts when I was very, very young, when my mom was diagnosed with cancer. I was three at that time, and the cancer took her really fast. The chemo wasn't enough, and she died when I was four. I was the last person she spoke to and she told me, "Goodnight. I love you." I went to bed and woke up in the morning and my father sat me down about six in the morning; it was still dark out, in the middle of January, and he told me my mom had passed away. I had never heard that term before, but I knew exactly what it meant; I knew that she was gone.

I see that event as being a turning point for my family forever onward – especially in the emotional health of my family, and for my father. He was very lonely after my mom died and had five kids to care for. I have three older sisters and a little brother. My sisters are much older, and helped raise me as a result of my mom's passing.

I was about six when my dad started dating Pam. I was really excited because I felt the devastating loss of not having a mom, and I wanted a mom so bad. I wanted a mom more than anything. So I saw Pam as a savior for my family, and a savior for me. I treated it with a lot of excitement and anticipation, and was eager to call her "Mom" and put her in that place.

Unfortunately, that wasn't the way things worked out. Pam ended up being probably the most abusive person I've encountered in my life. She left us six times in the first six months. There was lots of fighting; screaming, yelling, cursing.

My dad was a pastor and so we hadn't had exposure to foul language. That was really taboo, and all of a sudden we have curse words all the time. I learned all of my curse words from my stepmom. She would throw things, too. I remember her shattering a glass tabletop on our slate floor and barging into the kitchen where three of us were waiting for dinner, and *screaming* into my sister's face. It became almost a daily thing where it was either total rage or complete coldness. I was terrified of her.

My brother and I spent a lot of time together. My sisters were older and they got out – they moved away in one way or another as their age permitted, or even when it didn't; they left the house early. And it was just me and Jonah left to face it and deal with it for the rest of our childhood. For the next seven years, Pam was a terror in our lives, and she ripped our family apart in whatever way she could. My dad hated how she dealt with things. It really did a number on him because so much of it was directed at him.

The day that I stopped calling her "Mom," I had just turned eleven. We were on our way to my sister's recital and Pam was driving. My dad was in the passenger seat because he had been sick. There had been conflict about something, as usual. Me and my brother were in the back seat, and their fighting continued. My dad finally couldn't take it anymore and said, "Let me out. I need to get out of the car." She pulled the car over to the side of the road and let him out in the middle of town. My dad just started walking and me and my brother were left in the backseat with a totally crazy woman who was now enraged. She just sped off and we didn't know what to do. So we just sat totally silent, terrified. She pulled into a parking lot and spun around really fast and the car came screeching to a halt. She turned around and looked right at me and said,

"Karina, I want you to know this is *your* fault. This is your fault because you are so ungrateful. You're ungrateful for everything, and it's *your* fault our family is this way." I had just turned eleven and I remember burning with anger inside, and having this realization like, "No, this is *not* my fault. And I don't have the ability to tell you that, but I know this is not my fault, and there's something wrong with *you*."

She turned the car around and picked up my father. We drove back home and she left us that day; I think she was gone for like a year-and-a-half after that. They were separated. After she sped off, I remember saying to my dad, "There is no damn way I'm calling her 'mom.' I will not call her 'mom' again." I used a curse word for the first time ever in front of my dad, and I didn't care. (*Laughing*.) He said nothing. I felt like he knew she had crossed the line.

Pam hated me in particular. Jonah was very quiet and he was the youngest, so she didn't take as much issue with him. She would do horrible things in front of him, but never *to* him. But I was loud and outspoken, and I think she felt threatened by me, so she would tell my father that I was an evil child for things like not cleaning out the litter box. A couple of times she called me a "fucking bitch," and said that to my face. I was twelve.

But through those seven years they were together, my dad never left her, or never said, "No, this time you don't come back." He always tried to make that relationship work. I never felt protected by my father. He used to say, "Marriage comes first; children come second. Children are subordinate to a marriage." And that's the way it played out in our house. Even when me and my brother were sitting in my bedroom, huddled together, me covering his ears so he wouldn't hear the fighting and screaming, terrified she was going to burst in and terrorize us too – even with all that, my dad never stepped in. He never stood up to her for our sake and said, "No, you will not speak in front of my kids that way." She had complete power over the family and did an unspeakable amount of damage to everyone. I know this affected my father, and I think he never forgave himself for it.

The week before I was going to start high school, she attacked me. I caught her in a lie. I had known she was lying about things in the past, but always kept my mouth shut, because it wasn't my place, as I was told. But I didn't care that time and I stood up for my father; I was angry she was verbally abusing and lying to him. I stood up to her and got in her face, and I screamed and cursed at her, and said, "That's a Goddamn lie and you know it." She smacked me in the face and knocked my glasses off. She had a water bottle – it's like watching a kindergartner – she tried pouring water in my face and eyes. My father pulled her off of me at that point, and they started shoving each other, and I ran out of the house. That was the last interaction I had with her. I never saw her again; that was the day my dad said, "Never again. This is over." But it took that long.

The next couple of years were some of the happiest I've had with my dad. I was always happier when Pam wasn't around, but now she was really gone, not in and out of our lives. My dad and I had always been close, but this brought us even closer. I was in high school, and at that point a very compliant teenager. I totally adhered to everything my dad believed in, especially from the religious standpoint. I embraced being a pastor's kid, being evangelical and part of his ministry. I was very connected and reliant on my dad.

When I was sixteen my dad began a new relationship. He had not dated anyone since Pam, but began dating one of my friend's parents whose husband had died of cancer a few years earlier. A lot of the issues I had from the "Pam years" resurfaced fast and furious. I was afraid I would be abandoned again, that he would go right back to the same patterns he had with Pam. I was afraid I would lose my relationship with my dad, and afraid of being vulnerable to all those abuses again. I didn't have the words or maturity to voice that, so I started becoming very angry. That was when I began my rebellion, at seventeen; I started rebelling hard as a way of acting out against my dad and his new relationship with Susan. I didn't want her in my life; I felt so threatened. My dad accused me of not wanting him to be happy.

Around that same time my brother began exhibiting really disturbing emotional behaviors. He was really tanking and began cutting himself and had several suicide attempts that put him into a psychiatric hospital for more than six months. That was really hard; it was an added stress seeing my brother, who I always felt responsible for, seeing his arms totally ripped up because he was cutting himself. I remember he tried to hang himself with a belt from his ceiling fan, and the cops coming to our house and taking him away. (*Crying.*) That was really difficult for me at seventeen. I had no power; I couldn't protect him. I felt completely powerless. I was already in a bad state of mind, but this put me into a worse state, where I felt suicidal. It was constant obsessing on, "How can I get out of this? How can I escape?" And not having the emotional tools to deal with that at all.

So I became wrapped up in a relationship that I kept secret from my dad. Overall, it was a positive relationship in my life, but was a totally rebellious act. I was actively rebelling against my father, and moved away from the core values of my family and my religion. I lost my virginity, which I kept highly secret from my family because it was a very shameful thing. It was something I believed was never okay outside the context of marriage.

As time went by and my brother was in the hospital, I remember my dad taking this really kind of indignant attitude toward our behaviors, like, "What's wrong with you kids?" With my brother especially, just sort of like, "Why do I have to deal with this?" And it wasn't that he wasn't distraught by what was going on, but he seemed really disconnected from it. And not seeing the connection of what he was doing or not doing to give us a sense of security. Our behaviors were really quite normal for kids in our situation who had been through the kind of abuse we had experienced. My dad did not see the role he played in our behaviors and struggles. I remember him being so *bothered* with having a child in a psychiatric facility and another acting out at home, and that this was costing him money and time. And he really wasn't engaged in solving that. I don't know why it was so hard for him to see that, because he was a really smart man. I think he was emotionally worn out.

After I left for college, people in town were gossiping and there was an untrue rumor going around that I was pregnant. Susan, who was now my stepmom, caught wind of it, which resulted in my father and I having a *tremendous* blowout. He told me that I betrayed him, and called me a traitor. The lying was part of it, but it was about my decision to not maintain his values and remain chaste. He called me a whore and said I was acting like a slut. He said that I had ruined my reputation, that I had no integrity because I had been preaching all these things and then doing something else entirely. He really attacked my self-worth; that was very difficult coming from him, because that was not the nature of our relationship, at all. But he just could not handle that news. Our relationship was forever changed.

There was a lot of conflict and essentially an ultimatum. I had to break up with my boyfriend and never see him again, or never come home again. I don't think my dad ever expected I would not come home; I don't think he thought I would call his bluff, but I said, "Well, then I'm not coming home." So at eighteen, I ended up moving in with that boyfriend, and my father and I were estranged for the next three years. We still talked, but it was an incredibly tumultuous period of time. All the connectedness and closeness and love were pretty much destroyed. Our relationship was turned upside down.

Eventually, I decided that I needed to leave the relationship with my boyfriend, and just before my twenty-first birthday, I asked my dad if I could come home. He said, "Of course you can come home." (*Crying.*) He still loved me, but had I still been in that relationship I would have never been able to come home. But I wanted to come home; I missed my dad. I missed him so much and I grieved for the kind of relationship we had my whole life. I really wanted to fix what had been broken. (*Crying.*) I really wanted to reconcile and put it back together and get back what had been lost.

He had sold the house I grew up in, and he and Susan had bought a house together. I moved in but felt displaced; it wasn't my house. I quickly realized there were parts about this new stepmother of mine I had been never been privy to. There were some pretty negative qualities I saw right away. That really unsettled me. I tried really hard because my dad said he was happy. I kind of kept my mouth shut and tried to stay off the radar, but it didn't really work that way. I was faced with another summer of real depression. I had lost my romantic relationship and was finding that my new stepmom wasn't all that dissimilar from my old one; she just wasn't quite as noisy about it.

I tried to bond with my dad as much as I could that summer but it was hard because we were working opposite schedules. My dad had lost his church job and tried desperately to get another job, not just as a pastor, but also as a religion professor or history teacher. Nothing worked out and the only thing he was able to do was work at Home Depot. It was kind of below him intellectually; light reading for my father was Dostoevsky. (*Laughing.*) That was beach reading. He really struggled that summer and, I didn't realize it at the time, was really shutting down. I was struggling a lot with my own stuff, and I wasn't seeing everything with clear eyes.

At the end of the summer, I moved to the school I had transferred to. I would sometimes come back to the house, maybe for a day on the weekend. So it was my second semester at this new school, I was doing very well academically, and I was getting into finals when my dog got really sick. She was really old and she'd been our family dog since I was seven. Bella was a loved family pet, the perfect dog. She wasn't able to get around and became incontinent. I went home in early December to help care for her. We bought her those terrible little dog diapers. It was pitiful. I remember laying on the floor with her and feeling so sad. (*Crying.*) I texted my dad that I had figured out how to put the diaper on her, because he couldn't figure it out. I knew that would be the last time I would see that dog. (*Crying.*) I knew she would be put down soon. I said goodbye to Bella.

A week-and-a-half later I had my sophomore review, which is something that every music major goes through. They evaluate you on your performance and academic progress. My review was the day after Bella had been put to sleep. I had talked to my dad the day it happened to ask how it had gone with her. He had very little emotional response. He said, "It was fine. She was totally peaceful, totally at rest." He sounded very detached.

Despite my sadness at losing Bella, I did really well on the review. At that point, I had almost straight A's and had gotten really nice praise from my professors. I called my dad December fifteenth, 2007, at eleven twenty-one in the morning, to share my good news. He didn't answer and I left him a voice mail. The day went on and I talked to my sister on the phone and she said, "Hey, have you talked to Dad yet today?" I said, "No, I called him earlier but he didn't answer." She was like, "Okay. Susan is kind of freaked out. He was supposed to go to work and she can't reach him at work or on his cell." I thought it was a little odd, but that they would figure it out.

Susan calls me around three in the afternoon and said, "Have you heard from your dad? Have you heard from your father at all?" I told her I hadn't and she said, "I can't find him. He left in the morning, went to work, came home for his lunch break around ten-thirty and said he was going back to work. When I called the store they said he called out sick." My dad had been sick with a bad cold the last few days. She said, "He's not answering his cell phone and he didn't come home, and I have no idea where he is." At that point I knew something was up because now it had been a few hours of her not being able to reach him. I was mulling over where he could be and what could have happened. I remember saying to her, "Susan, have you checked your bank records?" She's like, "No, why would I do that?" I said, "You should check. If he went somewhere it would be in there."

I was getting ready to go to my restaurant job, and at that point I really started to panic. I realized something is not right

– my father is *missing*. This has never happened before. I got to work and was completely panicked. I walked in and said, "I'm sorry, I can't work tonight. My father is missing. I can't work." I started driving back to my home and I remember stopping in every bar, frantically asking about him. I thought maybe he's just freaking out and got overwhelmed and stopped for a drink, which wouldn't have been like him, but I had to do something. I didn't get anywhere with that and ended up back at their house.

Susan had called all the hospitals and hotels nearby. Now it's about five or six at night and I said, "Susan did you check your bank records? If you think he's flown the coop, he would have to have money." I finally got her to call the bank and they were like, "The only thing we see today are two purchases at two different Wal-Marts." I said, "We have to call those Wal-Marts right now. We have to find out what he bought." Susan seemed totally disinterested in calling. She said, "Karina, it was only $20 at each place; what could it possibly be?" At that point, I knew something was really wrong. I said, "What if it's bottles of Advil?" Her eyes got really wide and her face turned white.

I ended up calling the Wal-Mart and getting the purchase authorization numbers. (*Crying.*) I was kneeling on the floor holding onto a chair. I was just so anxious and at this point really fearing the worst and believing it could possibly be true. And the woman said, "The first purchase was three bottles of Simply Sleep and a legal pad. And the second purchase was two more bottles of Simply Sleep." (*Sobbing.*) My body – started shaking and I was saying, "Oh my God, oh my God." This poor woman on the other end, she had to have known what was happening. So then we called the police and even though it hadn't been twenty-four hours, they said, "This changes things."

My sister and her boyfriend had started driving around town looking for his car. They went to the second Wal-Mart, where he had purchased the last two bottles of sleeping pills, and they found his car in a motel parking lot next door. They called the police but didn't wait for them. They ran into the motel office and said, "We need to get into his room right now." They banged and banged on the door, and no one answered. My sister's boyfriend went and got a fire extinguisher and rammed and rammed into that door until he finally put a hole in it. He reached his arm in, opened the door, and my father was lying on his belly, on the bed, and he was dead.

We didn't know this was happening at the time it happened. My brother had now come home and the cops came to our house. The policeman took a call outside, and he came back in. He was such an idiot; cops are idiots when it comes to these types of things. Total morons about how to deal with people. He came back in the house and didn't even sit us down. He just went right to my stepmom in the kitchen while my brother and I were standing together in the hallway, listening at the doorway, watching what was going on. He just said, "They found him in a motel room next to the Wal-Mart and he was already dead." (*Crying.*) I'll never forget – my brother and I grasping for each other, clinging to each other, and just collapsing on the floor on top of one another, and the agony that came out of our mouths – just this awful, awful sob. I'll never forget how much my chest hurt at that moment. It was like bones were breaking inside of me. It was so overwhelming, and it's so shocking because it was just an ordinary day; it was just a regular day. And who would have ever thought our father would be dead like this? We had no idea that he was capable of something like that – that he was in that kind of state. (*Crying*.) It was – the most horrific – day of my life.

It's really important to me that I talk about the good person that my dad was. Because all of this tumult I've talked about, and the ways that my father wasn't present for me, is only half the story. My dad and I had been so close for so many years, and I looked up to him. I never had a mother; my stepmoms were no mothers in any way, and so he was really my only parent. I *admired* him. He was a larger-than-life personality. He was incredibly dynamic and charismatic, and really intelligent and intellectual – very deep. But, man, did he like to have fun and *laugh*! No one laughed harder at my dad's jokes than he did. (*Laughing*.) He loved his own jokes. And I always kind of liked that about him. My dad had the best belly laugh in all the world. He would laugh so hard that he would hold his breath and his face would get all scrunched up and red.

He loved entertaining, and would host all our family dinners; he was a fantastic cook. He cooked these amazing meals and you'd just think, "Holy crap, Dad. Who's going to eat all this?" (*Laughing*.) And he'd pack as many people into our house as he could, around that table, and tell stories about as loud and humorously as he possibly could. Unless it was a sad story, where he had a very important point to make. He was a fantastic storyteller; it was that total spectrum of emotion. (*Crying*.) I always regret when I talk to people about my dad that they'll never experience him, because he was such an amazing human being to me.

Up to that point in my life, everything that I had learned about anything, I had basically learned from him. Anything I knew about the world, or how to balance a checkbook, or music, or God – everything I had done and learned and experienced in my life, had been wrapped up in him – either in compliance or rebellion. In one way or another, it was totally about my dad. He taught me so many things, and was so fun a lot of times. Cleaning on Saturday mornings, we'd blast oldies; he'd dance like a total buffoon while he was vacuuming. And that was our thing together in the car; we'd sing oldies at the top of our lungs. He was just a really great person. And he was a fantastic dad; he didn't do his job in certain ways, but I would never have been the person I am without him. So it's been a real trial for me to reconcile this act of betrayal and abandonment with the love and honor I hold for him. I've been through so many fluctuations of horrible, horrible sadness and loss, and convulsive grief, and then severe, terrible anger. And then, sometimes, there's some peace and freedom from that pain.

I've grown in a lot of areas of my life, I think, because I lost my dad, and because I lost him this way. It's broken open some really important things that I don't know I would have discovered otherwise. Losing him this way, with so much pain attached, has both closed me off to my spiritual self, and then reopened me to an entirely different spiritual perspective. It's forced me to figure out what my life's meaning is. Because a lot of times I've thought my life has to not be worth much, if this is what has happened to me. And I must not be worth much if every parent I've ever had has left, most of them voluntarily.

I want to understand who God is and what this life is really about. I've come to believe that God is much broader than any definition I was taught growing up. Questions about my own life: Where do I go from this? What do you do with this kind of brokenness? It's like trying to put a mosaic together when all of your tiles have been obliterated. What do you do with shards of glass? They're not going to make a mirror. So trying to figure out my life has been a real challenge.

The biggest way that it's impacted me has been trying to hold on through the rollercoaster of emotions; feeling completely isolated at times, where it was like no one in the world could possibly understand me, because I don't know anybody who's been through something like this. And plummeting into anger and depression, and my own fights with feeling suicidal, because I just don't want to feel pain anymore. But then having spikes of joy and healing, and sometimes, peace.

I'm coming to a point now, where I can feel some compassion for him. One of the biggest blessings I've had since he died are my dreams. It won't be a dream *about* him, it's really a dream *with* him, where I'm asleep, but he's *so* real and *so* life-like, in a way that no one else I ever dream about is. We've had some *real* conversations in my dreams, where I've seen his pain and his agony and his regret at what he did, and the regret he felt in his own life.

I've gained some perspective that my dad did this, not because he didn't love me, which has been a really hard struggle to accept. (*Pause.*) Not because he didn't love me enough, but because he felt like such a failure as a dad. Because he didn't give us the things he wanted to give us. Just the other night, in my dream, he told me that. He said, "I haven't given you guys enough. I wasn't good enough of a dad." I said to him, "Dad, don't you see how great we're all doing? We're doing that great *because* of you, because you *were* such a good dad. And you don't have to feel like you didn't give us enough." I wish I had been able to say this to him in his life, because I always think it might have changed something. And I have to remind myself I had no control. But those feelings of inadequacy that my father had, he gave to us, because my family, my siblings, we all have to battle feeling like *we're* not enough, because he killed himself.

I know that I'm a deeper, more introspective person, and a stronger person. I do have a lot more compassion for people, but it hasn't been a linear journey to get here. I know there will be times when I will peak and valley. There has also been a tremendous amount of fear that has come with this; I'm afraid of having my own family. I'm afraid I'll make the same mistakes that my dad made, that my stepmoms made. I'm really trying to live with less fear.

This is not to trivialize the pain, the grief, or that I would do *anything* to have it be different, because I would – but my dad's suicide was the impetus for me to become independent of him and everything he believed. I could truly make myself who I wanted to be. He was my foundation; I built myself on him. So when he died, especially in the way that he did, taking his own life, so deliberately, with about three hundred pills and a bottle of vodka, alone in a hotel room (*pause*) – him dying, and dying in that way, literally ripped the foundation out from under me. The most painful and yet I think the biggest blessing that's come from it, is that I'm building my own foundation. Almost three years later, I feel like I'm *finally* building my *own* house on solid ground. I've put my life on track the way *I* want it to be, and not the way he or anybody else wanted it to be. I've graduated from college, supported myself, and done everything I need to do to reconcile this grief and make something of my life.

Exploration – Karina

1. The death of Karina's mother was a "turning point" for the family – especially in their emotional health. Was there a seminal event in your family history that felt like a turning point? How was your emotional health impacted, especially as compared to other members of your family?

2. As a six year old, Karina had longing and expectations that Pam would become a mother to her: "I saw her as a savior for my family, and a savior for me." Have you held similar expectations of someone, either in childhood or adulthood? How have your expectations of that person changed over time?

3. When she was eleven, Karina realized that Pam's tirades and accusations had more to do with something being "wrong" with Pam than Karina being guilty. Have you ever been unjustly blamed for something? Do you remember the first time you clearly saw the flaws of an elder and understood their shortcomings?

4. The family doctrine was "Marriage comes first; children come second. Children are subordinate to a marriage." Do you agree with this philosophy? Did your family have a credo about children?

5. Pam wreaked havoc on the family, and Karina's father was unable to stand up to his wife, leaving the children vulnerable and terrified. Did you feel protected in your family?

6. Karina's rebellion began at seventeen when her father
    started dating Susan. Did you have a teenage rebellion?
    Was there a specific impetus?

7. Karina wanted us to know that although her dad had
    faults, he also had some wonderful gifts. She fondly
    remembered him belting out oldies, and having "the best
    belly laugh in all the world." What is your most cherished
    memory of your dad? What is the quality you love best
    about him?

8. There was a dramatic shift in Karina's spiritual perspective
    after her father took his life. She said, "It's forced me to
    figure out what my life's meaning is." Have you had
    the experience of adopting an entirely new spiritual
    orientation? Has it helped you discover your life's
    meaning?

9. Because she didn't know anyone who had been through a
    loss like hers, Karina sometimes felt "completely isolated,"
    believing nobody could understand her. Has there been a
    time in your life when your pain cut you off from the rest
    of the world? What helped you to reconnect?

10. Karina's dreams helped connect her to her father and
    allowed her to "feel some compassion for him." Have you
    been able to experience compassion for someone who has
    caused you great pain? How did you come to that place?

11. Karina had some regrets about things left unsaid. Imagine
    any member of your family passing away tonight; is there
    something you wish you could have told them? What is
    holding you back from sharing that now?

Ann, 35

I guess it's been about a year since my husband told me he hasn't been happy in our relationship, and the reason why is because he's gay. He's the only person I've ever been with – I met him in college – so it was quite a shock to me. He said he wasn't sure at the time. He's like, "I think I might be; I'm not sure." And I really tried to dust it underneath the carpet. I was like, "Well this can't be possible, honey. How is this possible?" I mean, we were married nine years in May. How is this coming out now? I felt like I just tried to kind of not talk about it with him, and he tried to avoid it, too. In June, we went away for our anniversary and we came back and he told me he definitely is gay, and then he left me and my daughter. I'm still having a hard time dealing with the shock. At times I feel like this is reality, and other times I feel still in shock about it.

It's funny, because when I first met Rick, I really just kind of saw him as a friend, but he was the one who pursued me in a relationship. We went out probably for about six months and he actually broke it off with me because I think he felt a lot of pressure from school. But looking back now, I don't know if he really felt, even that long ago, that it was right for him. We took about a seven-month break, and after college we got back together. He graduated a year ahead of me; we stayed together.

Early in our twenties, before we even got engaged, we had just great, great times together. Looking back now – I remember, I don't know, we were so in love and had such chemistry, I thought. And even after getting married, I thought it was really great.

We had a really hard time having a child. I went through IVF three times in order to have her, because of him. He had a low sperm count and wasn't able to get me pregnant; that was a really hard time for *both* of us being diagnosed with that. I especially felt like I really wanted to be a mother; he felt like he really wanted to be a father. And now, looking back after all this is coming out, I think he was trying to do a checklist in his life, as far as what seemed right to him: I have to get married; I have to have a baby; this is what's supposed to happen in my life. So after three tries of IVF we finally do get pregnant, and have a daughter, Alana.

Through all those years we were together, up until the end, I never felt there was any type of sexual issue with us. Probably about a year before he told me, he started having issues. We would try to be intimate, but he felt like he couldn't get aroused with me. I was upset and was like, "Why is this happening?" Rick has juvenile diabetes and the doctor said that could be a side effect of the disease, so he gave him medication, but throughout that year, we were less and less sexual. I did feel like it was kind of almost like my fault in a way. But then he would be like, "No, it's because of my low blood sugar." So it would kind of make me feel better, but then after he told me he felt like he was gay, I was just like, I don't know, I was just so taken aback by it. I felt like a shock wave went over me. There are times when I look back and feel like it's not real.

I had known something was wrong for so long, not just in our sexual chemistry or connection. But he definitely had a lot of anger issues, and he was never really like that before. I mean, I knew he got angry at times, but especially with our daughter I noticed that he would kind of just burst out. It was Labor

Day weekend of last year, and we took Alana to the city, to see the sights. She was four-and-a-half, and I think she complained about being cold or something, and he just flew off the handle. He said, "You're not appreciative..." He kind of always dealt with it that way, to a four-year-old girl. So we drove home, and I was upset, crying, and she fell asleep in the back of the car. (*Crying.*) I just feel like he would get angry with her for no good reason. Since she was about two-and-a-half, he would not know how to handle her when she got upset or threw a tantrum like a two-year-old does, and take his anger out on her. I would get upset with him and start yelling, "She's a *toddler*. You can't treat a child this way. She doesn't deserve that."

I think he didn't have a great childhood. His parents were divorced; he is an only child; his mom was abused and his father was just not a nice person. It was a different childhood than I had. I attributed some of his behavior to that, that his parents didn't raise him the way I felt our daughter should be raised. And I knew he wasn't happy with his job – just unhappy in general. I look back now at some of the things he used to say to me. He used to be like, "The best part of my day is going to sleep." It's like, who really says that? Who says that about a relationship with his family?

So that day in the city he lost it on our daughter, we came home, I was really upset, and he's like, "I have to leave." So he left for most of the day, came back that night, and we were down in the basement and I said, "*What* is wrong with you; *what* is the problem?" And he just looked at me, and he told me, he said, "I think I'm gay." I just burst into tears. I was like, "*What?*" It really for me came out of left field. It really did. He said, "I've felt like this for a long time." Looking back, he feels that this is from his childhood. He can remember being four or five years old and feeling like he had those feelings, that he wasn't straight.

I didn't know what to do with it; I didn't know how to handle it. Even looking at myself, but then looking outside, my family, how would I ever be able to tell anyone this? (*Crying.*) I kind of felt like, what did I do wrong in this relationship? I took responsibility for what was happening in our relationship, for him being gay. Maybe I didn't do things right in our relationship; maybe I wasn't attractive enough for him. How would people even react to this? I'm really close with my parents; my parents really took him in as their son. (*Crying.*) And my friends; how would I ever be able to tell people this? I really haven't told many people.

There's shame, but it's kind of changing now. I really do realize that this is nothing that I have done. This is who he is, and these are the decisions he made, and there's really nothing I can do to change that. I guess it's just disappointment that this is what my life has become at this point. I go back and forth between sadness and anger about him, a lot. This is where I'm at right now. I'm really, really sad I'm at this point right now in my life. We have a beautiful daughter and I feel like I should be at a point where I should be really happy, that you have a family, and a good job, and your health. And it's just a complete turnaround.

He left, and that's the other part of the issue. He's living with someone else right now. This is a person who was our friend. Rick started a business with him and probably met him a year and a half ago. I knew Max was gay from the beginning; he was living with his boyfriend he had for over ten years. And eventually, Max lived with us for about a month because his boyfriend was jealous of Rick and asked Max to leave. The boyfriend felt something was going on with them. Rick swore to me that he had never done anything sexual with him, but I don't believe that at this point. I feel like I have to go get tested for any type of diseases I could potentially have. I mean, I just don't know who does this. This is who Rick is living with now. They've never admitted to having a relationship, but I can put two and two together.

I feel bad because my mom has kind of gone off the deep end, even more than I am. I feel like I've held it together. When I talk about it it's hard; I really don't talk about it that often. But she's like kind of obsessed. I know she's in pain, but she feels like he's totally done me wrong, which, I feel like he has too. But she's full of anger. She says, "The lies, Ann, the lies. For fifteen years he's lied to you." I do have anger at times, but I also have accepted that anger won't help me heal. I'm in that relationship, and she's not who I am; she's not in the relationship. I feel the anger, but then I go back into the memories of all the great times we had. It was real. My mom has asked me, "Didn't you know? How could you not have known?" Looking back over the years, I honestly can say I did not have any suspicion. It's kind of hard to look back, because I've felt, "Do all those previous years mean *nothing*?" And that was really hard to think about because for me they meant a *lot*. I look back and there were a lot of good memories. (*Crying.*)

I guess the feeling I have now is I want to give my daughter the best life possible. (*Crying.*) And I don't know how I'm going to tell her this one day. I worry about her; people find out, and kids can be cruel, and I feel like she'll have to deal with a lot, (*crying*) and she doesn't deserve that.

Telling Alana he was leaving was really hard. He actually wrote her a letter that he read to her when we were all together. I really didn't know how she was going to react, because she's five, but she understood a lot of it. She was really upset and cried a lot. I just don't want her to think he left because he was unhappy with her, so I tell her how much we both love her. She hasn't really asked that much, because in the past year and a half, since he started this business with his "friend," he really had distanced himself from *her* and me. He wasn't around a lot on the weekends like he used to be, and I think she was used to that; we would do things on our own.

He sees her once every weekend, and every other weekend she'll sleep over his place. I guess I feel like it's good he wants to take on the responsibility and relationship with her, but I am kind of worried, because she's really close to Max, too. He plays with her a lot and she likes him a lot, but when she leaves me, I mean, I'm lonely. I feel like Rick wants us to be this big happy family: me, him, Max and Alana, this huge happy family. And that's *not* going to happen for me. I'm not going to accept this person into my family. Not that I'm blaming this person, but he's torn my family apart, even though it's Rick decision and I really blame him. It's strange, but I almost have more anger toward Max.

I felt like I kind of was always independent before, but I feel like I'm so much more independent now. I'm in the process of buying Rick out of our house; I want sole ownership of our home. I want to raise my daughter the right way, give her a good home, and help her feel independent and strong in who she is as a person. So I kind of feel like it's my responsibility to lead her down the right path. I think I do see a change in Rick with her. I feel like he's gotten this rock off his back, and doesn't have something holding him down anymore.

I honestly have not even thought about getting into another relationship yet. I mean, I hope I do eventually. I think I will, because I'm lonely. I do recognize that. And I hope I can find companionship one day. My mom already told me, "If you bring a guy home, we're going to put him through a lie detector test." (*Laughing.*) I think I probably will have problems trusting someone again. I think it will take me a long time. I mean, I'm open to dating, but as far as getting into a serious relationship – I think it's going to be hard for me.

I need to be confident in who I am as a woman and know that I have the ability to lead a great life, and to move on from this. I really know in my heart (*crying*) that I'm going to be okay.

Exploration – Ann

1. Ann made a number of references to feeling so shocked that her sense of reality was compromised. Have you ever had that experience? What news caused it?

2. One of Ann's first responses was a deep sense of shame when thinking about telling her friends and family that Rick was gay. She asked, "What did I do wrong in this relationship?" Have you ever felt shame or taken responsibility for an issue that was beyond your control?

3. Ann said, "I should be at a point where I should be really happy…" Are there "shoulds" in your own life? How do these expectations influence your well-being?

4. Ann's mom was "full of anger" at the situation, while Ann felt, "I do have anger at times, but I also have accepted that the anger won't help me heal." How has anger helped or hindered your own healing processes? Have you had to set boundaries with other people's emotional involvement in your affairs?

5. Rick's announcement made Ann question her entire life with him: "Do all those previous years mean nothing?" How do you think Rick being gay changes their emotional history and the memories from nearly a decade of marriage?

6. Ann held Max responsible on some level for Rick leaving, and said, "He's torn my family apart." What role did Ann's anger toward Max play in this dynamic? Might she view him in a different light as she heals?

7. Issues of trust loom large in Ann's future. What do you think will foster a sense of trusting her judgment and other men again? What has helped you recover from the pain of a broken trust?

8. Contemplating Rick's role in the marriage, Ann said, "I think he was trying to do a checklist in his life..." Have you ever known someone to sacrifice their own happiness because of something they thought they had to do? What was the outcome for them? For those around them?

9. Alana was a great source of joy for Ann, and without Rick, Alana would have never been born. Is it possible to accept painful aspects of an experience in order to fully embrace the joy? How do you do that?

Emily, 29

It was my sophomore year in college and we lived on the same floor. This guy and me just clicked, instantly. It was good for a little while, maybe six months to a year. I mean, he had always had a temper and I knew that. He was the kind of person that would fight at a party over little things. I'm not a confrontational person, at all. I've never been physically violent with anyone. I think I liked that he was a very *masculine* guy. I don't know, there was just something about him. And in the beginning it was a very physical relationship – it was lust.

I guess it really started when I would try to break up a fight between him and someone else, and I would accidentally get pushed. The first time was at a party, downstairs in the basement of a frat house. He, for some reason, started a fight with this guy. I remember it was right after September eleventh. I can't tell you what happened, but it *erupted* and he's fighting this guy and I remember he grabbed the guy's shirt and pulled it over his head. I was trying to pull him away, and he turned around and pushed me. I was just shocked. Then I just kind of let him go and he obviously got kicked out of the party. That was not the first time he had been kicked out of parties, and I was always the one to go with him when he left. Alcohol was always involved; college parties – there's always alcohol there.

We would go home and he would be fired up about it for days after that. I would try to calm him down, but... I always thought he was wrong in situations like that. Nothing anyone does to you should cause you to hurt them physically. Ever.

There was a big part of me that loved him and wanted to be in the relationship with him, so I kept telling myself when things like this would happen, "The good so outweighs the bad." We just had fun together, we really did. I think it all came down to: He really loved me and was very passionate about me and our relationship. And I *liked* that. I liked that I was the center of someone's universe, even if I had to deal with all this crap in between.

I have amazing parents. They're still together. I had a great childhood. But to the guy that I dated in high school, I was always the afterthought. I always came number two. Now I realize I dated him because he was the captain of the soccer team, and I liked the status that came with that. But I was always second. In college, I was number one with this guy – I was the living end. And I *liked* that.

After multiple times of him getting in fights, I slowly started to hate going out with him because I always knew this was how my night was going to end: Him getting kicked out of a party, me following along and having to deal with the repercussions – for days. When I asked him about his anger he would say it came from his bad childhood. His parents divorced before he was ten and it was a horrible relationship between the two of them. When I would question him, that's when our fights would start. When I would try to get him to think about what happened, he would make up these stories in his head that weren't reality. It's not what actually happened. From someone who was on the outside and saw everything, he was completely wrong. And when I would challenge him on that, that's when his anger towards me began.

I had always dealt with that anger, but it was never directed at me. And then it started. The fights at the party didn't stop; they continued. And then later on in the relationship, he would fight best friends for questioning him about fights he had with other people. He mostly just pushed me around a lot. At that point, I was still in it because I was far away from home and he was all I had. I had one close girlfriend but I never talked to her about what was going on. I was ashamed. I wasn't raised to be that kind of person, to let myself get into a relationship and let someone do this to me. So I hid it. Well, I thought I was hiding it. Everyone knew. Oh God, *everyone* knew. Because in the dorms, people would hear us.

Junior year he moves out of the dorms; I still lived in a dorm. That's when it got really bad because he had a room completely to himself. When we would come home from parties, after a fight, that's when he would start to get really physical with me. It would start with just grabbing me on my upper arms, so hard I would have bruises from his fingers. I would try to cover them up. Thank God it was cold; it was easy to hide the marks under long sleeves. Then it escalated – if I tried to walk away from him, he would pull whatever clothing I had on; I had burns from clothing rubbing on my neck. Those were harder to hide. At this point, he wasn't actually hitting me; it was just a lot of throwing me around, holding me down. I think I thought I could make it better. I thought it would eventually stop. I always got the, "I'm so sorry, I can't believe I did that" the next day. Once the rage and the alcohol went away he would realize what he had done and was very apologetic. It was just a habit. It was constant, and it happened all that year.

During that time, people close to us would ask me questions. They all knew because they could see it on me. He slowly broke me and the person that I was. I would completely, emotionally shut down. Just turn everything off. I didn't want to deal. I *knew* it was bad. And I would completely just shut it off. Stop talking, stop thinking, go off into my own little place. I would sit and watch TV and just zone out. That's when the depression and anxiety started. I didn't really have a way to deal with it. Even he saw it. I would have panic attacks out of nowhere.

At the end of junior year, his father wanted him to go to school closer to home. I actually thought that would be a really good thing because then we would be separated. It would have been done. I thought there was no way I could end it while we were in the same place. I was scared. I was scared of him being physically violent with me if I tried to end it. I think I started to realize at a certain point, "I'm not going to be able to stay in this relationship." But I didn't think I could break up. I mean, he would throw me across a room when I would try to leave an argument; I could only imagine what would happen if I tried to leave the relationship. I was at school, six hours away from home, I mean, I lived there. I had nowhere to go.

My grades started to really suffer. There were classes I registered for and didn't even go to. Then I would think, "Well, it's too far into the semester. I can't go now; I have to just drop it." Needless to say, my father was not very happy with that. I was never a *great* student. I was always the type of person who really had to apply myself to do well. I had to really work at it. There were times in my life when I worked harder than others, (*laughing*) but my parents couldn't understand what was going on. I played the part at home very well. I faked my way through the depression when I saw them. I couldn't confide in them and it killed me. My mom and I are extremely close, but I didn't tell anybody how bad it was. My parents hated him, but I didn't know why. Maybe on some level they knew. They just didn't like him.

He convinced his dad to let him come back to school. So he was back. Over that summer it was better. When we were at home, either on breaks or for the summer, things were good. We would see each other weekends, at our parents' homes, and just have arguments. It was quiet for the first couple of months. Then there was a *huge* blowup at his mom's house, and his mom saw him grab me. I ran out of the house and drove around for a while, but came back. I *couldn't* leave. I don't know why. There was a piece of me that was still invested in him.

At the end of the summer, something happened in the car. It was the first time he really smacked me – in the face. We were at Burger King, and food went flying and hot coffee spilled on me. I just stopped and cried. I knew that it was bad. He hit me without provocation. I probably said something that set him off, but I'm sure it was over nothing. I wanted to say what I wanted to say. I started to speak up and it got worse.

We went back to school for the beginning of senior year and we both had apartments. Our doors were directly across the street from each other. In the beginning it was fun; everybody had their own apartments, all of our friends were nearby. It was *really* fun. But he lived with four guys and I lived with four girls, and that's when people started to realize. We just couldn't hide it. One time we were fighting in his bedroom and there was a living room full of people. He had thrown me up against the door and I fell and hit the ground. That caused my second concussion from him. One of his friends came in and tried to stop it, and he ended up getting into a fight with him. It was really bad.

During this time, my panic attacks got really intense. At that point, I knew people knew, and that was really hard for me to deal with. I don't know if it was shame or embarrassment. I'm not that kind of person. He knew I was having panic attacks, and said, "Well, you'll just go get on some medicine." So I decided to see a therapist. He was this awesome guy, really young, wore Birkenstocks with socks. He was just really cool. But the boyfriend took me there and would sit in the waiting room because I didn't have a car; he had the car.

So I go to talk to this guy and I *couldn't* tell him. He said, "What is causing you to be so anxious?" I'm like, "I don't know." I kept thinking if I told him the truth, that what's going to happen is he is not going to let me leave with him. And then what kind of scene is going to be caused in the waiting room of this doctor's office? I couldn't do it. I *couldn't* tell him. And he knew. The doctor kept trying to dig and dig and dig. And I just had this wall. I couldn't tell him.

That first semester was really bad. The fighting continued. It's all a blur, but it was happening every day. I started to fight back. It's so hard to explain... If it's going to happen, then we're going to go for it. I didn't know if I would hit him because I needed to physically fight with him; I was really angry too. And if I did that, it would get worse. I have a very sharp tongue; when I want to hurt someone, I can. I would never initiate an argument because I knew where it was going to go. But once we were into it, it was my only power. I would yell and bait him into things, and push his buttons. That was my only defense.

There were times when I would not go to class for days at a time. And I didn't sleep really at all, didn't eat much. I would have severe panic attacks and would not leave the house because I thought, "Well, why?" I was checking out. I dealt with the stress by cleaning; at five o'clock in the morning I was cleaning the inside pockets of the television with a Q-tip. It was bad. I was completely losing it. Friends tried talking to me about it, but I was pretty shut down. It became the elephant in the room. Because of my roommate, we never fought in my apartment. I felt safe there and guess I didn't want to leave.

There was a weekend at the beginning of March, second semester of senior year. I came home to be with my best friend from high school. We were both twenty-one, and decided to go to an upscale bar in our town. Well, I see this guy at the bar, and I thought he was so cute. Eventually he came over to talk to me, and this person is now my husband. The whole time I was like, "I have a boyfriend." He was like, "I don't care. I want to call you." I was like, "Okay." I gave him my number at school. And I went back to school and there was a message from him on my answering machine and I was *ecstatic*. I called him and we ended up talking for hours on the phone. The whole time, I kept telling him, "I have a boyfriend; I shouldn't be doing this." It was the only time in two years I had been happy. I told him, "Maybe next time I come home we can hang out." He was like, "All right, I'm good with that." Talking to him made me realize I could be happy. It shouldn't be like it was with the boyfriend. My mom kept telling me, "Love should not be hard. It should be work, but it should not be hard."

Then it was St. Patrick's Day. Everybody at school's drinking and happy to be outside 'cause the weather is finally getting nice. I wasn't drunk. Every once in a while I would have a crazy night, but I just wasn't a big drinker. I came back to my apartment and my roommate had her boyfriend and his friend there. So I go in my room, get my pajamas on and I sit out in the living room. We were just hanging out. I'm getting ready to go to bed and my boyfriend comes to the door. I opened the door and he starts shouting, "I thought you were going to bed!" And I was like, "Well, they were just hanging out up here..." – and he punched me in the face, and walked away. My roommate saw it. I shut the door, locked it, turned to her and said, "I'm done."

So I called my best friend from high school at one o'clock in the morning and told her *everything*, 'cause I knew if I didn't tell someone right now, and have them listen to how angry I am, and get it all out, I might not do it. I knew by telling her, she would never let me forget it, ever. She'd been my best friend since sixth grade. She would tell my parents and then it would be completely out of my hands.

The next morning I called my parents and told them everything. I told them, "This is what's going on. I need to come home." My mom cried and my dad was so mad. Two days later my dad was there with a truck and moved me home. It was a big, big thing.

I told the boyfriend in person the day after he punched me: "I'm done with this. I'm going home. I'm never going to talk to you again." He was crying and begging me to stay. I just said, "I'm done. I can't do it anymore." He knew it wasn't good. He knew it was a mess. It was just bad, all of it. I left school the next day.

When I came home I was a mess – because I had to talk about it, had to actually realize how bad it was and tell people. My mom. That was hard. (*Crying.*) I didn't want her to feel like anything *she* had done led me to this. You would think that as a parent, especially because now I am a parent, you'd want to teach someone not to do this. My dad's pain, too. My parents are perfect for each other. My mom's very loving and caring and emotional. And my dad just isn't, but she brings out a loving side in him. So my dad was just angry and didn't understand how I could let it get that bad. I didn't know either.

I needed counseling. I knew I couldn't deal with this and get over it. I mean, I still don't think I'm over it; I don't think I'll ever completely heal from it. I went to counseling once a week and there were times when my parents would come, too. Things started to get better. I played a big role in what happened with this guy and I let myself get sucked in. I don't want to play the victim again.

A couple days after I came home, my mom said, "Go upstairs and pack your suitcase; we're going to Florida. You and me and my friend Donna are going to go meet up with Aunt Sissie and have five days at the beach. Just a girl trip." And it was *exactly* what I needed. They let me talk. And now, I have an amazing group of girlfriends who I can talk to in the same way. I never really had that when I was younger. We do girls' night once a week and it's awesome.

When I got back from Florida I called Sean (my husband now) and said, "Well, I'm not going to be home in the summer. I'm actually going to be home sooner than that." And he's like, "Well, do you want to hang out?" I was like, "Sure." None of my friends were home and I knew if I sat at my house I would be depressed. Sean and I were not serious. I used him in the beginning to get out of the house, and he took me to dinner. That's how I thought of Sean. I thought, "Well, this is fun. I've never really been out on a date. I've never had somebody come to my house." And I knew, I knew I was a mess. I told him the whole story, so he knew too. I was like, "I am a broken person. And I'm not ready for a relationship." I told him, "I don't want to be your girlfriend; I just want to hang out with you." He was fine with that. He wanted that. I think we dated for a month before I even kissed him. And I knew it was not right for me to jump right into another relationship. But I remember telling my best friend, "If I let this guy go, it's gonna be a *huge* mistake." He really brought me back to life.

The boyfriend never stopped pursuing me. My parents screened my calls; I wasn't allowed to pick up the phone. But he would have someone else from college call and then get on the phone. He was relentless, calling at all hours of the night. We went to the police station, and I don't know what they said to him, but I never got another phone call from him after that. He sent letters but I never got them because my mom checked the mail and threw them away. But at that point, he was six hours away from me and I just didn't care. There are times, even now, when it still comes up. He found me on Facebook before I blocked him. The first time he did it was when I was pregnant with my son. And there was so much I wanted to say, but decided that not responding was more of a message than any words I could ever put together.

I will not take shit from anybody at this point. Now I speak up. I've been through a lot in my life, I think at a very pivotal age. It made me a really strong individual. I would never give up what happened to me because it brought me here. (*Crying*.) And I *love* where I am. I have an amazing husband and marriage, and the most beautiful little boy ever. I really like the person I am. When I love something, my whole heart is in it, because I *appreciate* things now. I appreciate how much my parents love me, and I appreciate my husband and my friends – I just love what I have right now. I'm in a really good place.

Exploration – Emily

1. Early in the relationship, Emily rationalized her boyfriend's fighting with the thought: "The good so outweighs the bad." Have you excused a loved one's bad behaviors only to later see them escalate?

2. In her high school relationship with the soccer captain, Emily "was always second." Of her college boyfriend she said, "He was very passionate about me...I *liked* that. I liked that I was the center of someone's universe..." Do you need to be held in a similar place in relationship? How much would you tolerate to stay there?

3. When she started getting pushed around, Emily justified her continued involvement by saying, "I was far away from home and he was all I had." Have you ever felt that dependent on someone? If you were Emily's friend and knew what was happening, what would you have said to her?

4. Emily felt ashamed of her situation and said, "I wasn't raised to be that kind of person...to let someone do this to me." Have you had the thought, "I'm not that type of person," about things that have happened in your life? What do you think is at the root of Emily's inability to break away?

5. During her junior year, Emily said, "He slowly broke me and the person that I was." Do you believe a person is capable of "breaking" another? Have you ever felt this trapped in a situation?

6. Although she was incapacitated at school, Emily "faked" her way through the depression when she was home with her parents, saying it "killed" her not to confide in them. Was there a time in your life when you chose to wear this kind of mask? How difficult was that for you?

7. Emily eventually engaged in the fighting by "yelling and baiting him into things." She perceived her involvement as her "only power" and pushing his buttons as her "only defense." Do you agree with her assessment? Were there other ways she could have defended herself and reclaimed her power?

8. After she came home, Emily had to deal with her parents' pain as well as her own. Have you ever had to share an emotional ordeal before you even understood it yourself?

9. When Emily's mom took her on a "girl trip" to Florida, Emily said, "They let me talk." After that experience, she found "an amazing group of girlfriends" she could talk to "in the same way." How important are your friends in helping you cope with life's challenges? How has the nature of your friendships evolved over the course of your life?

10. Emily quoted her mother: "Love should not be hard. It should be work, but it should not be hard." Do you agree with her guidance? What is your philosophy about what is necessary for a loving relationship?

Bronwyn, 65

I think both of my parents, oddly enough, were pretty prudish when it came to having sex outside of marriage. My dad was not prudish about dirty jokes or that sort of thing, but was more uptight when it came to you personally. When I was a sophomore in high school, I had sex at this boy's house. Of course his parents weren't home. Somehow my parents found out I was there and they drove over to pick me up. I had already had sex and showered when they showed up.

The secret is, after we got home, my mother came into my bedroom and asked me to pull down my pants, and she sniffed my crotch. This was *way* past boundaries. I had thought maybe I was going to get a spanking, or who knows. I would've never have guessed that she would sniff me for semen. I had taken a shower and we used condoms, so there's nothing she was going to smell. I felt that it was really something she should never have done, it was very emotional on her part, and it was really an infringement of my privacy.

That's the only time she's really ever done anything like that. I think she was just fearful I might get pregnant. She could've asked me, and I could've said, "We used protection." But she didn't ask me anything; she probably couldn't. My grandfather was a minister, and women were pretty conservative in those days. She was brought up very differently than I was. And in all other ways she really brought me up as a feminist. My mother was the ultimate feminist, but not when it came to sex. I think she did believe that sex was for marriage – if not for having children, it was just something women did to please men. Not until my thirties did I discuss this incident with my mom. I think I said, "You know, it was a real breach. You've been so perfect in every other way, but that was really bad."

I think I probably shared less with her after she did that. I was much closer to my dad. My dad was such a character. He was a lot of fun, and I know I was his favorite. He was just so much fun. He'd leave the bathroom door open, be sitting on the toilet, and say, "Pull my finger," and he'd fart. Stupid stuff like that. I was more like him in personality; he was outgoing and had a great sense of humor. I was brought up with lots of dirty jokes.

I've always liked being with guys. When I was in fourth grade I was the only girl in this club we called "the sneakers club." Basically we sneaked around in people's back yards. (*Laughing.*) I was always like a tomboy, but in a good sense. I always had guy friends. I got my period in fall of sixth grade and I was pretty much fully developed by the time I was in seventh grade.

I did petting in junior high and lost my virginity as a freshman in high school. I never felt that I was doing it to please the guy. I was always very popular. You hear about kids these days, the young girls go down on the guys, but there's no reciprocity; I never felt that. I was always popular – I just liked sex. I wasn't promiscuous; I would see one guy at a time, and they were mostly older.

The first boy I had sex with was a senior when I was a freshman. He was on the basketball team, so it was kind of cool. I just thought sex was fun. I didn't really talk about it with my friends; I'm sure some of the other girls were doing this. It seemed good to me at the time. (*Laughing.*) After this thing with my mom, it could've gone either way, but I became more sexually active. It was probably in the making before that even happened, but I think that incident just propelled me forward.

My mom was so good in most ways. She was always available for homework; she was a teacher, so I was proud of her. But I think I kind of felt she was out of touch when it came to sexuality. And I suspect she probably didn't enjoy sex very much. I think it was more of a duty for her, so we just had no common ground on that.

I used to taunt her, because I'm fairly busty and she was flat-chested. I would make these moves. *(Shimmying breasts, laughing.)* Hubba-hubba. *(Laughing.)* So she had a lot to contend with, with me. She didn't laugh. No sense of humor about sex at all. I feel sorry for her, really. She missed out. I'm sure she was one of many in that age group. And in every other way she was very feminist. My parents very much treated me as though as I should do as well as my brother. My dad was a coach when I was younger and I felt I could say, "Dad, you're spending more time with Don, teaching him how to hit a golf ball." My father would stop, and spend more time with me. In a way, I was kind of spoiled. And then when I got out into the working world, I had no idea that women didn't have it as easy as men.

I had sex with a number of people before I met my first husband in college. He was Italian-American from Port Lee, New Jersey, which is how I got to the East Coast. He didn't want to have sex before we got married, and I think that was a big mistake for me. Because I don't think I would've ever married him. He wasn't reciprocal about oral sex, and he was a premature ejaculator. I knew enough that I would've known better; that was a mistake I made. At least I was smart enough not to have kids with him, 'cause then I would've felt I had to stick around for a lot longer. I don't think I ever told my mom why I split up with my ex, I mean the sexual part. I don't know that she would've even understood that.

I was cheating on my first husband. He was very jealous and I figured if he's going to be jealous, I might as well act out. (*Laughing.*) I had a great time with my boss; we had "nooners." I loved the sneaking around and the risk of it. I think that's one of the things I liked about sex when I was younger – the risk. Although I was always careful about protection. I never wanted to get pregnant.

I moved to New York after my first marriage split up, and my parents were visiting me. My mom was getting something from the car and my dad was walking me into the building and was telling me, "Just because a guy takes you out to dinner, you don't have to sex with him. He won't buy the cow if the milk is free." Stupid stuff. I turned to him and said, "But Dad, I like sex too." I'll never forget the look on his face in that moment. He was surprised. That's why I think they didn't have a really robust sexual life. I don't think he was ever with another woman; I think he probably didn't get much, and what he did get, was pretty much the missionary position.

So I had this affair, but I waited longer than I would have, probably, to leave the marriage, because I wanted to make sure I was leaving because I was unhappily married, not hoping to hook up with this other guy. He was British and about eight years older than me. He was great; the day I left my husband he came over with a rented car and drove me to the airport to get home to Illinois. He introduced me to a lot of things, culturally, and also like, I didn't know what a dildo was; I was really naïve in a lot of ways. So he was a great person for me. One of the other things I liked when I was having the affair with him is that I was married and he was single. (*Laughing.*) The reverse of what usually happens.

He lived in England, and I would see him for a few years after that, but I was seeing other guys. In a way, I was like a man, with the notches on the belt. I had sex with three different men in one night. Not together – separate encounters. (*Laughing*.) That was kind of fun. And then I picked up a guy on an airplane on my way to L.A. on a business trip; a black guy. I had sex with him the second night we were together. I went to his apartment. Maybe it's a risk thing, because I think now, "God, the things I did."

Down in Brazil with my friend, I met a guy who was watching us play tennis, and stayed in his house with him for two nights. I can't even remember their names, I mean, that's terrible. The guy seemed nice. I thought my friend was prettier than me, but Brazilians really like thin women, and in those days I was very thin. So I was the one he chose. He was great; he chauffeured us around Brazil and took us to Mardi Gras, the real Mardi Gras, that we would have never felt safe to do otherwise. Maybe I used these guys to a certain degree.

The fact that I came of age in the Sixties and Seventies may have had something to do with it, but I think it has more to do with being a risk taker and curious. I took risks in a lot of other ways, too. I liked to have sex with different ethnic guys. I had sex with a Sikh, guys that weren't circumcised. I never had sex with an Asian, but would have liked to. I had sex with a guy that would come before we even got undressed – twice! I never had a threesome, but would've liked to have been with two men at the same time. I experimented with a woman, but it wasn't something I wanted to do again. She's still a friend.

Eventually, I moved out of New York and met Michael. After a year, we started living together. My mother knew that we were living together and she was very upset about that. My father had passed away by then. So I was about forty, and

Michael and I are living together, and he has these two small children. And my mother says to me, "Living together outside of marriage is a bad influence on the kids." I said to her, "Well, Mom, I think it's more important that we treat each other well, that we're egalitarian with each other. These are the important influences on children, especially girls." So I didn't agree with her on that either.

One time we went down to visit her in Florida and my mother said, even though she knew we were living together, "I'm very uncomfortable with you and Michael staying in the same bedroom." Which is silly. I was forty-two. I didn't really know how to handle it. I was seeing a therapist at the time, and he suggested we just say, "Thank you, but we would prefer to stay in a hotel, then." So we did that, and after that she was okay with us staying with her.

I've been monogamous since I met my husband over twenty-five years ago. I never thought I could have a man as my best friend, and Michael really is my best friend. I guess because I had so many sexual encounters with so many different guys, I was kind of done with running around. It took me a long time, but the oats were sown. I couldn't cheat on him. He's such a nice guy, and I'm very lucky that after a lot of frogs, I finally met the prince.

I was also lucky, probably because of my father, that I was comfortable in a male environment and able to get mentors who kept me under their wing professionally. I was in a meeting, when I was around thirty-two. I was the only woman in this big meeting of the Retail Trade Association. This one guy, who looked like Buddy Hackett, pulled out this picture and said, "Oh my God, this is a picture my mother gave me when I was reaching puberty." He passes it all around this room; there's about thirty-some men in there and *me*, most of them quite a bit older. And they were very uncomfortable. It gets to the poor schmuck next to me and I look over and see it's a boy with a superimposed hose where his penis would be. Remember, this is thirty-five years ago. They're all looking at me to see my reaction. Luckily, because of my father, I just said, "That's not the Jim Levine I know." (*Laughing.*) And that was it; I didn't have any other problems. I was lucky in that way; my mother would never be able to handle that.

She died at ninety-six, and I would say, in just about the last five years, she always liked to tell me things when it was dark and I was driving. After my dad died, I introduced her to one of the guys from Montgomery Ward. I would go out to see her every holiday, and I would invite George along to keep things a little lighter. And they started dating. She never wanted to remarry because she was like, "Oh I don't want to be pushing some old guy around in a wheelchair." But they went on a few vacations and he would go down to visit. She was living in Florida and he would call her every morning, so it was nice for her to have him.

So about five years ago, we're in the car and I'm driving, and she says, "I wanted you to know I had sex with George." Maybe that was her way of kind of saying, "I hear you. I accept what you did," without really saying it. I'm sure it took a lot for her to tell me. And that's why she did it in the dark. Just a few years ago, we had another one of those conversations, where she said, "I'm really glad I didn't accept George's proposal for marriage." (*Laughing.*) It still makes me feel good. There's some closure about it.

I think it's only after my father died that my mother and I became closer. I remember one time she was visiting me in New York, and she was showering, and she said something about did her breasts have enough uplift to them. (*Laughing.*)

So maybe that had to do with me shimmying around as a kid. I was a pistol, I really was. I was the cheerleading captain, but I got suspended from cheerleading because I was cutting class. Maybe all this is part of the same thing. (*Laughing.*) In sixth grade, I was very proud of the fact that I got a checkmark for talking too much. Girls didn't do that. It's probably why I was very successful in business – they couldn't say anything that would embarrass me, and I could swear with the best of them.

I always had a lot of respect for my mother. I don't think she really wanted to go back to teaching, but my parents always made it seem like that's what she wanted. They didn't want us to have any debt; we didn't have any student loans because they paid for everything for us. They lived way below their means so we didn't leave school with debt. She was always available for homework; we never had housekeepers. My dad helped a little, but she basically did everything. They didn't fight at home; it was a very happy environment. It's what makes you walk into a room and feel like everybody's going to like you. I got that from my parents.

Exploration – Bronwyn

1. Bronwyn felt her mother's act was "really an infringement" of her privacy. Was your privacy respected when you were new to sexual exploration? How do you decide how much privacy to allow your own children?

2. When she was in her thirties, Bronwyn finally shared her feelings about her mom's "breach," letting her know "that was really bad." Have you needed a lot of time to pass before confronting a family member about an emotionally volatile issue? Did addressing it years later have positive repercussions?

3. Bronwyn was raised believing she should do as well as her brother, but encountered a different mentality about women in the working world. Did the way you were treated in your family prepare you for the outside world? Were you expected to be as successful as your siblings?

4. Confidence seemed to be a gift of Bronwyn's from her earliest days, and she was even able to tell her dad that she liked sex. Could you be as forthright with your father? Have you ever discussed your sex life with either parent?

5. Bronwyn was a sexual adventurer and proud of her varied experiences. At one point she reflected, "Maybe I used these guys to a certain degree." What are your feelings about her sexual activity?

6. The car was a place Bronwyn's mom felt safe discussing her own sexual adventure. The revelation that she had sex with George and had no intention of marrying him

brought comfort and closure to Bronwyn; she seemed to feel less judged. Have you been forgiven or accepted by your parents years after a perceived transgression?

7. At the end of her story, Bronwyn credited her parents for her confidence: "It's what makes you walk into a room and feel like everybody's going to like you." How did the ways you were treated in your family contribute to your sense of self-worth?

Lisa, 45

It was the summer between fourth and fifth grade. Daddy put me on a train to Indiana. He had gotten me one of those single beds in a sleeper car. He worked for Penn Central and knew guys on the train who would keep an eye on me. I was excited 'cause my parents sold me on the whole thing. I'm one of six, and since I was usually surrounded by my annoying little brothers, my mom and dad were saying, "You're gonna be on the train by *yourself*." It was a really big adventure.

So off on the train I went; I was staying with my grandparents for about six weeks. I was very close with my cousin Christy, who is two years younger than me. She and Aunt Trudy lived a couple minutes from my grandparents. My Aunt Trudy was my favorite aunt when I was growing up. She's just fun. She's the youngest; my dad has a bunch of brothers and sisters. I would stay with her and my cousin Christy for a few days then go back to my grandparents' house, and we did this back and forth thing for a couple weeks.

I didn't really know my grandparents very well. They lived out there and never came to stay with us. If they came east they'd stay with my aunt who lived about a half hour from us. They were family. We had fun, but my grandfather was always very touchy-feely with all my cousins and it made me uncomfortable a lot of times. So I kind of stayed away from him. It wasn't that I didn't like him; I was just uncomfortable. I would just stay away from him.

My aunt was taking Christy and my other cousin on an outing. We had been running around a lot, going here, going there, and I was like, "I don't really feel like going anywhere today." My grandmother still worked, so she went to work. I had been talking the night before, I don't know how I got this in my head, about milktoast. My grandmother heard me talking and she made it for me in the morning before she left.

When I was nine, I was already physically changing. I got my period when I turned ten. But that summer I was starting to get boobs, and I had gone through a growth spurt so I was almost five feet tall.

It was just me and Granddad. They have this old Fifties kitchen table and this ranch-style house. He was mumbling something like, "Oh, your grandmother made you milktoast." When I came into the kitchen the milk was in a pan on the stove, and the toast was on a plate on the side. I sat down to eat and he's watching me for a minute or two then picked me up from the kitchen table and was spinning me around the room. I'm like, "Put me down, put me down." He's talking about how to make the breakfast and slurring his words. It's *nine in the morning.*

I don't know how he ended up getting me on the couch; I don't remember that. But he did. And he was on top of me on the couch. And he stank like nasty, nasty bourbon. He was on top of me and kept kissing me, sticking his tongue in my mouth. I didn't know what to do. I didn't know what to do. I had never even kissed a boy yet. And then he started talking about he could see my breasts starting, and he put his hands all over my chest and under my shirt. And then he stuck his hand down my pants and put his fingers inside me. (*Crying.*) I did not know what to do. And the whole time he's asking me if I like it. "Do you like this? Do you like this?" I wasn't answering him. He even said to me, "Do you want me to stop?" I didn't know what to do; I wasn't saying yes, I wasn't saying no. I was supposed to be good. I was supposed to listen to the adults. If I'm bad am I going to get in trouble? Meaning like if I talk back to him, am I going to get in trouble with my parents, because then my mom would be all manic and crazy.

All this stuff's goin' through my head and then he said, "I want to take you to the bedroom because I don't want anybody to see us in the window." And then he picked me up again and took me into his bedroom where he sleeps with my grandmother, where he's been sleeping with my grandmother for God knows how many years. He kept doing basically all of that. The only upside I can say about it, is he couldn't get it up. (*Quiet laugh.*) So *that* didn't happen. But everything else did.

I remember getting up, going into the living room, pulling myself together, and telling him, "I'm going to the playground for a little while, okay?" He's like, "All right." Like there was nothing goin' on. I put on my flip-flops and walked up to the playground and I *stayed* there until five o'clock, stayed there for six hours, until my grandmother came home. I was on the swings. They had these big, long swings. I was on them, swinging all day. He didn't come lookin' for me either. I can only assume that he passed out. I hurt, but it was like – I felt, (*whispering*) "I can never tell anyone this ever happened." This is my father's father. My father, who I *loved*. I remember the only thing I could do was just go numb. I just shut it down. (*Pause.*) I couldn't fight back. I didn't even know how to do that. I didn't even know what the hell was goin' on. I didn't even know how people had sex.

At five o'clock I went home. My grandmother said, "Oh, you had the milktoast! What'd you think?" I'm like, "I didn't like it." (*Laughing hard.*) Yeah, I wasn't really crazy about that. I honestly don't remember a whole lot of that night. I do remember the next day. That morning, Aunt Trudy said, "I'm goin' to the drugstore." I said, "I'm goin'." (*Laughing.*) I was then, pretty much attached, as much as I could be during the day, to my aunt. But I was afraid she would find out; I thought it was my fault. I thought it was something I had done.

It was common knowledge in the family that my grandfather was an alcoholic. He had been diagnosed with cirrhosis of the liver but he "stopped drinking." Well, he didn't stop drinking – he *never* stopped drinking. He would just drink when nobody else was around, which was apparently when my grandmother went to work.

I watched him with a different eye after that. I watched him when he would call over my cousin Christy, and insist that she sit on his lap when she's just in her sleeping t-shirt without underwear. Everything became like, "No Christy, why don't we go play dolls." I was worried about Christy because she *lived* there. But I couldn't warn her – couldn't even go there.

The night after that, my grandmother came in and announced to me that instead of taking the train back home, Granddad was going to drive me back east from Indiana. I freaked out and started crying. My grandmother said, "Why are you so upset?" I told her I was homesick and I really wanted to go home.

Meanwhile, back at the ranch, everybody's in denial about his extreme alcoholism. Me and him alone, in the car, driving back east. *His* idea. Honestly, I didn't know what the fuck to think. I started playing out in my mind how it was gonna go: Well, I could sit really close to the passenger side. I'm already thinking chess moves. I had been doing that around him anyway, prior to all this happening. I could pretend I'm sick or sleep in the back. It was definitely a feeling of "I'm on my own."

My mother was also from Indiana and her parents lived nearby. But they didn't really have a relationship with my dad's parents. My mother's mother was a wonderful woman. She was a Christian Science practitioner who was very high up in the Mother Church in Boston. She travelled the world teaching Christian Science. At that point in the summer, she wasn't travelling. The next day was a Saturday, and at two in the afternoon my Grammy showed up and said, "Hi, I'm here to collect Lisa and all of her things." My grandparents were like, "Oh…really? She's supposed to stay another few weeks." "*No*, she's coming with me." I was *ecstatic*, relieved, and plus she's my Grammy who was amazing and awesome and I *loved* her.

I spent the next ten days with her at her apartment. We hung out and she took me shopping, and I went to see the cousins on my mother's side. She took me to church, bought me beautiful clothes and showed me her amazing fan collection. She didn't ask me anything.

Now my visit with my grandparents has been cut off by three weeks, so my big sister Diana came out and spent a couple days with us, then she and I came back on the train to her college. I got to hang out with my sister at *college* for a week. Went to my first keg party. (*Laughing.*) Then my brother came and took me back home.

But home wasn't the same place. Literally. My mom had moved from one town to another about forty miles away. I never got to say goodbye to my friends, and now I'm trying to meet new people and make friends, with all this other hoo-hah going on. I didn't say anything to anybody about it. I didn't say anything to anyone. But things started happening. I would just shut down and hide in my bedroom. I wrote a lot. And school – I couldn't concentrate in school. My parents were having trouble and Dad was floating in and out. And now when Daddy's around, I'm weird around him. Because my first thought was, "His father's like this and I trusted him. Is Daddy like this?" I was afraid. My father is a big guy and he'd come and pick me up and hug me real close; it's just what we did. (*Crying.*) And he didn't do that with the others; he just did it with me. And then I was thinking like, "Whoa, okay. Wait a minute. That's weird." 'Cause he's not doin' it with everybody; he's just doin' it with me. I remember him noticing it once. When I was about eleven or twelve I remember him saying to me, "Are you starting to go through that *girl* thing? Where it's not cool to be around dad anymore?" And I said, "Well, kinda." But there was still that weird thing. During this time period he was in and out of the house. Where we were really connected when I was little, now we weren't. My mother didn't notice anyone's emotional changes because she is who she is. I think she's bipolar.

The first time I tried to commit suicide, I was twelve. It was very dramatic. (*Laughing.*) It was an overdose of Tylenol – fifteen of them. It was actually after a fight with my mother. We fought viciously at that point. She was just *nuts* and I wasn't takin' her shenanigans anymore. I fought back and it was bad. I ended up telling her about the Tylenol because I got scared. She took me to the hospital and that was the first time I got my stomach pumped. We were fighting, I was mad, and I'm like, "*Why* do I live?" It wasn't like I was waking up every morning thinking of what happened with Granddad. I was just waking up and going, "What is the friggin' point of life? I don't get it. Because this is not fun."

Had another growth spurt, now I am the tallest girl in my entire class and I have boobs. It's about seventh grade. Fortunately, that only lasted for a year, then the other kids finally started catching up. The fourth time I tried to kill myself, I had to go to the hospital again. I was fourteen. My mother took me, and instead of pumping my stomach they made me drink Ipecac and then said to my mother, "Your daughter is severely depressed. She's told us this is a multiple suicide attempt and we recommend she get help immediately." They checked me into the state hospital that night. I was there for two weeks while they figured out what to do with me. It was an interesting group; there were kids like me hangin' out with the criminally insane. I was transferred to a private institute and was there for five months. I still didn't say anything. Nobody had a clue. Nobody could figure out what was going on with me.

My doctor was an amazing man. They brought me in on a Saturday, and he sat across from me, and we're talking and he's writing everything down, and I go, "What are you writing?" At this point, I'm fourteen and have a little bit of an edge to me. (*Laughing.*) He showed me. The first line said, "The patient is a fourteen year old woman." That's all I read, and I'm like, "He called me a *woman.*" He doesn't see me as a little girl 'cause I'm not a little girl anymore. That earned my respect and then I could talk to him. And I did. I talked to him about all kinds of stuff; I talked to him about my crazy mother, my parents' drama, never getting along with my little brothers 'cause they're superstars and I'm "dork girl." Everything. Except (*pause*), I don't even know what to call it. Was I raped? Was I molested? I don't even know what the fuck it was. I really don't.

Dr. Layne had had us in a couple family meetings and he was saying, "I really believe that there's something core that has gone down, but I don't know what it is. And she's telling me it's you (meaning my parents)." My parents had somewhat reconciled at this point. Dad had moved back in after I was in the institute. Before landing in there, I had been skipping school all the time. I guess they wanted to make sure I didn't have a learning disorder or something, so they did a bunch of tests on me, including an IQ test. They were like, "You have this 131 IQ." I'm like, "I *get* all this stuff, I just don't want to go to school." (*Laughing.*)

My older sister Diana would come to see me religiously, at least once if not twice a week. She'd bring me Archway cookies and other goodies. So one night my sister came to visit. At that time, the institute was a very lovely facility. They had a big lobby with these open stairs and a little fireplace kind of tucked under the stairwell. If we could get that spot, Diana and I would hole up under there and it was great 'cause they'd have the fire going and it was cozy. (*Pause.*) My *sister,* (*crying*) my sister was not buying any of what everybody was saying about my issues. She just finally said, "Lisa, did somebody do something to you?" (*Crying hard.*) Nobody had ever asked me that question. They assumed what was done was my mother. "Has anybody ever done anything to you?" And I said, "Yes." And then she said, "Lisa, did Granddad ever do anything to you?" And I just lost it. I'd been holdin' it for four and half years at that point. I was like, "Yes." And she says, "Did it happen that summer when you were out there?" And I'm like, "Yes." And she's like, "Goddamn it! I *knew* it." And then she told me it had happened to her.

Nobody had ever posed the question the way Diana had. I just couldn't hide it anymore. After we talked, my sister immediately called my doctor and told him. Within that week, Dr. Layne and I went through it, pretty much the way I just told it. That was the first time I actually talked about it, so it took a little longer. I was embarrassed. The whole thing was just embarrassing and gross and dirty. After I told him, I felt like somebody had taken the rock off the lid. Like there'd been a boulder (*laughing*) and somebody moved it so I could open the lid. Unfortunately, it wasn't just Granddad at this point, it was a whole bunch of other crap comin' out of it. But in this instance, I was with Dr. Layne for four or five hours, just letting this whole thing out. He said, "You know, we have to tell your family this. *You* have to tell your father this." I'm like, "I don't know if I can do that." How am I gonna tell the man I love most in the world, and I know I'm his favorite (*laughing*); how am I gonna tell him that his father did this to me? I was afraid of hurting him, and I didn't want him to think badly of me. I kept sayin' to Dr. Layne, "Why didn't I stop him?" We spent some time on that.

Then we did it, in session, with my parents and Diana. I don't remember how I delivered it, but I didn't go into detail. I do remember that Diana and Dr. Layne were helping, not by putting words in my mouth, but by supporting me in saying it. Through my entire childhood, my father never cried. That day he broke down and cried in front of me. (*Crying.*) I just never thought I could ever hurt him. And I never wanted to. I felt like I broke his heart. He then came to me and wrapped me up in his arms, and we all cried together. Everybody thought, "This is great. Now we have something we can work on." And now I'm on the fast track to get out of the institute.

The back-story, even bigger, is of how my sister saved me, back when I was nine and in Indiana. Diana was always the one who saved me. She always is. My mother and sister were talking on the phone; Diana was still away at college. Mom says, "Oh Granddad's going to bring Lisa home. He's going to drive her out from Indiana." And my sister Diana said, "Over my dead fuckin' body," and proceeded to tell my mother something she hadn't told her, or anyone, *ever*. It happened to Diana when she was *twelve*, on a visit to Grandmom and Granddad's. My mother believed her, called her mother and told her; my grandmother hung up the phone, got in her car and drove to my grandparents' house and picked me up.

My mom never asked me anything. There was a whole lot of, "We don't talk about these things." There was a lot of cover-up behavior *always* with my parents. I was happy to be home; she was happy to have me home. By having Grammy come get me, they probably felt they had avoided that. Even after I started losing it, my mom said nothing.

We got through the big family session, but I was still depressed. I still didn't see the point in living. I was glad that I finally got that out, because I was withholding it so much that it was difficult to express myself in any way. Because I was always afraid it was gonna come out. So while that was a catalyst, I wasn't done with trying to destroy myself. I had learned a new trick at the institute; I started cutting. Then cutting got deeper. I would be so depressed, kind of like in a trance. I'd use dirty knives, or a piece of a soda can. I would feel better when I saw the skin split – a sense of relief.

Eventually, I got the cutting under control because I wanted privileges. There was a cute guy in the boys' unit, and I wanted to go outside and make out with him. (*Laughing*.) I was still a teenager. I got up to full privileges and then the next step was to try going home and into therapy once a week. So all that happened and I was released, and I went back to school.

Everybody knew I had been in the hospital. I had a couple friends, but was definitely an outsider. I was being bullied before I left, and when I came back they started in on me again.

I ended up overdosing at school; this time it was my mother's sleeping pills. Nobody knew it. I went home and passed out on my parents' bed. They came home and put me in my bedroom. I woke up at two in the morning, and got into my last major cutting episode. It was a pretty big one. My mother found me the next morning in the bathroom. I went after my legs, my arms, my face, my chest. Two hundred and thirty-six stitches. (*Pause.*) Yeah.

I still couldn't answer the question: Why is any of this worth it? What am I gonna do? Go to *college*? I didn't want to go to college. I couldn't even get through *school*; school was so hard for me. Trust some guy and hope he'd take care of me? Like that's gonna happen. So then I'd have to take care of myself. I couldn't see a way out. There was no way out. I was involuntarily committed to a psych facility in the city. Dr. Layne was on staff there, too. It would go back and forth. I'd have a good time – play Rummy, make people laugh. The better things I like about myself now were there then; it's just who I am. But I could go so black. It would be so black that I couldn't figure out why, so I would make up a story of some tragedy that happened, because I could not figure out why I was so dark. Then I stopped caring about figuring out why. On top of everything else going on, I was a hormonal fifteen year old. (*Laughing.*)

I was there for another four months. We kept working on it. And then after my birthday in September I was out. But I cut again, and was back at the institute in November. There was group therapy, art therapy, and the whole intensive thing.

That Christmas, I got a day pass. And my grandparents, my dad's parents, were visiting in the next town. Meanwhile, back at the ranch, my father had shared the story with his sister, and she checked her daughters. Because now we knew it had happened with Diana, me, and another cousin. Diana is now like Joan of Arc. She said, "We're not gonna let the bastard get away with it anymore." (*Laughing*.) So the whole family knows, more or less, *except* for my grandmother and my grandfather, who now has about a sliver of liver left. He was there visiting and the families were expected to get together. And there wasn't going to be any of this "Well, we're not going to go," because we *always* went. If we didn't go it would look weird. It would be talked about and nobody wanted to discuss anything. They just wanted to have a good time, have the kids get together.

The first thing that happened Christmas morning, after my parents picked me up from the hospital and brought me home, is that they gave me a guitar. (*Crying*.) They knew I was writing, they could hear me singing, 'cause I'm always singing and they knew the one thing I *loved* was music. It was a Yamaha classical guitar, so it had the catgut strings and a big, wide planking neck. Not really conducive to a woman's hands. (*Laughing*.) All I knew was that it was a guitar, and I was thrilled.

I went to my aunt and uncle's with my family, and my father did not leave my side the entire day. He wanted to make sure I was safe. It didn't bother me that two rooms over was my grandfather. It was the first time I saw him, but it was okay because of my dad.

My parents took me back that night and I went up to my unit and brought my guitar with me. I had my own room then. They had taken me off the adolescent unit since I was a little susceptible to suggestion. (*Laughing*.) That's how that cutting thing went. One kid did it, then it went like wildfire. I took the guitar into my room, shut the door, and thought, "Now this, *this* I could turn into a reason for living." (*Crying*.) I'm like, "I will learn this, I will write, and I will sing." And I remember praying to God: "Listen, if we can do this, then I won't cut anymore. I'll try and live. This gets me excited." And it did; it was the only thing that did.

Music... For some reason it's easier for me to talk about my grandfather than it is for me to talk about how I feel about music. At that time, I could walk into my bedroom, shut the door, and in that room with me was Bruce Springsteen, David Bowie, Chrissie Hynde, and all of this great energy, and the stories. Some of them I could relate to because of what I had been through, and some of them were just so Romeo and Juliet, some of them were romantic dreams – they were *everything*. The fact that I had a guitar meant that maybe I could be part of it, too.

Initially, I wanted to be Bruce Springsteen. I was writing about stuff I had *no* idea about. Cars and livin' on the mean streets of suburbia. Yeah, we kicked a cow last night. (*Laughing*.) I'm sixteen, seventeen and very wrapped up in my life with boys. So I wrote a lot of stuff about love, or "I don't get you" and all of that. Through writing and singing I could finally speak to people and express myself. It was a better outlet than cutting; by the time I was done with high school I hadn't cut in a couple years.

I went to the shore for Senior Week and met a guy. He was one of these guys on the boardwalk hawking the softball-in-a-basket game. He ended up getting me into my first band. I wish I had made more of a profession out of it. I was all about the art; I wasn't gonna do it for money. A friend convinced me to go to L.A., but I wasn't able to get to the level I wanted. But I did have amazing musical experiences. I met great artists and was truly shaped by the music; I learned who I was as a singer.

There are people who like music and there are people who really love music. And then there are people like me, who need it to keep their heart beating. Because I have that, in some capacity, whether I'm performing, or listening, or trying to find something new, or digging back into old stuff and asking, "What does this mean?" Like really putting myself into it emotionally – it is just the *fabric* of who I am.

My instrument is my voice. I wish I had had the patience to actually play a musical instrument, but for me, it is more about the emotion and the feeling and the lyric side, and wondering, "Where was the person's mind when they did this?" Or maybe it's just a fun song and it makes you *feel* good. But it *always* makes you feel something. And that's huge, because for a long time I wasn't feeling anything.

Exploration – Lisa

1. In recalling the trauma of being molested, Lisa remembered the fear and confusion she felt wondering what would happen if she were "bad" and "didn't listen." Have you been in a terrifying situation where you didn't know what to do? As time has passed, what thoughts and feelings have surfaced about the way you dealt with the ordeal?

2. On the swings, Lisa decided to "just go numb." Has there been an incident in your life that compelled you to emotionally shut down? How long was it before shutting down started to take a toll?

3. When Lisa finally returned from Indiana, "home wasn't the same place." In what ways do you think the move exacerbated her challenges? Have you been uprooted at a fragile time in your life?

4. Lisa's first suicide attempt was not something she associated with being molested. She remembered her state of hopelessness: "I was just waking up and going, 'What is the friggin' point of life? I don't get it. Because this is not fun.'" Have you ever felt deeply depressed and not known why? Did you later come to understand the reasons for your despair?

5. In his case notes, Dr. Layne referred to Lisa as a "fourteen year old *woman*" and won her respect. Do you remember the first time someone referred to you as a woman instead of a girl? When did you first *feel* like a woman?

6. Lisa was thankful for Diana's enduring, loving protection. Is there a Diana in your life?

7. Lisa's mother never questioned if anything happened to her daughter, even after Diana revealed she had been molested. Lisa said, "Even after I started losing it, my mom said nothing." Why do you think her mother did not ask Lisa whether she had been molested?

8. What feelings arose when you read that the family brought their daughters to the holiday party with Granddad? Was the way the family denied the devastation this man caused indicative of how our culture deals with child molestation?

9. Lisa continued to struggle with depression until her parents bought her a guitar and she finally had a reason for living. Is focusing on wellness and joy as important as dealing with problems and pain? Have you embraced one approach more than the other with your own challenges?

10. In talking about music, Lisa said, "And then there are people like me, who need it to keep their heart beating…it is just the *fabric* of who I am." Is there something in your life that elicits this kind of passion? What describes the "fabric" of who you are?

Kat, 42

I grew up in Laguna Beach, California. It was a gated community with sort of Ozzie and Harriet neighbors. The women were all California blondes, except for my mother who looked exactly like Cher. She had been a ballerina and owned a dance studio. She was this beautiful, beautiful woman. And she was schizophrenic. So I grew up in this seemingly perfect neighborhood with a schizophrenic mother. No one knew except for maybe a couple of neighbors. Definitely no one in my world knew.

I was about seven or eight when I knew something was different. She would be talking about the aliens coming down to grab her, hearing voices, asking me if I heard those voices. I was like, "No." I knew she was different, that there was a label for her, but it wasn't explained very well. I remember asking my Dad to explain "schizophrenic" and his answer was, "a chemical imbalance." That was supposed to be the only explanation I needed, and I got the message I shouldn't ask too many questions about it.

At nine, ten, I was her best friend and confidante. She would share all her secrets with me. They were mostly secrets about her love life. She would say how she had lost her virginity to Lloyd Bridges and slept with other celebrities. And that she was "Miss Hawaii." Her stories were mixed in with her worries about aliens so I never believed anything she said. She was very private but she'd share her secrets with me. I happened to be one of those ten-year-olds who listened, so a lot of people shared things with me. Even neighbors. Another woman told me her husband was having an affair and she was so confused. I listened and observed and was a confidante to the neighborhood women. At that time I thought I wanted to be a therapist.

I was never really a kid. I was quiet, a good listener, and someone who was *responsible*. I always had a sense of responsibility – and guilt. I always felt guilty that my mom was that way. She was very manipulative and controlling. I felt like there was no one else who was going to be responsible for this woman except for me. When she couldn't explain herself, I was her voice. I think even at that young age I felt some compassion too, because I was really her only ally. Dad completely checked out.

I have two younger brothers. One is a year younger and the other is ten years younger. My mom loved taking classes and dragged me to Las Vegas so she could have a singing lesson. No one knew it, but she got pregnant there and when we came back, my dad found out and didn't believe in abortion. So she ended up having the baby, raising the baby as one of our siblings. Then she started saying she was with Dean Martin. We actually think the father was one of Dean Martin's bodyguards. I don't think it was Dean Martin. My dad ended up raising my little brother as his child, and none of us knew he wasn't my dad's kid until years later.

During her pregnancy my mom would say, "I'm having this child so you won't get pregnant and have kids at a young age." And that was a constant mantra of hers. "I'm doing *this*, so you won't do *that*." It breaks my heart, that this mantra was said throughout my childhood. I don't have kids. I'm forty-two. I really wanted kids. But throughout my life, even into my thirties, my mom would say, "Don't have children, don't have children, don't have children." She was constantly projecting her thoughts onto me. I knew she wanted fame and success, but because she had a family, her dreams were shattered.

Growing up with a mom who had that type of personality, I had no idea that it shaped my life, until now, really. I always thought, "I'm okay. I have my own life now." I never went to therapy after growing up with this crazy, eccentric, beautiful, dynamic woman. I never realized I was attracting toxic people for basically my entire life. They were mostly alcoholic people with a lot of *drama*. And Mom was all about drama. She was like an entertainer type of personality. She was a very loving and protective mother, but not in a normal way. One thing about my mother is that she was always very complimentary. So from a young age, she built up my self-esteem, in all aspects – for looks and personality. But at the same time, she could take me down with just a few words.

I remember one night when my mom woke me up at three o'clock in the morning because she was hearing voices and freaking out. We were in the kitchen and she really wanted to know if I could hear them. "Are you sure you can't hear the talking, the screaming?" I remember sitting there thinking, "*Why* am I in this family? Why am I with this woman?" It was one of those quiet, still moments and there was some sort of divine intervention that happened. My mom's ranting faded into the background. It's like an angel spoke and said to me, "This is not forever; it's temporary." I was ten when the angel came to me, and since that time, at hard times in my life, I've had interventions like that happen.

There were a couple incidents with the law that probably contributed to my dad ending the marriage and having her committed. (*Laughing.*) I kind of laugh about it now because telling this stuff feels like someone else's story. So my mom was driving with my little brother in the car; he was probably two. There were no seatbelts at the time, and a car crossed in front of her, she slammed the brakes, and my brother went flying and scraped himself on the dashboard. It wasn't awful. She was so mad the driver had pulled out in front of her that she followed the guy to his office. She went in with a knife and slashed his wallpaper. It turned out he was a therapist; he wasn't very happy. He filed a complaint and restraining order against her. It was my brother's birthday when the police came to the door. My mom opened the door and two officers tackled her. She started screaming at me, "Get the camera, get the camera!" She was frantically yelling at me to document it. I was trying to do whatever I could to make my mom happy and prevent her from going to jail. I felt scared and responsible because I couldn't find the camera. I was so angry at myself that I couldn't find the camera. I just wanted to help her. She had studied karate and was a black belt; they were all literally wrestling and one of the guys had to call for backup. She was hauled off to jail on my brother's second birthday.

So when I was twelve, my dad put my mom in a – they don't call them insane asylums anymore. (*Laughing.*) She went into the crazy house. He asked the three of us kids, "Do you want to go to Hawaii?" We thought we were going on vacation. We packed our clothes and said goodbye to my mother. Intuitively, I think she knew I wasn't coming back for a while. So we went from a gated community in Irvine Cove to a small trailer in Hawaii. Maybe there was a mattress in each room and a kitchen table.

In my twenties and up into my thirties, I attracted a series of alcoholics and addicts into my life. My very best friend was an alcoholic; she's been sober for about five years. Loves drama; a little crazy. And then I met this guy, Mike, when I was twenty-nine. We were together for ten years; married for three of those years. He was also addicted. He would come home at all hours of the night and I put up with it for years and years. I didn't even realize what I was doing. The final straw was when he had an affair. That was what really broke up the relationship, but it was a blessing. I was divorced in January and my mom died a month later in February.

On February fifteenth, I was sitting in a town council meeting. I was there on business, doing public relations for the town. I had given my presentation and was sitting quietly listening to another person speak. At four o'clock, I felt something go through my body. Literally, something moved through my body. It was sadness and anger and love and compassion – every kind of feeling you can imagine ran through my body and I just started bawling. I am not usually one to cry and here I was just losing it, for no apparent reason, in this professional setting. Tears were just pouring down my face and people were asking if I was okay. I had no idea what was going on and all I could say was that I just felt really, really sad.

The next day I went to work and my brother called and said, "Mom died." And he said it kind of like that, so matter-of-fact that I said, "I'll give her a call." And he said, "No, no, Kat. You can't call her. She's dead." She had died the day before. And I think I was just in shock. But after a while, my heart realized everything happened for a reason and it couldn't have been better timing. My brother and I supported her financially and emotionally. So when she passed it was kind of like, "Go have a life now. Go be who you want to be." I was thirty-nine.

Losing the marriage was very hard. Losing my mother was also hard, but there was a sense of relief with it. I walked into my boss's office and said, "I can't do this anymore." At that point in my life I had been working really, really hard. I call it "caught in the vortex." I was working, I really wanted children, then my marriage failed and my mom died. I felt like I was at the top of the castle and then the bottom brick was pulled out and I was in the rubble. Completely in the rubble. I felt like I had nothing.

I sold the house and we divided the assets. In April, I threw my stuff into a storage unit, bought a half-around-the-world ticket, and went travelling for four months. I started my trip in South Dakota, went to Hawaii where I had family, went to New Zealand to say goodbye to my in-laws, then went to Australia, Bali, Thailand and Hong Kong. When I came back to San Francisco I started a business.

Feeling like I had everything, and then nothing, was probably the start of this awareness process. I saw a therapist three times, but most of my therapy was through writing. A year after my mom's death, Memorial Day, was when I hit my lowest point. I was *angry* with my mother. I was sitting in my apartment, writing in my journal, and all of these emotions came out. There was a lot of anger. I didn't even know I had anger. I never realized how angry I was. And I was so sad. I was literally *crying* and *angry* and *writing* and in my apartment for four days. When I came out of my apartment after those four days, I felt like I had forgiven her. I had forgiven her for not letting me be a child, forgiven her for imposing her views and mantras all those years. I had forgiven her for her craziness. It was a big four days. Letting go of all that anger felt good. Afterwards, I felt so much lighter.

Something else helped me after she died, when my brother and I were cleaning out her apartment. We found a "Miss Hawaii" banner and a letter that said she was part of the pageant. I googled the year to find out if she actually won. She didn't, but she was definitely a contestant. We also found mementos from Lloyd Bridges, like notes that said, "To my love" and old snapshots of him. (*Laughing.*) I'm pretty sure she did lose her virginity to him. We were shocked and laughed; it was as if her secrets were finally unveiled. Finding these things helped me understand that there was some truth to her stories – it wasn't all lies and toxic words. I realized that at one point, my mom's life was probably pretty normal. It just happened to be before I was born.

I felt like my mom was misunderstood because of her illness. I guess, in some ways, I felt sorry for her. Those little pieces of her history that we found were all that remained of her story and life. It made me realize that our *life* is our story, and that's it. It's not stuff; the stuff means nothing. Because of her death, I have simplified my life. I feel content and practice gratitude every day.

There's constantly new awareness around this. Right now I'm realizing I don't have to be a people pleaser; I don't have to make everyone happy. I don't have to be responsible for everyone, and I know that some things are out of my control. The most important thing for me now is to have balance. Balancing work and play and life. I don't need to bring toxic and dramatic people into my life anymore. I'm very much a free spirit so I attract crazy people. (*Laughing.*) Right now, I don't mind chatting with them for five minutes, but they don't have to stay. I want to attract good, healthy people into my life. I just need to be more aware.

Exploration – Kat

1. No one in Kat's young world knew her mother had schizophrenia, and Kat remembered her neighborhood as "seemingly perfect." Have you had the experience of thinking everyone else's life was "perfect" while yours clearly was not?

2. Her dad explained schizophrenia as a "chemical imbalance" to eight-year-old Kat and she learned to not ask "too many questions." How would you explain this kind of mental illness to a child? What would be the most important information you'd want to convey?

3. At ten years old, an angel came to Kat while her mom was ranting, letting Kat know it was a temporary problem. What was your reaction to reading about that pivotal moment? Have you ever had a similar experience?

4. Carrying guilt and responsibility for her mother, Kat felt she was "never really a kid." Did you grow up feeling responsible for other people in your family? Were you allowed to simply be a kid?

5. Kat reflected with sadness on her mother's "don't have children" mantra. What was the mantra you often heard growing up? Did it directly influence the course of your life? What feelings does it evoke for you now?

6. Kat said of her mom, "I know she wanted fame and success, but because she had a family, her dreams were shattered." Do you believe this was the reason her mom

could not realize her dreams? Have you ever been made to feel responsible for someone else's unhappiness?

7. While talking about her childhood, Kat laughed and said, "Telling this stuff feels like someone else's story." Are there events in your life that sound too unbelievable to be real? How does talking about them change the experience for you?

8. Kat's world was turned upside down when her mother was institutionalized and her father moved the family to a trailer in Hawaii. Was there a time of complete upheaval in your childhood? What helped you get through it?

9. There were a lot of stressors in her life, and after her mom died, Kat felt like she was "completely in the rubble" and had "nothing." This very low point became the impetus to radically change her life and start to heal. What was the lowest point in your own life? Was it a springboard for transformation?

10. On a four-day writing jag, Kat accessed anger she didn't even know she had. What has been your best therapy in tough times? Were you surprised by what you discovered about yourself?

11. Kat continued striving to find balance in her life. She came to understand that she was not responsible for others' happiness, and that toxic and dramatic people could visit but need not set up camp. What helps you find balance and attract healthy people?

Lily, 19

I started a new school in seventh grade. It was a private middle and high school. In the eighth grade I was in PE class playing flag football and met a boy named Paul. He probably said something like, "Will you be my girlfriend?" (*Laughing.*) And I said yes. So we started dating when I was thirteen.

My parents had always been very strict. I always had guy friends, but wasn't hanging out by myself with boys, and always had a curfew. They were strict; I had never dated before eighth grade. This was my first relationship, so I was really excited. All my firsts were with him – first kiss, all that. Paul was the sweetest kid, ever.

The next month, my mom and I were working on a big fundraising carnival for Camp Ronald McDonald, which is for cancer patients. There was a really cute boy there, my year, and my mom thought he was so sweet, and he was a nice Jewish boy, etc. When my mom and I were driving home, she was like, "That boy is so cute, you should keep in touch with him." *Blah, blah, blah.* I was like, "Yeah, he's cute, but I'm kind of already dating someone." I told her his name and I think she was surprised and intrigued but didn't say much about it; but she was interested. At that point, she had no idea that Paul was black.

A week or so later, my mom wanted to see what Paul looked like in the yearbook, so I showed her his picture. Obviously she could tell he was black, (*laughing*) and she seemed surprised but didn't say much. She was, I think, holding back a response to it.

My parents have always been such generous people, giving to many different organizations and causes, and devoting their time, and being just generally very kind, caring people. It never occurred to me that this would have been an issue. I had no idea my parents would've felt this way, so strongly, about it. My family is religious, traditionally Jewish, and maybe I was naïve, but I really had no idea this was going to be an issue.

They sat down with me a few days later. Clearly, my mom had discussed it with my father. My parents sat me down and told me I wasn't allowed to date him, that this was not okay, not acceptable. I was really surprised. My parents framed it as: They were really upset because I wasn't allowed to date *anyone*. That was their justification. I reminded them of my mom trying to fix me up with the boy from the carnival. And once she finds out I have a black boyfriend, now I'm not allowed to date anyone? Right? Mmm, a little fishy. We had this really long, heated conversation and I was struck by the complete racism of it. In this conversation they said, "We are proud of our heritage, proud of our background and history." And so I have to date someone Jewish, and I have to be proud of who I am and keep that in the family.

We're conservative Jews but always very traditional. My mom came from Egypt, grew up in a close-knit Middle Eastern community and is very close with her siblings. My dad had a more religious upbringing and all his siblings are Orthodox Jews. I guess because of the combination of the close-knit family and the religion, they've always been very tied to their heritage. I didn't realize that would get in the way of me dating someone who wasn't like us.

I was so pissed off because my parents were trying to pass this off as if this was a normal thing. I said, "Be with the times. This is absolutely, just completely racist." I did not agree with it, and I wasn't okay with it. They pretended it wasn't racist and tried to cover that up. That was what really pissed me off the most, that they come off being like, "We're not racist, that has nothing to do with it, what are you talking about?" But then at the same time be like, "You're going to get a reputation for only dating black guys."

I didn't agree with it, but after practice a couple days later, I told Paul we couldn't go out anymore. My mom came to pick me up from practice, and she saw him with me and just immediately freaked out and said, "*What* are you doing? You said you weren't going to do this anymore." I said to her, "You know what? I just broke up with him and I did it for you. This doesn't make any sense, you're racist and this isn't fair, but I did it."

So I had planned on ending things with Paul even though I disagreed. I don't remember how much later it was, but after about a few weeks Paul and I started talking and hanging out and just seeing each other at school. I really, really liked him. I had never gone against my parents, at least not in an extreme way, so I guess, for me, the push was that I just really didn't agree with how immoral it was for them to insist on this. That was what made me not obey them. My relationship with Paul was under the radar so he and I kept dating. Had it made sense and been fair, I might have gone along with what my parents wanted.

In ninth grade, I was hanging out with Paul after school and my mom came to pick me up. She was walking through the school looking for me and comes into the locker area and sees me standing there with Paul and just *screams* at me – right in front of him. She doesn't acknowledge him and just orders me into the car. I got in so much trouble. Throughout all the Paul conflict, which lasted through twelfth grade, I probably was grounded for a good two years. I would be grounded for four months at a time, with no phone. So after this time in ninth grade, my dad came into my room and *ripped* the computer wires out of the wall, I got my phone taken away, and I wasn't allowed to hang out with any of my friends for four months.

Looking back, (*crying*) this was the foundation for my relationship with my parents, and my relationship with myself, too. I became seriously depressed. My parents' response was to just scream at me and take everything away from me, which didn't do anything. The communication was completely lacking. There was no acknowledgement of feelings. It was their way or the highway. I was feeling completely powerless, completely pissed off. I also struggled with self-image issues. I was a teenager; didn't like the way I looked, didn't like my body. And then I was having all this shit from my parents that I was so disrespectful and was a terrible child. I basically just ended up resenting them completely and really wanted nothing to do with them.

I think they only were able to see me in this one way. They were completely caught up in seeing me as the rebellious child and couldn't get past that. All those things led to me sinking into a deeper depression and I didn't have anyone to speak to. I shut down and didn't tell my parents about anything. I had a lot of really good friends in middle school, and they knew what was going on the whole time, so we talked about it a little, but I've always been someone who's kept things to myself. I don't like to involve other people in my problems; I don't like people to feel bad for me. I just don't want everyone knowing my business. Even with close friends who were supportive, I've always been more to myself.

So I was depressed, grounded and really pissed. I started cutting myself. And throwing up. I just hated myself. I hated myself so much and I hated them more than anything. I used to cut my wrists and legs at night before I'd get into bed. I'd be so sad, I'd sit in my room and cry. It was my fault too, because I was completely blocking them out. My entire eighth through the first part of tenth grade years, I had to figure out how I could see Paul without my parents knowing – somehow meet up with him somewhere. It was just a very *tense* time. I was always worried my parents would find out and I'd be punished for months.

This pattern of me breaking their rules by seeing him and then getting grounded for months continued until tenth grade. At that point, finally, my parents sat me down. They said, "We're not dumb. We know that you're still dating Paul and we realize you're going to do what you want, so we're letting you make the decision." It wasn't like, "Go have a great time, we give you our blessing." It was more like, "We understand you're going to do this no matter what we say, so just do it." They didn't want to be involved; they didn't want Paul at the house. They were still not for it at all, and didn't want to talk about it.

I always just felt so bad for Paul. Obviously, it was hard for me because I had to deal with my parents, but I always felt so bad 'cause I didn't want to tell him my parents didn't like him because he's black, but he knew what was what. It really hurt him a lot. He'd get pissed off at them and be really sad. When I told him we were allowed to date, he was happy for me since I was no longer going to get in trouble, but he didn't want anything to do with them.

Things didn't really improve at home. I feel like the dynamic between us was already set. This condition that I could date Paul but they didn't want anything to do with it was still there. Even though it was allowed, it was something that was not talked about. I was still harboring a lot of resentment, but more than that, I couldn't even tell my parents when I was happy. There was a big part of my life that I couldn't talk to them about.

My parents were so caught up in seeing me as the problem child, that I was treated differently than my brother and sister. They really did treat me differently. There's always been a lack of communication, but this made it so much worse. I was dealing with depression by myself, I had no one to talk to, I didn't trust anyone, and I'd constantly get in trouble with my parents. *I* was the problem. They didn't see that they were at all part of the problem. *I* was the one who was not listening, and *they* were the parents and therefore got to make all the rules.

Eventually, Paul started coming to the house and it was really awkward. He'd talk to my mom and she would pretend for a couple minutes, but it was very uncomfortable. That was difficult for us, and I would be like, "What am I supposed to do?" There's be blowups occasionally where he'd be like, "Your parents are racist – fuck them." He also understood I was dealing with even more on my end. Paul and I ended up dating through senior year, until I left for college. It was a very loving, very sweet relationship. It kind of had a natural ending when we had to go our separate ways after high school.

My parents just dealt with it so wrong. I was thirteen years old. The way they handled it deeply affected me and it's obviously affected my relationship with them since. I get along better with them now, but I'm still very apprehensive when I'm around them. I don't really like involving them in much, just 'cause I don't like having things thrown back in my face. I just don't really trust them. I cringe when my mom tries to hug me. It's been better, but back then I couldn't even be around her. She'd try to be affectionate with me sometimes and I couldn't handle it. Until this year, I didn't talk to them about my emotions.

I guess I've always been really strong in my convictions. I don't really let other people tell me what to do. If something doesn't make sense to me or doesn't seem fair, I don't do it. I've always been really independent. My parents would always tell me how terrible I was, and what an awful daughter I was. My dad called me a whore so many times to my face – it just made me hate myself. That's the biggest part of it I think. It's just really affected my relationship with myself. I hated myself for doing that to my family and I also hated what they were doing to me. (*Crying.*) I don't know, I felt terrible about it. Even though I thought they were wrong, I still didn't feel good about it. It caused so much stress for me in every part of my life.

This past March, my mom and I went to Cancun. We stayed in this really nice hotel for four or five days, just the two of us. We were at dinner the last night, and we were having this conversation that started out about her and my father. My father is a very difficult man. I think I was actually applauding her for staying with him this long. He's very stressful. She's in some kind of therapy now and somehow we ended up talking about the whole Paul issue. I really don't remember exactly how it happened. But I said to her, "That was crazy. That was just so wrong." And she admitted to me, she was like, "You know what? Your dad and I handled it wrong." She said, "Looking back on it, it caused so much more pain than good." I haven't spoken to my dad about this, because he would definitely not say that they were wrong. But my mom, she was like, "You know what? Looking back on it, we were wrong. We shouldn't have put that pressure on you when you were so young, and been so strict about it." She said, "It really just caused so much pain for this family that we shouldn't have handled it that way." That was the first and only time I've ever heard that in the past seven years. I thought, "Finally." I told my sister about it and she said, "Wow, I can't believe she said that, admitted to it." Because my parents are not the type to do that. It was just so, like, "Wow, you realize it now. Maybe you should have realized it like five or six years ago."

It's not even the resentment from the Paul thing that holds on. That kind of just led to so much other angst between me and my parents, with school and all sorts of things. That was the foundation for our entire relationship these past six or seven years. I definitely can see a difference in our relationship now, since I've been off at college and out of the house. But being at home still makes me so anxious. Being at home doesn't feel like home. My mom really does try to be caring, but her way of cheering me up is to say, "Everyone has problems." I'd be like, "Yeah, okay, I understand everyone has problems, but here are *mine*." It's not her lack of compassion or sympathy, but she thinks saying that helps, and it doesn't.

I'm definitely the biggest disappointment in my parents' lives. I'm taking this semester off and I probably just let my parents down every step of the way my whole life. And it sucks, because I'm a good person. What sucks more is that I have been mentally gifted since I was young, so my parents have always had the highest of hopes for me. That's part of the reason I'm treated differently. They just expect so much from me, and I've resented that. The happiest I've ever seen my dad was when I got an eight hundred on my SATs. My dad was just so happy and proud of me. I've always tried, but let them down.

Over the past couple of years I've gone through a lot of transitions and struggles, and my parents have become more compassionate and caring. In February, my dad took me to the Super Bowl, which was a lot of fun. It was just the two of us in Miami, and the last night we were in the hotel room, he just started asking me about how I feel, and I started talking to him. That was the only time we had ever spoken about my feelings – I started crying and told him how unhappy I was. (*Crying.*) It affected me 'cause I was like, "Wow, we've really never done this before." Things are moving in a better direction, but there's a long way to go.

Exploration – Lily

1. Lily perceived her parents to be very strict as she wasn't allowed to date before eighth grade and always had a curfew. Were your parents strict? Did you feel they were fair?

2. Her parents expected Lily to date someone of the same race and religion, and came down hard when she violated those unstated rules. In your dating experience, were there rules that were stated and others that were known but never discussed? Did you learn any of the rules by crossing boundaries?

3. Lily was incensed by her parents' racism. Was there strong prejudice in your family toward certain groups of people? How did you feel when you became aware of it? Are there people of particular races, ethnicities or affiliations you hope your own children will not date?

4. Being "depressed, grounded and really pissed" led Lily to start cutting and throwing up. Was there a time in your life when you resorted to self-harm? Do you understand why you made that choice?

5. After Lily's parents gave her permission to continue the relationship with Paul, they didn't want to hear anything about it. Lily said, "I couldn't even tell my parents when I was happy." What do you think of her parents' decision? Are you free to share your full range of emotions?

6. In reflecting on her parents' discipline, Lily said, "They didn't see that they were at all part of the problem. *I* was

the one who was not listening, and *they* were the parents and therefore got to make all the rules." What is your philosophy about setting rules and disciplining a child?

7. Lily disobeyed her parents, and believed they thought she had squandered her intellectual abilities, earning her the role of "problem child." What role did you play in your family? How were you treated differently from your siblings?

8. Lily recalled, "My parents would always tell me how terrible I was, and what an awful daughter I was. My dad called me a whore so many times to my face…it just made me hate myself." Was name-calling part of your family dynamic? How did that impact you?

9. During their trip, Lily and her mother had a conversation about the "Paul issue." Lily's mom admitted that she and her husband "handled it wrong," which was an important revelation for Lily. Have your parents ever apologized for mishandling a situation? Do you admit to your own children when you could have done better by them? How has that affected your relationship?

10. At the age of nineteen, Lily's dad finally asked about her feelings, and she "started talking to him." This seemed to be an important step in healing and moving forward. Does your family take time to acknowledge one another's feelings? Do you take time to acknowledge your own feelings?

Susan, 68

O ne of the issues that has really shaped who I am today is the fact that I became pregnant as a college student, and I had not intended to become pregnant. This was back in the early Sixties, so it was at a time when not only was abortion not available legally, but contraception was not easily available. I was raised in a family where my parents spoke openly with me, saying, "One day you will be having sex, and don't get pregnant unless you plan to." I think that's one of the reasons it's hard for me to talk about it. They're deceased now, but I think if I had told them, they would've been very supportive. I actually was aware of them helping two other young women find abortions at that time. So they were not against it, but they would've been surprised and disappointed that, with all of their good care in raising me, something like this could've happened.

My boyfriend and I were living together while we were in college, during a work period over summer. Our friends and my parents knew we were living together, which as I look back on it, is kind of remarkable for that day and age. I had been using contraception; I think it was the diaphragm. I had missed two periods and I was never irregular, so I figured I was probably pregnant. I really didn't know what to do, didn't know who to turn to. I knew that abortion was illegal; I wasn't at all sure I could find somebody to help me. I did not know at that time as much as I subsequently learned about how to find out about it.

My boyfriend didn't suspect I was pregnant. I didn't share it with anyone; I was all by myself. I felt a sort of embarrassment:

"How could this happen to *me?*" I had been using contraception so there was really no reason to be embarrassed. But I had believed that there's no reason to be pregnant if you don't want to be, and here I was pregnant.

I knew I didn't want to have a child at that time – I wanted to have a child at some point. I think I may have heard about coat hangers; I'm not quite sure what I had heard, but I did suspect that it might disrupt the pregnancy. (*Pause.*) I inserted a knitting needle into my cervix – but nothing happened right away. I didn't think it had been effective, and I was going to have to figure out what to do.

Two weeks later, I went home for a visit. I was about to get on the bus to go back to school, carrying heavy luggage, and I just fainted right in the middle of the bus station. As I came to, I was in the manager's office – and I was bleeding. I had had a miscarriage. It may have been a miscarriage that I was going to have naturally; I don't know. But I suspect it was because of what I did. I had a rush of mixed feelings: "Am I going to be okay?" And, "Thank God I'm not pregnant." And absolutely not a mini-second of remorse that I was not pregnant. And that maybe I was going to be able to get on with things and no one needed to know. But I didn't get on the bus; I went home.

My parents may have suspected something because I just slept for the next two days. They didn't need to know I was pregnant; we didn't talk about it. I was not conflicted about my decision to end the pregnancy. There was no remorse or regret that I had a miscarriage. I was experiencing great relief and maybe, "No one needs to know." I guess I never got over that; I really haven't talked about it much.

There's no doubt in my mind that that experience is among the reasons I spent much of my career working for women's reproductive rights. It was about seven or eight years later that

I started counseling women with problem pregnancies, helping them make the decision whether or not to continue, and helping them find a way to get an abortion if they wanted to end the pregnancy.

The most rewarding counseling experiences I had were with the teenagers. We did not require them to bring in their parents. If they called or walked in for the appointment, we asked if they wanted to bring their parents in. We talked with them about how they could talk with their parents. But they usually chose not to. For so many of them, this was the first life-determining decision they made on their own. I could see them growing up in front of me, with the confidence of, "I can make a decision that is going to impact the rest of my life, on my own." And that was wonderfully rewarding as a counselor.

I'm so grateful to have survived the method I used to end my pregnancy. I have subsequently learned a whole lot about what happens to people who do what I did. They can have terrible infections they can't recover from. So I feel grateful that didn't happen. And I don't mind the person that I've become. (*Laughing*.) And I do think that clearly shaped a big chapter in my life, professionally. These days I spend a great deal of time with people who are a half or a third my age, helping them with career decisions, helping them figure out who they are, and how to have confidence in themselves. And I think that probably also finds its roots back in those days, when I was giving myself guidance as well.

I have one child. The year before he was born I delivered three months early. It was hard; it was a very wanted pregnancy. She lived for about three days. There's a very rational, pragmatic part of me, as well as a profoundly emotional part; the rational part, as I was going into the hospital, asked the doctor if there was any chance at all that there could be survival. He said, "Very, very little; it's way too early." I said, this rational side of me, "Well, let's not do anything extraordinary to keep it alive." About an hour after I delivered, he said, "She's really struggling to live. I have to do everything I can now or the nurses are going to turn me in." And so then of course all the hormones kicked in, I got very emotional, and we started trying to figure out how to keep this little thing alive, who was just over a pound. Her intestines were distended outside the umbilical cord. So after three days we agreed to try the surgery. And she didn't survive it. That was very hard. The feelings of regret and sadness were overwhelming.

My son was born two months early, but he was big and hearty. Six years after he was born I got pregnant again, unplanned and due to bad contraception. I think if I hadn't had the three-month-early delivery, I probably would've continued it. But I wasn't going to go through that again. This time I had a legal abortion, and it was very easy.

People comment on how I have a great deal of compassion. I think it's really easy for me to put myself in someone else's place, and understand where they are and what they're going through. It probably comes out of a collage of experience, but what I went through in my early twenties may have contributed to it. I'm kind of known as a surrogate mother and mentor to many young women. The fact that I didn't have a daughter meant that I could borrow other people's daughters. (*Laughing*.) My whole life has become about helping people.

Exploration – Susan

1. Susan did not tell her parents about the pregnancy, and remembered, "…they would have been surprised and disappointed that, with all of their good care in raising me, something like this could've happened." Has the fear of disappointing others prevented you from sharing something important?

2. With abortion being illegal, Susan "really didn't know what to do, didn't know who to turn to," and wasn't sure she could find somebody to help her. Have you ever felt this isolated? How did you navigate your way through?

3. After miscarrying in the bus station, Susan reflected, "I was not conflicted about my decision to end the pregnancy. There was no remorse or regret that I had a miscarriage." Have you gone through the experience of terminating a pregnancy? What feelings followed that decision?

4. Susan felt her experience was one of the reasons she spent much of her career working for women's reproductive rights. How have challenges in your personal history influenced your career path?

5. Before legal abortion, many women died or became sterile in their efforts to end pregnancies; Susan felt grateful to have survived the method she used. Reflecting on dangerous or desperate actions you've taken, is there a feeling of gratitude for having survived? Do you know people who weren't as fortunate?

6. Susan spoke about the pregnant teenagers she counseled and recalled, "For so many of them, this was the first life-determining decision they made on their own." What was the first life-determining decision you made?

7. Feelings of "regret and sadness" overwhelmed Susan after her premature baby died. Have you gone through a similar loss? How did you cope with your grief?

8. Where do you stand on the issue of legal abortion? Have your feelings on the subject changed with time or circumstance?

9. Susan saw one of her roles being a "surrogate mother and mentor to many young women," noting that her life has become about helping people. Have you had the opportunity to mentor someone? Is helping others an important aspect of who you are?

10. Susan described herself as having "a great deal of compassion." She said, "I think it's really easy for me to put myself in someone else's place, and understand where they are and what they're going through." What experiences in life have contributed to your sense of compassion?

Tess, 51

This is a story about the first person I ever fell in love with. And I've never told anyone. I was thirty-one and had already been married eleven years. I got married very young, right out of school. I met this guy while I was working. He was a doctor; he was brilliant. He had gone to law school first, then to medical school, and when I met him he was doing his residency in internal medicine. I was already in the process of separating; the marriage was basically over. So that's where I was.

I met him at work and he was also separated. I fell *crazy*, madly in love – and that was the first time in my life. Truly, truly cared for this person. Needless to say, we saw each other, had a relationship. It was like magic, what you read about. It was like, when I would see him from a distance, not expecting to see him, my heart would pound. It was really, really intense. The passion was just so incredible. I had never experienced that in my life – nothing like it.

The reason I never told anybody about this is because after our relationship developed, and I guess he loved me and trusted me, and I loved and trusted him, he started wearing women's underwear. Maybe five months into the relationship, he sat down and said, "I need to share this with you. And I need to know your reaction." And then he just showed me. He had on a garter belt with black stockings, a pair of Victoria Secret panties, and a silky camisole. I looked at him like, "What's up with that?" (*Laughing.*) He said, "I just have this need; it helps me feel sexy; I love feeling it against my skin, and it makes me feel good. This is what I want." I said, "Okay." (*Laughing.*) I didn't know what to say. He said, "How do you feel about that?" I said, "It's interesting." And that was it. Of course, there were questions racing around my head: "What makes somebody do this?" I had never heard of this before. It was still kind of weird for me. It wasn't real mainstream. I remember learning all this weird stuff in school when we did our deviant sex course, but nothing really prepared me for this. I came right out and asked him, "Is it because you feel you are a woman?" He said, "Absolutely not. I just love feeling women's things on me." It was a fetish.

And yet, that was only underneath; on the outside he was perfectly normal. And he confessed to me that he sometimes had to wear these things because he *needed* to. He didn't know why; he just had to. Sexually, everything was normal. I mean, he didn't want me to pretend he was a woman, nothing like that. When he would undress, they were on. But they of course, came off. It was really weird.

You have to understand, I came from the straightest upbringing you could imagine. I was one of these kids who never did anything wrong, never got in trouble. I never even drank or did any kind of drugs in college. I was really well behaved, very straight. I didn't have sex until I got married. So for somebody like me, it was *shocking*, shocking. This is the part that amazed me: I loved him so much, I didn't care. Does that sound crazy? I *accepted*, and that's when I realized: "You know what? I really love this person." Initially, I thought it should bother me, but it didn't. That was the thing that bothered me – that it didn't bother me. This experience taught me total acceptance; it taught me really what love is. And then my acceptance, I think, made us closer. He *loved* the idea that I was accepting. It was really great.

Our relationship lasted another two years, and then he was done his residency and went to Maine. At that point, he had two small children and his wife was putting pressure on, and he couldn't stand it, and he went to Maine and decided to go back with her. It was terrible. I was devastated, devastated. Depressed. That's when I went into therapy. I was so depressed; that was the only time in my life I thought I would want to kill myself. He had even asked me to marry him. I thought I had found my soul mate. In fact, he even referred to me as his soul mate, even before that terminology was mainstream. While he was in Maine he tells me that because of the children, he can't deal with it; he can't leave them. (*Whispering.*) He can't do it. It got so bad that even his mother called me and said, "What are you doing? You're a home wrecker." It was bad; it got nasty. And I thought, "You know what? I don't need this."

So we parted ways but it took me ten years to get over it. It was the lowest point in my life. And after I went through that low, I swore to myself I would never let myself get that low again. *Ever.* That's when I took charge of myself. I realized that I had the strength. I went into therapy, I learned meditation; I just *knew* that I could take care of myself. I figured it was about time I started falling in love with *me.*

But there's more. In 1995, about five years later, I called him, just to see how he was. He told me he was very unhappy, still miserable in the marriage, and would I meet him for the weekend? I said no. I wouldn't meet him. I couldn't do it. I said, "The reason I'm calling you is for closure. I wanted to tell you I'm finally over this." And it was good; it was closure for me. I just needed to tell him he was my first and true love. It would always be that way, but it's over.

In 2007, I googled his name, just for the hell of it. I don't even know what made me do it; I just had a feeling. His obituary came up. I was...Oh my God, I was in a state of shock. So much so that I called his brother, who I had never spoken with. His brother is a congressman from a Midwest state. I left my name and he called me back immediately. I knew that his brother knew about me. I said, "What happened?" He said, "He killed himself." I said, "Why?" He said, "Well, these last few years he was in a terrible mental state. He went to some psychiatrist who told him he needed to be a woman." He asked me, "Tess, do you believe that?" I said, "No, not at all." He said, "I never did either, and I told him, 'Don't listen to them and get another opinion. Go *talk* to other people; this is nuts – this isn't you.'"

And then I explained to his brother, I said, "You know, he had some fetish issues." He said, "Yes, I know. He told me. He confided in me." Then his brother said to me, "So he went and had the start of a sex change operation." I said, "You're kidding!" He said, "No. And a year later he blew his brains out." Yep. I was a *mess*. I cried; I was an awful mess. It was sad. This was his choice. Not my choice. He made the choices. I was *left* with his decisions. It wasn't my choice; it wasn't what I wanted. But it didn't really matter at that point, I guess. I had already been through so much hurt; at that point it was just sadness. The other thing I said to his brother, I told him, "I loved him. I genuinely loved him. I want you to know that." He said, "I always knew that."

I know it had something to do with his mother. She had sexually abused him as a kid. During our time together he confided in me that he had dual personalities. We talked about that a lot. I'm sure that he did. He was locked in a closet as a child, he was forced to wear girls' clothing, he was molested.

Unfortunately, he never really got the help he needed. And I'm telling you, a brilliant person. Sad.

I think this relationship taught me a great deal of tolerance and understanding that I never had before. It also taught me the power of love – total unconditional acceptance that's real. Learning that you don't have control. There are some things that are out of your control. You can either accept it, or feel bitter. You have to move on. The only way I'm gonna be happy is to make myself happy.

It was out of my control. I have to accept what it is. I just feel badly things didn't work out. When you care for somebody you want the best for them, even if it's not you.

I dream about him sometimes. I thought of him as a tormented soul. He certainly didn't have peace while he was alive. I feel he's at peace now. That thought is very comforting.

Exploration – Tess

1. After separating from her husband of eleven years, Tess fell in love for the first time. When did you first fall in love? Was the timing unexpected?

2. The early part of Tess's relationship was "like magic." She remembered, "When I would see him from a distance... my heart would pound. It was really, really intense." What is the most passionate relationship you've experienced? How was it different from others?

3. After love and trust were established in the relationship, Tess learned that her lover had a fetish for women's undergarments. Have you been surprised by a partner's disclosure? In what ways did it impact your relationship?

4. What was your initial reaction to finding out about the fetish? Did Tess's reference to her lover being abused as a child impact your opinion about his behavior?

5. Tess recalled, "...the part that amazed me: I loved him so much, I didn't care...this experience taught me total acceptance; it taught me really what love is." What has taught you the most about love?

6. When Tess's lover left her to reunite with his wife and children, Tess went into a painful depression. She remembered, "...that was the only time in my life I thought I would want to kill myself." Has there been a time when you have considered ending your life? How did you climb out of that dark place?

7. After going through a long depression, Tess vowed she would never sink that low again: "I realized I had the strength. I went into therapy, I learned meditation...I figured it was about time I started falling in love with *me*." If you decided to fall in love with yourself, would you be treating yourself differently than you do now?

8. Five years after he left her, Tess's former lover asked to rendezvous for a weekend. Although she considered him her "first and true love," she turned him down. What has been the most difficult boundary you've set with someone? Why was it necessary?

9. Toward the end of the story, Tess reflected on her disappointment with the way the relationship ended: "There are some things that are out of your control. You can either accept it, or feel bitter." Have you struggled with acceptance of others' decisions? What has helped you release feelings of bitterness?

10. Tess thought of her lover as a "tormented soul" and was comforted by the belief that he was finally at peace. Do you know someone who committed suicide? How have you come to terms with that action?

Elise, 50

It took me a few years to become pregnant with Sam. I went through all the infertility stuff; I had surgery, my husband had surgery. We put a lot of effort into having this baby. When I finally got pregnant, it took me a while to accept the fact that I was really going to have a baby. When I had him I was really, really happy. Being the first child, the waited-for child – I'm sure I spoiled him. I took six months off work, then when I went back two days a week, I had a nanny because I didn't want to send him to daycare. Everything was organic, I breast-fed, all that shit. He seemed like a fine, normal baby.

Then I got pregnant again and had his brother. They're two years and three months apart. When James was born, Sam immediately had a very negative reaction. He would try to rip the baby off me when I was nursing, and yell, "No feed him!" He was completely devastated that I had another child. It was like I totally broke his heart. That's when I started noticing negative behaviors. He was constantly beating on the baby and being really nasty to his brother. He would tell me to "shut up" if I told him to stop.

I consulted with a psychologist about him being so aggressive. I tried a bunch of behavior stuff with him like a reward chart. I tried ignoring him when he was saying terrible things. I tried spanking. I tried putting him in his room, and he would beat on the door and make holes in it. My friend, who is a special-ed teacher, told me if you're trying to extinguish a behavior it's going to get worse before it gets better, and that I'd have to be very consistent.

He went through a phase where he would say, "Shut up, you idiot" to me. He was three or four. I felt angry and scared, wondering why is he doing this, why is he so angry, what's wrong with him? Is it my fault that I'm not parenting him right? Did I spoil him too much? We had to put a lock on the outside of his bedroom door. Every time he said, "Shut up, you idiot," I would stop whatever I was doing, carry him upstairs and lock him in his room, because he wouldn't stay there otherwise. This would sometimes happen ten times a day, and I did it for weeks. It slowed down, but didn't stop.

It got to the point that he was so oppositional with me, I realized I would have to apply some kind of behavioral intervention every time I was with him – and I didn't have the energy to do that. I took him back to the child psychologist and while talking about these issues, I realized that I probably needed to be talking to the psychologist more about my relationship with Bill because it seemed like the marriage was starting to fall apart. We wound up going for therapy and Sam got sidelined for a while. We did split up and Sam continued acting the same way he always had.

When Sam was seven he went on medication for depression. The psychiatrist said he was depressed. That was really difficult because you don't want them to be on something when you don't know what it'll do to them. I was just so desperate. I spent money on psychologists, psychiatrists, testing for learning problems. Bill would come with me to these appointments but never really spoke much, so I always felt like I was the one putting out all the effort. Bill wasn't very good at following through on parenting things, so I definitely felt like I was battling this pretty much by myself, and that Bill was more of an obstacle than a help.

Sam did a bunch of stupid stuff in ninth grade and ended up getting kicked out of private school. He hacked into the school's computer system, among other things. So he wound up going to public school in tenth grade. He was into computers and I thought he was going to be one of those depressed kids who sat in his room all day and played video games. He went on a mood regulator and gained a ton of weight. He was always a skinny, skinny kid and he actually became fat and started wearing all the black Goth stuff, and had a Mohawk. I took him off the medicine because I was worried what it was doing to him. He lost twenty pounds in a month.

When he went to public school he became more social and started to make all these friends. Sam is very charismatic. He is a leader and not one of these kids who sits in the back and sulks. He's more like a smartass. But his new friends weren't academic; they were the ones who were going to get into trouble.

The worst trouble was about a year and a half ago. It was a Sunday morning and I was making pancakes. When I went to bed the night before, he was already in his bed. So I'm making breakfast and there's a knock at the door and it was the police. The cop said, "Were you aware that your son was in an accident last night?" And I said, "Nooo..." I thought it was a mistake 'cause I knew Sam was in bed when I went to bed. Then the cop said, "Is that your car out there?" And I said, "Yesss..." I was just confused; I couldn't figure out what was going on. He said, "Did you know your car was in an accident?" I put it together that Sam must've taken my car while I was asleep. Apparently, Sam had gone to a party in the middle of the night and hit a couple of cars on his way out of the party.

After that, I started hiding my keys in my room at night. He wound up doing it again. He was disappearing all night, hanging out with this one kid. He would leave and tell me he was sleeping over the kid's house. The kid had a prescription for Xanax, and they were snorting it and going out and ripping off cars. First they went to unlocked cars and took radios, GPS receivers and things like that. Then I guess they started breaking windows to get in, and they would pawn these things.

The third time Sam was arrested, he stole my keys while I was sleeping, took my car and went to some guy's house. They stole beer out of his garage, noticed his car was unlocked and took his wallet. He was a retired police officer and his badge was in his wallet. Sam used the guy's credit card to put gas in my car. So the cops show up at my door with a search warrant, and Sam's not even home. Four cop cars are in my driveway, and they're ready to tear my house apart looking for this guy's badge. That was the worst moment. I was so afraid; I knew he did something really bad and was in a lot of trouble. And here were these cops that were going to search my house, and I was just *scared*. I called Sam and said, "You better get home right now."

He swore to the cops he didn't have the badge. They tore apart his room and didn't find anything. They went to the other kid's house and found the wallet and the badge, and some other things they had stolen. Since this kid was already over eighteen, he got the major punishment. But Sam still had felony charges. I told him the first time he got arrested that I wasn't going to hire a lawyer again. So I did not hire him a lawyer. Then I went through a lot of guilt, questioning what was the best thing to do. Because he is young and stupid and impulsive and he has a problem, should I try to protect him and minimize the amount of trouble he's in?

In the meantime, they put him in some kind of after-school drug treatment thing for an hour every day after school. It was obviously not working. Instead, it was just introducing him to more kids who were doing the same stuff. I told myself, "I've got to let him take the fall for this. If I protect him it's just going to prolong the situation."

I know that all my friends would've gotten a lawyer. But I also know that sometimes you have to hit bottom before making a change. It takes a lot to admit you have a problem, and unless Sam got it in his head that things were really bad, he wasn't going to be motivated to make any changes. At the time I didn't know it was this pill thing that was motivating him; I thought he was just stealing because he liked stealing.

This third arrest was a violation of his probation, so they put him in a place that was like a jail, but for teens. Even though there were no bars, he wasn't allowed to leave or it would've been an escape charge. He was there for ten days. I felt really bad when I visited because he was incarcerated with all street kids. But part of me was happy to have a break because it was so stressful to live with him. Every night he went out I wondered if I was going to get a call from the police, or if he was going to be dead. For those ten days, at least I knew he was safe. James didn't miss him at all. And I really didn't miss him either. You know, I felt bad, I felt guilty, I felt sad, but I really didn't miss him.

When they let him out, he had an ankle bracelet and was on house arrest. A probation officer showed up at random times to make sure he was home, and Sam had to call in. That was really hard because he was not happy about being on house arrest. He would have friends over and I would allow it, because if he were just by himself he would make me crazy with his unhappiness and would pick on me. So I'd let him have friends over but that was hard to deal with 'cause they'd be out in the garage drinking and smoking pot. I didn't trust them and would find that things were missing from my house. Sam stole from me a million times. I have a safe in my closet where I locked any kind of medication and my car keys. It was really horrible. I have been through a lot with him.

For years, Sam blamed me for everything that was wrong with him. He had a lot of anger toward me, and would often do really mean things. He once took my watch and threw it off the balcony. I would go to work crying. Part of it was I didn't know how I could live with a kid like this all the time 'cause it's so much stress, and part of it was I didn't feel like I had any support from his dad. I was wondering if this was my fault and questioned how much of it was because Bill and I split up. He was there physically, but he was not emotionally supportive. Maybe Bill blamed me, too.

Sometimes I would feel guilty. I have a lot of friends, who, once they had kids, their lives became all about those kids. Everything they did, every night would be sitting with their kids doing homework. If they had a kid with a problem, it was all about going to parenting groups. Part of me envies those people and feels a little guilty, but I'm not that way and I can't do that because I will have a nervous breakdown if I devote all my energy to this child. I just can't be that person. I need to do things for myself in order to maintain my own sanity. I had to accept that, and that's still a battle I have with myself. How much attention can I give? How much is it selfish for me to go off and do things by myself? I've always been kind of a loner and I need a lot of time to myself, to recharge. I give myself pep talks and say, "You're doing the best you can; you love your kids, but this is all you can do."

I think that deep down I felt like it had something to do with issues on my father's side of the family, with some undiagnosed bi-polar or mood disorder. It was pretty clear it was genetic because it had started so young with Sam. I felt like even though Bill and I split up, we had a very good breakup, I think. There were not a lot of really bitter feelings. Even though there was a time when I was very sad, probably clinically depressed for a short time, overall, we maintained a friendship.

I would ask the psychiatrist every now and then, "Do you think Sam is a sociopath?" Sometimes I think he has no empathy; that he's this oppositional, antisocial person who will wind up in jail for the rest of his life. And the psychiatrist would say, "No, I think he does have empathy, and a tough exterior, probably because of insecurity." So I would go back and forth, and I would feel sympathetic if I thought it was insecurity, but sometimes he would be so evil that I would think I just have to protect myself from him. If I asked him to do anything around the house to help, he would just say, "No. I'm not doing it. I don't feel like it. Fuck you." He would call me "bitch" and say because he was my son I had to take care of him. Before he went into detention we had our worst moment, where I felt physically at risk. I think he destroyed every framed photo that summer; I'd come home and there'd be glass all over the floor, or he'd grab something and throw it.

Part of me wonders if he's really ever going to be able to live independently. I used to think it's possible he'll be with me the rest of his life. Because we had so much trouble getting along, he actually lived with his dad three years ago, for a whole year. And it was great. My life was very calm and I really didn't miss him. That was before his dad moved in with his girlfriend into a really tiny house.

Sam screwed around and failed some classes senior year of high school, but now he's making them up. After he finishes the course work, he'll be graduated, I guess, and then wants to go to Community College. But I'm not in any hurry. I don't want to send him away or try to get him in some school just to make it look good that he's in college somewhere. I just feel like he's not ready. Until he makes the decision and figures out what he's interested in, I don't want to throw money away.

Day to day, I'm trying to not make any kind of predictions. I went to see the psychiatrist a couple weeks ago to get another prescription for Sam's ADD medicine, and said to the doctor, "What do you think? I think sometimes he's going to wind up living with me for the rest of his life." He said, "Well, you know I don't have a crystal ball or anything, but I really don't think so." I've gone through every scenario in my head about what could possibly happen. A year ago I really thought he was going to wind up in jail. What I'm thinking more now is that he's going to wind up having a substance abuse problem for a long time. That might be something he deals with the rest of his life. The thing is, whenever I make predictions, 'cause I tend to be negative or catastrophic about things, it doesn't do any good. Things usually turn out better than I think they will.

I feel like as long as he can be respectful to me, then my role is to support him. I've said to him, "I'll always be here for you. If you want to seriously get yourself together, if you need to go to school, or whatever kind of support you need, as long as you're trying to do the right thing, I would never kick you out. But you have to follow some basic rules: You can't steal and you can't be doing illegal stuff while you're living here. If you are willing to stay within those rules, I will never abandon you."

It's easier now to have compassion for him. I think that was marred. I can relate to him better because it seems like he's more of a human being. I see that side of him that actually is a good person. A lot of people probably would've kicked their kid out, but there was always that part of me, as a mother, that knew he was struggling. There was that self-preservation thing, too. I kept saying to people, "I'm not going to let him drag me down." I felt like if I was too compassionate or too invested in him, I might wind up losing it. I still have the problem of him doing things I wish he wouldn't do, but compared to the way it was, it's so much better. I almost feel like he's a straight-A student. (*Laughing.*) Most people would be appalled if they knew their kid was screwin' a bunch of girls and drinking beer. A lot of eighteen-year-olds are doing that; they just don't share it with their moms.

People have ideas of how things are going to be; they plan things out in their heads about their lives. I think the experiences of having my marriage fall apart and having a child like this made me realize you don't have control. I've been reading a lot about Buddhist philosophy during the past year, and it was helpful in confirming the belief that you really don't have control over anything. It's just an illusion. It was very freeing for me to realize it wasn't all on my shoulders. That all I really had power over was myself; to try to work on myself and how I dealt with things.

I felt a lot of judgment from anybody I talked to about Sam. Unless it was somebody who had a problem child and had been through something similar, I felt very judged. I remember saying to a psychologist that people pat themselves on the back if their kids turn out good, but I think it has a lot more to do with just who the kids are, and even what's inherited genetically, than it does from their parenting. People want to give themselves credit. If I give myself credit for James being such a great kid, then I have to blame myself for Sam. And I don't feel like either one of them is a result of anything I've really done directly. I remember telling somebody I'd given up on the idea, when Sam was seven years old, of really controlling him and having a direct influence on the outcome of his life.

I realized the most important thing to me was to have a relationship with Sam, and not be combating him all the time. Everybody seemed to be telling me to clamp down on him and be a stricter disciplinarian. I thought if I do that it will just destroy his relationship with me. At the root of all this, I think he's just very insecure and he needs to feel that I accept him for who he is. There's a part of me that says I know Sam better than anybody. I need to go with my intuition with what I think is the right thing for him.

I see other parents with kids that are just a little bit younger, and their kids haven't gotten into any trouble. I see the expectations parents have, like, "Oh my God, if my kid did that I wouldn't be able to take it." Because of what I've been through, things don't seem that big of a deal to me anymore. I realize I can handle even the worst thought: that my child might be in jail for the rest of his life. You can't know how things are going to turn out so there's no point in catastrophizing or worrying. You can't predict what's going to happen, and strangely enough there's peace in that.

Exploration – Elise

1. Sam began acting out after his younger brother arrived on the scene. Elise wondered if she raised Sam "right" and questioned whether she spoiled him too much. What exactly does "spoiling" mean in your family culture? Did the arrival of a second child cause problems in your household?

2. Elise felt Sam blamed her for "everything that was wrong with him," and vented the worst of his anger towards her. What were the ways you coped with your children's anger? Did they blame you for their struggles? When you were a child, how did your family handle anger?

3. Do you agree with Elise's idea that kids are less influenced by parenting than most people think? If we take credit for our kids' successes, should we blame ourselves when they run into trouble?

4. Elise's experiences of a failed marriage and challenging son fostered a belief that control is an illusion. Do you believe this, too?

5. Elise said, "It was very freeing to realize it wasn't all on my shoulders…all I really had the power over was myself, to try to work on myself and how I dealt with things." Have you had a similar experience of letting go? How did focusing on yourself change things?

6. Elise felt she knew Sam better than anyone else and said, "I have to go with my intuition with what I think is the

right thing for him." Do you trust your own intuition to that degree? In what instances has it served you best?

7. There is a classic female conflict in Elise between her needs and the needs of her children. Do you feel this tug in your life? How do you carve out the personal space you require?

8. When Sam was arrested for the third time, Elise made the difficult choice not to hire a lawyer. If Sam were your child, what decision do you think you would have made?

9. Elise arrived at a place where she felt, "You can't predict what's going to happen, and strangely enough, there's peace in that." In thinking about your own life and family, does finding peace in unpredictability resonate with you? If not, what has helped you find peace in your most challenging relationships?

Caitlin, 51

I was ten when I was diagnosed with diabetes. From the beginning, I had to take injections. At the time, you're a kid, so it's not so traumatic. It was just something else I had to do. I didn't really know what this was going to mean for me for the rest of my life. It was just – now I was sort of special and needed to do these other things.

For the next twenty years I lived pretty normally. Being a diabetic, you have to do certain things, and it's a pain. You have to eat a certain way and you have to take your injections. It's just something you have to do. I was not one who was highly disciplined; never have been. So, even though I knew that I needed to take care of myself, I was never really fanatical about it. I tried not to let it be the guide to my life. It's something I have to deal with, but don't want it to take over my life. I think even during my twenties I felt the same way, and probably didn't take very good care of myself during that time. Part of me knew I had to take care of this, but at the same time it's something I didn't really want to do, and I didn't do the best job. As a result, in my late twenties I started having problems with my eyesight.

The first big thing happened when I was on a plane to Florida, for my *honeymoon*, and one of the blood vessels in my right eye burst. I freaked out. I was blind and there was nothing I could do. No one could see it; it's in the back of the eye, but I suddenly lost vision in that eye. I was freaking out, "Oh my God, my eye, I can't see through my eye." We landed late at night, and I had to fake being okay checking into the hotel. I didn't go to a doctor because I think I knew there was nothing they could do. What happens is that your body eventually reabsorbs the blood, so I could kind of see out of it a couple days later.

Later on, it happened again and I ended up having a detached retina. They had to put a bubble in my eye to keep the retina from completely detaching, and for *three weeks* I had to have my head down, hanging down towards the floor. They were hoping the retina would stay attached. I had a lot of sad incidents that happened with my right eye. To this day, the retina is partially detached and I have to wear a contact over the eye or I have double vision.

My left eye at that time was fine. Basically, I was using my left eye for everything. But over the next twelve years my vision in that eye got progressively worse. I had laser treatments, but still thought of it as my "good" eye. While the laser treatments help prevent blood vessels from bursting, they unfortunately compromise your vision.

During those years, driving was increasingly more difficult because, one: I'm driving with one eye and have no depth perception, and two: the laser treatments sort of erase things, so you don't see as clearly as you used to. So I had a lot of strategies for how I would drive. I would have to think about where I was going and how many lights there were. I couldn't read the signs. So I would create a route that involved traffic lights that I knew really well and wasn't heavily travelled. I didn't want to hit anybody and I wanted to be safe.

In my early thirties, I knew I had to make a career change. I had been working in the technology area of education at the time, doing video work and highly visual stuff. I met somebody who said the visually impaired field was an area that needed teachers and might be getting some funding. I knew my vision was compromised and thought maybe I'd be a good role model, and I was already working in education. So I went back to school to be a teacher for the blind and visually impaired.

I had to drive to school. It was difficult. I have to say, I don't know how I did it, really. There were times when I would be driving and would go by somebody and didn't even see them. Oh my God, I could have hit that person. They were in the shadows on the side of the road. So part of my strategy was that I would try to drive in the middle of the road. I couldn't anticipate something happening very fast so staying in the middle was the strategy. When I was going to school my vision was okay, and I knew I could get through. But as time went on, it became worse, and then I altogether stopped driving at night because it was really difficult.

Before I adopted my son, I worked as a teacher for the blind and visually impaired. When my husband and I moved to Boston, we knew that we needed to move close to where there was public transportation. There was a high likelihood that my vision would decline, so we purposely bought a house on the T so I wouldn't be completely stranded. There was forethought in a lot of the actions and decisions I made at the time. But when I got the teaching job, I didn't realize that much of it would be itinerant and that I would have to get to different places. Although I liked being in the blind community because a lot of the people are very caring and understanding, I didn't think this all the way through. As a teacher, I'd have to get to all these different schools. I mean, there are visually impaired teachers who are working in the field, but they get people to drive them; they're not behind the wheel. (*Laughing*.)

My impairment is totally invisible. You can't tell. Maybe you could look at my right eye when the contact is in and think,

"She has a weird iris." But on the whole, most people don't know that I can't see. And it's a major barrier to having people understand that I'm visually impaired. It's terrible. I tell people, but they don't understand, they don't remember. Some people get it, but the majority of people don't really get it. I can't see people's faces clearly, so I don't recognize them. As my sight has gotten worse, it's really difficult to know who people are. I end up recognizing them by the way they speak. People don't really adjust their behavior because they know I can't see. (*Laughing.*) Weirdly enough, that's including my family. I'm talking about things like writing notes bigger, using a bold pen, or being more descriptive. When they're making reference to something "over there" I can't see "over there" so they have to give me a little more to work with. (*Laughing.*)

My relationships are really limited because I can't read people's social cues; I don't know what the expression is on their faces. I've lost all of that. Even though you can *tell* people, they still think you can see. I look perfectly normal. If I was carrying around a white cane it would be more of a reminder. People don't accommodate for me as they would for somebody who looked obviously disabled.

So I ended up being declared legally blind. When you cross the line into legal blindness, they report you to the Commission for the Blind so you can get services, but they also tell you that you can't *drive*. I will always remember when the doctor said, "I'm going to have to tell the Commission that you'll have to give up your driver's license." I felt *angry* about it. I'd been fighting it for so long. It just wasn't fair. I guess I felt angry at life, not the doctor. Just, why do I have to go through this? It's so hard. I got a call from the Commission and I didn't want to talk to them. I thought, if I do have to talk to somebody, I want somebody that has a disability; I don't want to talk to somebody who doesn't. I wanted to talk to somebody who would understand how I felt.

I still had my driver's license; it wasn't expired and I continued to drive for about another year. It wasn't like the Commission was after me; I think it takes them a while to deal with all the administrative processing. I didn't have a gun to my head or anything; I didn't have anybody saying, "You have to give it up." So I kept driving.

For a long time, I would do these strategies, and even say, "I'm not going to drive," 'cause I want to see how it's going to be. "I'm going to try and take public transportation to wherever I'm going. I'm just going to see how that goes." I can't even tell you, it's just such a hard thing to give up; it represents your freedom and your independence. It just limits what you can and cannot do, and you're going to be dependent on other people. For all of those reasons, I was fighting against having to give up my license. I really tried to wean myself off the car and use public transportation, and ask people for rides.

There were times when I just felt I had to get somewhere or I had to do something, so I would take the car out. And yeah, no one would know. I don't know if people saw me, but maybe they did. At one point, I think I said, "If I'm telling people that I can't drive, but then they see me drive, what is *that* telling them?" You can't have both. I even remember that I would drive the car somewhere, and park it in a place that wasn't with all the other cars because I didn't want anybody to know I was driving. I mean, here I am asking people for rides and, jeez. I do remember being caught having to lie a couple times where someone would ask me if I had a ride home, and I would say, "Oh no, no. I'm going to walk," and I actually had the car. The car was parked somewhere else. I felt guilty. I felt that I was kind of two-faced. I'm sending out a confused message. I didn't want to give up the car; I wanted to drive, but I knew it wasn't a safe decision to do that. I was always in jeopardy taking out the car.

When my son was a baby, I think my eyesight was okay, but it wasn't perfect. I was driving up this hill and the sun was right in my eyes. I didn't see one of those lawn trucks parked on the side of the street and I plowed into it. Maybe if I had really good eyesight I would have seen it, but I didn't see the truck at all. No one was hurt, and the car wasn't really damaged, but it could have been worse. My son was in the car at the time; it could have been a lot worse. You'd think that would have been a turning point, but I continued to drive. As time went on and my son got older, he could talk and tell me things. I would say, "Well, what is the color of the light up ahead? Do you see anything on the side of the road?" Totally, totally irresponsible. I was doing it so I could continue to drive, continue to do the things I had to do. I don't think my husband knew that my son was giving me directions.

I finally thought, if I'm going to give up my license, this is what I'm going to do: I'm going to go away. I went on a trip to San Francisco with my mother, and we were going to be away for a week, and I wouldn't be driving for the whole week. I thought, well that's a good plan. I'm going to be away, and this'll be a turning point where I come back and I'm not going to drive. I made a pledge to myself. I won't say I was one hundred percent not driving after that, but I will say that I drastically reduced my driving by ninety percent. I don't want to be responsible for somebody else's death.

Life without a car is horrible and huge. It's very difficult because it has impacted my son, my husband, our whole family dynamic. It's not easy to ask people for help; it's not easy to ask people for rides. My son is affected because we both have to ask people to help get him places. He just finished middle school and was the only walker. He's had to be more independent, had to learn public transportation, had to learn to get places on his own. I'm proud of him. Rarely does he complain he can't get somewhere. But my husband has had to pick up a lot of the slack.

I think I have more of an appreciation for the environment. I'm always walking or biking places, and I use public transportation. So I guess, if anything, I've become more of an advocate for anti-car and anti-big-gas-guzzling vehicles. I've been forced into the alternative and have become more conscious about it. I maybe would never have thought about it before. Because I'm forced to walk places, it's probably made me a healthier person. I've maintained my weight and I'm not as lazy as I could be. There's also a sense of relief that I won't harm or kill someone.

It's still frustrating in social situations. It's hard for me just having relationships with people. That's the hardest part right now. If you wanted to take a class or wanted to go to something at night, all the plans that it takes to do that – sometimes you just don't want to go through all of that, so you just don't go out. I just can't get out to meetings at night; my community is limited. Really, our society is not a good place to be visually impaired. You're always educating people; it's tiring.

I made a major change when I wasn't driving: I searched for work inside the city so I wouldn't have to take a car. Now I work in Boston on a federally funded technology program, working with people who have disabilities. So, for me, I don't know if I would have had that experience if I didn't have the visual impairment and stopped driving. It's an extremely satisfying profession because I work with people I can relate to, and they can relate to me. It does my psyche a lot of good to give back and work with all kinds of people. I think having a disability myself breaks down lots of barriers; I know where they're coming from.

It's been seven years since I gave up my license, and honestly, not driving totally sucks. I compare it to an addiction. I dream a lot, and in my dreams sometimes I'm driving. I used to have more of those driving dreams, but now they happen less. I *love* the dreams when I'm driving. It's wonderful; I love driving. I miss it. Anytime I go to an amusement park, I make sure that I drive the bumper cars. I always search out opportunities where I can drive; I'll even drive the car out of the garage or drive around the neighborhood and come back. I mean, it's not good, but that desire hasn't gone away. If I had good vision right now, I'd be back in the car in nothin' flat.

Exploration – Caitlin

1. In her youth, Caitlin said she didn't want diabetes to be "the guide to her life" and felt it was something she had to deal with, but didn't want it taking over her life. Has disease or illness ever threatened to "take over" your life? How were you able to prevent that from happening?

2. Caitlin persevered to get her Master's, and employed numerous strategies to help her drive to school. Do you support the risks she took to enter a field suited to her disability? Have you taken calculated risks in order to change your life?

3. The outside world generally did not perceive Caitlin's blindness. She felt this was a "huge barrier" and said, "…people don't accommodate for me as they would for somebody who looked obviously disabled." Is there anything more she could do to help bridge that barrier? Can you empathize with the frustrations that even her own family "forgets" she can't see?

4. When the doctor informed her she would have to eventually give up her license, Caitlin was angry and only wanted to talk to a disabled person: "I wanted to talk to somebody who would understand how I felt." Do you agree that only another disabled person could empathize with her situation?

5. Besides feeling a sense of loss regarding her freedom, Caitlin expressed frustration at "having to be dependent on other people." Would you be comfortable asking

people for transportation help? How important is a sense of independence to your overall well-being?

6. Although she felt it was irresponsible, Caitlin made the choice to drive so she "could do the things I had to do." Are there pressures in your world that would make you want to employ a similar strategy? How do you feel about Caitlin asking her young son to help navigate?

7. Caitlin seemed to love her current job and understood how her impairment and giving up the car brought her to that place. Yet seven years later she said, "Honestly, not driving totally sucks." Are there similar dichotomies in your own life?

Angie, 36

It all started when someone took my mom from us. She was murdered and our house was set on fire. I had just turned sixteen years old. One of the neighbors came to school and mentioned there was a house fire, nothing else. I was brought home from school halfway through the day to watch my house burn to the ground, and I had no clue that my mom had been in there to begin with. I didn't know about the murder, or anything that had happened. I came home to fire engines and ambulances. At one point I was worried about my clothes; I was sixteen and was like, "Oh my God, my prom gown is in there." I was thinking of such little things – my curling iron, my clothes. I didn't put two and two together until I had seen somebody come out on a gurney and they were covered with a sheet. My mom's car is in the driveway and I'm just frantic; I don't know what to think. Nobody is talking to me and I'm asking everyone, "What's going on? What's going on?" All they said was, "Calm down, calm down, it's going to be okay. We'll figure this out."

My little brother comes home from grade school; he's twelve and all I remember is him crying. A fireman comes out with our little baby puppy and I remember saying, "They got this puppy out and they didn't get my mom?" They gave Steven the dog. The gurney had already come out and I was thinking it was her because her car was in the driveway. (*Crying.*) My dad arrived and I remember him just leaning on my mom's car and just crying and crying. He was hugging us but I don't remember if I asked him anything, or if he answered me. The next day we were homeless and motherless.

At that point we knew our mother was dead, but we did not know she was murdered. My dad kept it from us; we thought she had burned in the fire. And I had such unbelievable shock, like, "How could they get a puppy out of there and not my mom?" How could that be? All my dad did was cry; it was really hard to even face him and ask him. My dad didn't want the TV on, because it was all over the news. He didn't want any newspapers in the house. He kept us from finding out the truth as long as he possibly could; he really had a lid on this.

We didn't hear it from him. We were staying at my grandmother's house and I overheard my relatives talking. My mom was the baby of nine, so there were a lot of aunts and uncles, and we heard them talking and learned that she had been stabbed to death. She was strangled, stabbed in her chest and throat, and set on fire, with the house. She was dead before the fire was started; the fire was to cover up her murder.

She was a good person. We were really close. (*Crying.*) Nobody could even imagine that this had happened to her, of all people. This was the most shocking thing. She was an RN in a doctor's office, and her patients couldn't believe it. I didn't even think it was true. Nobody wanted to discuss it with us, nobody. I didn't even know how to process it, how to put my ducks in a row to even count them. I didn't know where I was going with it. When we upped and went with my grandparents, I was cut off from all my friends; I didn't have any support. My Dad's mother lives miles from our house, where all my friends were. The next time I saw somebody from my gang of friends, it was them sitting across from me at the funeral parlor. Back then we didn't have cell phones or internet or anything; we met at the street corner or the park to talk.

So I had nobody but my brother. We just cried and held each other. (*Crying*.) I tried to tell him that everything was going to be okay, that somehow it would be okay. I was trying to make myself believe that, too. I was like, wow, this little boy is twelve years old; what am I going to do? Our lives were falling apart in front of us. She was the one that kept us on track. It's your mom, you know? She did *everything* for us. We didn't do anything. She didn't have a lot of friends; she didn't go out a lot. We were her life – her kids, her garden, the dog. She was a really good person.

We were never allowed to grieve. Even in the passage of time getting over this, for the longest time my dad didn't want to talk about it, didn't want to bring it up. It hurt him so much, but I don't think he realized how bad it hurt us not to talk about it. It's a little different now, but he suffered so bad. He didn't want to talk about it in *any* way.

I can remember right after my mom's funeral, being carted off to the police department for questioning: "Who are your friends, this that, give me names of this, who was at your house, who's *ever* been to your house…" I mean, I'm like, "All my friends have been to my house. Are you nuts? Are you crazy?" We're kids. And the drilling of like, "Where were you? How'd you do this? When did you do that? How did you do this? Who were you seeing? Where were your friends?" They took the whole funeral parlor register, and took that book and went down that list and asked me who they were, what they were to me, how did they fit into my life. I was on autopilot. But I sat there and answered them. I think most of my life has been on autopilot, from that day forth.

Being kids, we just sucked it up, and said, "Dad's doing it, we gotta do it too. We have to be strong for him." We have to not cry in front of him, not let him see how mad we are, and how hurtful it is. We didn't want him to hurt any more than he needed to hurt, either. Yet, we were just kids. I just completely shut down. We were at my grandparents for a good month, and back at school about a week afterwards, with my father driving us. My friends didn't want to talk to me about it. It was, "I'm sorry for your loss; I can't believe this…" No one asked questions. I think they were afraid to hurt my feelings. I did speak touch-and-go with some of my girlfriends, but not much. I think I just tried to swallow it; didn't even chew it first, just swallowed it. I was trying to do what I could to keep me and Steven going. Poor little thing – he had no clue, being even younger than me.

We eventually moved to a furnished apartment and got back in a routine. Our house was being rebuilt. I heard all this talk about how that wasn't a good idea since it was a murder scene. But my dad *insisted* on building this house again. I didn't want to go back there. I was scared. I did not want to go back to that house. This person knows something about us, and we have no clue who this person is. He could have seen my pictures on the wall; I don't know what drawers he's gone through. I don't know if he knew she had children. That kind of stuff went through my head. I think my dad put a cap on us even harder, not wanting us to talk to anybody about it.

I do remember my dad taking us to one or two sessions with a counselor. And that was the end of it. I couldn't even tell you if I told the truth or if I even spoke aloud. I can't remember if I spoke out loud because I didn't know what I could or couldn't say, or what I should or shouldn't say to hurt my dad. It was a whole group therapy: my brother, my dad and me. And it was clear he didn't want us talking. I don't know what the reasoning was for the counseling. It was an absolute waste; it was awful.

Before we were to move back into our house, my dad sent both of us off; he separated me and my brother. He sent my brother to Washington State to stay with my grandparents, and sent me to my mom's side of the family in Florida. We actually were separated which was horrible; it was awful. I remember I wanted to be with my brother so bad. I just wanted to be around my friends and family and I was sent away for almost the entire summer. I was very resentful. That was the last time my dad ever separated us.

My dad, himself, rebuilt this house up from the ground. Eventually, (*whispering*) we did move back in there. My brother would not go back into the room where they found her dead. *I* ended up staying in that room. I just tucked the fear away. If I didn't think about it, then it's not here and it's not happening. It didn't work out so well. I just tried to keep on going.

The investigation continued and then it hit a dead-end. I guess after the fact, maybe my dad got angry that this had happened to him. I guess he wanted it solved and wanted closure. We did a taping for Unsolved Mysteries and they came to our house. We got to speak about it with him a little more freely, but to this day it's still walkin' on eggshells with him. The words of her being "stabbed" or "murdered" has never come out of my mouth to him, never. Absolutely, never. When we were fresh into this, we didn't even try to say her name because we didn't want to hurt him.

We ended up resenting him a little bit because he started dating fairly quickly after losing my mom. We were like six months into this ordeal. When I came home from Florida there was a girlfriend on the scene and I thought, "We walked on eggshells for you. We didn't even mention her name or talk about this because we thought it hurt you so bad. And now, you're obviously okay with this." But we never said anything;

we didn't *ever* talk back to our dad. It's just the way it was. My mom was the softness; she was the reasoning in our family. She was the one who said to him, "You're being too hard on the kids." My dad went to work, made the pay, came home, handed over the check. She was everything. She was the glue that held everything together. When this happened, our family literally fell apart. I mean, *fell apart.*

My dad started drinking pretty heavily, and when I was still sixteen, I got involved with drinking and drugs. That was another big thing that separated us even more; I wasn't the good little girl I had always been. I started going out drinking, smoking cigarettes, smoking pot. I did whatever was out there that my friends were doing, too. It helped a little, but I was going down a pretty bad road; I was drinking and getting high all the time. Me and my dad were constantly fighting. He would say he was protecting us, but he wasn't. He had no clue how to help us. He didn't even know how to write a check. When I say my mom was everything, I mean *everything*. She did *everything*.

I didn't graduate high school. I got pregnant and dropped out halfway through my senior year to have my son. He's seventeen now. When I got pregnant, me and my dad stopped talking, of course. My brother called me every single day, "Did you have that baby yet?" He was so young. I was turning nineteen and he was just a kid. My brother is my best friend, forever. We're three thousand miles away and we still talk every single day. We're each other's therapy. That's how we get by in life.

I think me getting pregnant at an early age was almost a blessing in disguise because I could've been dead if I hadn't thought I needed to clean up my act. That was a very big thing that kicked in when I got pregnant. I thought, "Oh my God. I have to do everything and anything to protect this baby, and ensure that I'm here *forever*." That probably was a very big moment in my life because then I became, I'm not gonna say a "freak," but I became anal about everything. I didn't let anybody babysit my kid; I was the only one who could care for my kid and care for him properly, I thought.

Not having a mother to help me with him was hard. I was really resentful to my husband's mom because she was there. I wished it was my mom helping me. She would have been a great grandmom. So the depression started all over again. I didn't know how else to handle it, except the way I did the first time, just sucking it up, not talking to anyone.

My husband and I were together about a year and a half before my son was born. He knew how my mom died and was very therapeutic in the beginning. But later on, we started having awful arguments and disagreeing on just about everything. Once we started having problems and I wasn't sure I wanted to stay, he would throw it in my face: "Your mom's going to be disappointed if you break up our family." So I was staying with him just because I wanted my family to be strong and together. As a child, my mom was taken away from me without me saying it was okay, without an option. I didn't get to say, "Please don't do this to me. Don't leave us." So I felt that guilt, for a long time, to stay with him. He was verbally abusive and even took it to the level of, "Your mom's ashamed of you – she would never want you to leave." I stayed in that very unhealthy relationship for about fifteen years. I had to get really *strong* to get out of his claws.

I have more fears in the last ten years than I've ever had in my life. They just keep surfacing. I think I can control everything. I won't get in a car unless I'm driving; I have to drive just about everywhere. If I am in the passenger seat I'm just about to have a panic attack. I am an absolute control freak. Things have to run like clockwork for me. I think I'm gonna be here forever, here for my children. I just know how important it is to be in my children's life as long as possible.

Some people might think that sixteen is on your way to being an adult, but it's not a lot of time. There are things that happen every day that remind me she's not here. My son is going to graduate this year; I'm sure that's gonna be hard. Every holiday is a trauma for me. It brings up everything I dread to even think about. I think by tucking it away I can make the hurt go away. I just keep on going. I think that's why I'm so regimented.

For the longest time, I had nightmares. All I could see is that white gurney. And now I know it is her. I can dream that day perfectly, and I've dreamt it over and over. I keep thinking, "Do I remember something? Was there somebody that I did miss? Or was there someone in a crowd that I overlooked? What could I do to solve this?" I think I'm trying to search for something that might not even be there.

The fact that this person still has a life, if he or she still has life, and the fact that this person still gets to celebrate holidays... I don't know this; he could be rotting in a jail cell right now. But my take is that my holidays are spent being upset and grieving, and some piece of shit is out there celebrating a holiday with their family. Or maybe not; maybe they're just pissing it off. Whatever it may be – but they're still sucking up life while we're missing our mom, and we want her here. I was angry at the situation; this person took what was important to us and didn't give a crap. The mind is crazy. I can consume myself with this; drive myself up a wall.

I think closure would be good only due to the fact that I would know this person is off the street and would never do this again. To this day, I don't know if it's a he or she, I don't know if this person has a family, I don't know if this person knows who *I* am, or my little brother. That gives me fear. And that I have children in this world too – that scares me. I think if I do something wrong, make a mistake like yell at a guy in traffic, he might kill me and take me away from my kids; it just sparks *craziness* in my head.

It just takes that little thing to set me off, and then I have to work it back down and get it under control. I'm really good about tuckin' it away; that's the one thing I *can* do. But the bad thing is that it's just being put under the couch; it's not being addressed. I make it gone; I make it disappear. Until the next issue, the next trigger. I've had them for the last twenty years; I'm sure there's going to be plenty more. I am going to be here for as long as possible. Nobody's gonna hurt me or take me away from my children. I just *have* to be here, no matter what, I have to be here.

Exploration – Angie

1. Angie was never directly told that her mother had died, or that she had been murdered. The gurney and her father's crying led Angie to the reality of the death, and overhearing relatives was how she learned of her mother's violent demise. If her father was incapable of talking about it, who could have taken on that responsibility? What would you have said to her?

2. Grieving was not an option for the children since their father did not want the subject of their mother's death brought up. Angie said, "…I don't think he realized how bad it hurt us not to talk about it." Have you ever felt your voice silenced in grief? What did you do with the ensuing pain?

3. Angie's friends didn't know how to talk to her about the tragedy. She said, "I think I just tried to swallow it; didn't even chew it first, just swallowed it." If Angie were your friend, would you broach the subject? How would you be present for her?

4. Angie was forced to return to her house, and to spare her little brother, she slept in the room where their mom had been murdered. What has been your most courageous act? What was the impetus?

5. Like her father, Angie escaped into alcohol and other drugs to cope with her emotional pain. In the wake of living through such a violent trauma, was there was any other path she could have taken? What would have had to happen for that to occur?

6. Becoming pregnant at sixteen was a turning point that Angie called "a blessing in disguise." Have you had an experience that was "a blessing in disguise"? At what point did you see the blessing revealed?

7. Angie's husband exploited her mom-centered vulnerabilities to control her actions. Have you been involved with or witnessed this kind of emotional manipulation? What did you learn from it?

8. Twenty years after her mother's murder, Angie had "more fears...than I've ever had in my life." Do you think a person can recover from a trauma like this? What counsel would you give Angie in helping her live a happier life? Is confronting her father an important component?

9. Despite all her trials and pain, Angie found the strength to leave her husband and begin anew. Do you know someone who has overcome enormous odds and moved forward in life? What was the source of their strength?

10. Angie's brother was a solid, loving connection throughout their ordeal, and continued to be her "therapist" and best friend. When the going gets tough, is there someone in your world you can always count on? How was that bond forged?

Carson, 22

I was a junior in high school and had just broken up with my first "real" boyfriend, and my friend Nick says, "Well, if it makes you feel any better I know somebody else that really likes you." I had a crush on Nick for a while; he was cute and really flirtatious. A couple of days later we were talking, and I was trying so hard to get him to tell me who liked me, and instead of telling me he *kissed* me. Yeah. Pretty smooth for a sixteen year old boy. That started our relationship. We had spent a lot of time around each other; I knew his family, he knew mine. So we started dating. Things were going pretty well, but I sort of always had this feeling that I was a little bit more into it than he was. I just knew that I really, really, really liked him. That's the simplest way to put it. I didn't really know how or what he felt. I always kind of knew something was amiss.

He had dated this girl, Lizzie, and his parents had made him end it because they didn't like her. The whole school had known what happened and it was kind of a scandal; everybody felt bad for this girl. It was unfortunate. Our school was small; twelve hundred total from pre-school through twelfth grade. I knew that Nick and Lizzie were friends, but they weren't really supposed to be hanging out outside school. They weren't supposed to be spending time together one-on-one.

I remember at Christmastime my present was a diamond ring. No boy had ever given me anything so beautiful in my entire life. We were at Disneyland and the snow was falling, and he gave me the ring, and I was just so happy. I definitely felt in love with him.

About five and a half months into it I could kind of feel... I was starting to get really stressed out. I was working on applications to colleges because I was originally thinking of playing college sports. So I was starting to send in videos; I was playing club volleyball, which was about fifteen hours a week. And I was writing essays for colleges, and going crazy with recruiting.

Also around the same time, I was on the Honor Committee, and this huge cheating scandal broke out and I had to expel a couple people I had known for more than ten years. So shit was hitting the proverbial fan. My high school advisor, who was like the coolest woman alive, had just been fired and they wouldn't tell us why. It was one of those springs where everything terrible that could've happened, did happen. My sister was going away to college so my parents were starting to freak out about that. Everything was getting worse and worse. I remember feeling extremely overwhelmed.

A bunch of us were hanging out at my friend Johnny's house. It was kind of unusual for me to be there, because basically since Nick and I started dating, Johnny had been acting really cold to me. So Nick called me inside and said, "I don't think this is working out. I think we've been unhappy. I think it's time for us to break up." I was devastated. I said, "I've been really stressed out lately, but I think we can work through it. I agree with you that things haven't been great but I've had all this stress, and when summer comes a lot of it's going to go away." And he was like, "No, there's no convincing me." And he cried; whatever. I was bawling.

I thought it might have something to do with sex. I had had a lot of pressure, not from him, but from mutual friends, in terms of the sexual department. I had a lot of insecurities there; I didn't know what the hell I was doing. And Nick was really closed off about it. We had fun, a lot of surface fun. Looking back, it was really only deep on my side, I think. I think I knew that. I wasn't shocked when he broke up with me – I was just sad. I wasn't really doing anything sexual with him. I knew it had part to do with that, and part to do with just, "Well, he is just cooler and cuter than me. I just don't deserve someone who is like him."

That weekend I just sort of walked around kind of numb. He and I still talked; we decided we were going to be friends. We had been really good friends beforehand so we decided we were going to work on being friends. It was going to be hard but it was important to both of us. He saw me down when we broke up and said, "I feel terrible about hurting you. It's important to me that we stay close." I was like, "Okay. Whatever." This happened on a Friday night. That Monday, I remember having a break at the end of the day, sitting near him and being like, "Why am I subjecting myself to this?"

On Tuesday afternoon, someone came up to me and said, "Look, I have to tell you something." This was just sort of a random person. She said, "I was sitting at a table with a bunch of girls, and one of them said that Lizzie had gone for birth control and that Nick and Lizzie have been together for months." I can remember exactly where we were standing. I just fell over. I sat down on the floor and started crying.

My volleyball teammates and other friends ran up and sat with me and said, "You know, we've been trying to figure out a way to tell you for months." One of them had written me a letter, but hadn't figured out a way to hand it to me. The girls I played volleyball with said, "Every time we saw you we wanted to tell you, but we didn't know how. We knew how bad it would be." They were amazing to me; it was guilt I'm sure, but I spent the next three days at friends' houses. They said, "The only thing you can do is keep busy and don't think about it. It's just miserable; he's not worth it."

It's funny, because my mom had tried to warn me earlier in the day that Nick was cheating on me, even before that girl told me. I was furious at my mother for implying this, absolutely furious. It turns out a friend of hers had seen Nick and Lizzie together, and shared that with her. Mom tried to gently let me know and I was just having nothing of it.

So that day, Nick was at a baseball game. I can remember what I was wearing. And I remember shaking. I went up to his car when he got back and I said, "Somebody came up to me and told me this today." And he completely denied everything. And I said, "That's absolute bullshit. I don't believe you." Then he said they kissed a few times but absolutely had not slept together. I just remember really, really wanting to slap him, but I was just too shaky to even know what to do.

I was angry for a month straight. I just remember I was *so, so* angry. He wouldn't even look at me. His mom called me and said, "Look, Nick wants to talk with you. We totally understand if you want nothing to do with him ever again, but he does have something to say." His parents really liked me. They still have a picture of us in their garage; kind of strange. (*Laughing.*)

I called my friend Johnny's mother, who's like a second mother to me, and said, "What should I do?" She said, "Well, if you think you're going to get some closure from it, you should go." This was also my first exposure to the concept of closure, which is like super-strange to think of now, because it seems to be such a standard thing in a relationship, but I had no idea what any of this was about.

Nick's parents grounded him for four months and pulled him out of school for a week. They took away his cell phone and his car. It was awesome. (*Laughing.*) They actually talked about moving for a while. They hated Lizzie, and they liked me, and they were just so furious at their son. They wrote me a letter a couple months later and the letter said, "We hate what he did. We know that when he was with you he was the best person he'll ever be."

I went over to see him and he said, "I can't even look at myself for what I did. I know that I hurt you and I have absolutely nothing left. I miss you like crazy. I need a friend; no one will talk to me; no one wants anything to do with me." I said, "I appreciate everything you've said today. I know it's hard to own up to what you did, but I absolutely cannot be your friend." Which was the first time I think I really stood up for myself with a boy. Which was awesome.

It was hard; for a while there I remember waking up every single day and it was the first thought in my head. You wake up and you're like, "Oh yeah, that *did* happen. I have to go to school today and see this person." I had teachers approaching me, telling me I was going to be okay. I had people I had never even talked to in school walking up to me saying, "He's such an idiot, you're so much prettier than her. You shouldn't care." I tend to look at most of my breakups like there's a winner and loser; I think it stemmed from that time. I remember feeling, "Well, I won. Everyone knows what he did. Everyone in this school hates him for what he did." I *wanted* to people to dislike him for what he'd done.

Ultimately, it was awesome because two weeks after we broke up, Johnny walked up to me and said, "The reason I haven't talked to you for the past six months is because I was in love with you and you were dating my best friend." So that was pretty awesome because then not only did I win, but I got to date the guy's best friend.

How I am now in my relationships is that I'm a trusting person until you cross me. If you hurt me once, there is absolutely no going back – it's over. After Nick and I broke up, I vowed to myself that I would never let a boy take advantage of me again. I've gotten a lot better about cutting all ties. It's pissed off a lot of ex-boyfriends. (*Laughing.*) If I could talk to that younger version of me, I would definitely say, "Keep your guard up a little more." It's something I maintain now.

I think that that relationship had ramifications for me emotionally and in terms of my sexual comfort level. I'm happy I was not more sexually active with Nick, because I think it saved me from a lot of hurt I've watched my friends go through. One of the things I was really proud of myself for, was that I didn't give in to the pressure; the pressure to go at least a few steps farther than I was comfortable. My friends were having either oral sex or intercourse. I don't remember Nick pressuring me directly; it was more my knowing that I was behind a lot of our friends, and behind his expectations, and feeling pressure to do whatever I could to save our relationship. I remember thinking it wasn't possible that somebody like him could like me as much as I liked him.

Looking back on all that sexual stuff, you sort of inherently know if you're comfortable or not. You can try to convince yourself otherwise, but something in you knows. The biggest flaw in our relationship was that we were both so insecure and so closed off about everything. I think if we had just talked openly, maybe things wouldn't have gotten to the point that they did. Maybe he would've felt comfortable sitting me down to say, "Look, I'm actually still in love with Lizzie. I shouldn't be dating you; it's not fair to you." But we were both so immature; we both were so insecure. Neither one of us could sit down and have an honest, open, emotional conversation like that. I suppose that's why you go through these relationships – you learn the importance of communication.

That experience forced me to tie emotions to sex. The trust issues don't just accompany the emotional stuff; they relate to the physical issues, too. There is no such thing as sex without emotional ties for me. For whatever reason, it's manifested that way and that definitely has been positive. I felt like I've really known and trusted each one of my boyfriends in college.

It also changed how I interacted with boys, how I flirted with them. Ever since then, I've been very defensive. I definitely put way more importance on sitting down and talking things out, which has served to drive future boyfriends absolutely bonkers. (*Laughing.*) But it's so important for me to not ever feel like there's a distance. It's also led me to confront people I feel have done me wrong. Off the bat, I absolutely don't trust boys at all. My heart is definitely not on the table.

Now that I verbalize it, it does make more sense to say – I do have trust issues with every guy I meet. I'm hard on them; I definitely have high standards. If I'm comfortable enough to enter a relationship, then I better trust them. My point is that if they can make it through, if they don't mind putting up with the fact that I'm *not* going back to their room at two in the morning after a drunken night, if they actually care enough about seeing me to pursue me in a respectful way, that's when the trust develops.

Exploration – Carson

1. Carson "always had this feeling" that she was more invested than Nick and "knew something was amiss" early in the relationship. What role has intuition played in your romantic life?

2. Sexual insecurity and believing Nick was "cooler and cuter" were Carson's initial explanations for the breakup. She took it a step further and thought, "I just don't deserve someone who is like him." Self-blame is often a female default mode of thinking. Why do you think we're so quick to do this?

3. Carson was furious when her mother tried to tell her Nick had been cheating, but immediately accepted the news from her peers. What factors do you think were at play in her response? How do you take news from different people?

4. The concept of closure became "a standard thing" for Carson. What has to happen for you to have a sense of closure? Do you need closure in order to move on?

5. When Carson definitively told Nick she could not be his friend, it was the first time she "stood up for herself" with a boy, and she called the experience "awesome." Do you remember the first time you felt a sense of personal power in a relationship? How do you think it impacted future relationships?

6. Carson viewed breakups with the sense that there is a "winner and a loser." Do you agree? What factors play into those roles?

7. If Carson could talk to her younger self, she would counsel, "Keep your guard up a little more." What relationship advice would you give your younger self?

8. The breakup with Nick has led Carson to confront people who have done her wrong. Are you comfortable confronting people who have not treated you fairly? When is confrontation most challenging for you?

9. Nick risked (and lost) a lot by being with Lizzie. Has a romance ever compelled you to take a huge gamble? Was it worth it?

Merle, 66

Growing up, there was my brother and me. We were indispensable to each other. We were best friends and did everything together. I was always protective of him; he was always protective of me, even though he's a couple years younger. I always thought I had a really good childhood, a healthy childhood. My parents were loving; my father adored me, my mom was wonderful. She wasn't there a lot because she had a business and was very busy. I was brought up with the business. My dad worked as a plumber, but I don't remember him working that much. We would go everywhere together. He was really proud of me. I think I was speaking before I was a year old and I read really early, too. From a young age, I always felt safe, certainly when he was around.

My mother had a large family; she had two brothers and three sisters. One of the sisters, Aunt Helen, lived near us and we would go there on Sundays. It was a family thing; other aunts and uncles would come and we would all congregate around this big, huge, long table. My Aunt Helen did nothing but cook. She was four hundred pounds with shoes cut out for these hideous bunions she had. No teeth in her mouth. She never went anywhere and would send the kids out to do the shopping. She was kind of sad; their house was really pathetic, looking back. My Uncle Abe was about ninety-pounds and looked like a troll. He was an ugly, little man and smoked Chesterfields that were always tucked into his sweater-vest. Supposedly he was a carpenter, but every window in the house needed a piece of wood to hold it up so it wouldn't smash down on your fingers.

If it wasn't every week, it was at least two or three times a month that we would be there. My Aunt Helen would cook and make all the things my mother liked. She would make cake for her and paté for my cousin Sonny. It was cows' feet in the jelly. Oh, it was disgusting. They liked it with pumpernickel, butter and a slice of onion. There was always chopped liver. Helen would be up early, baking challahs and danish.

Helen had three children. Irv was the middle child and about eight years older than me. My father liked him because he was into woodworking and guns. Whatever a man sees in a boy, my dad did like him. But Irv was my problem, and was a problem for years. I think it started because I loved to read. I read every book my mother used to bring home, from *Marjorie Morningstar* to *Peyton Place*. I would read stuff that was *way* over my head, but I just liked to read. I loved going to the library; the children's librarian at the city branch was always recommending books to me. I was not allowed comic books. My mom would've thought it was a waste of money and that I should read a *book*. But I loved comic books, too.

My cousin Irv had comic books, *lots* of comic books. Scary ones, which I loved, and *Little Lotta*, and *Superman*. They were always kept in Irv's bedroom, down at the end of a real long hall. So I would go *down* this hall, and go into the bedroom, which I was allowed to do, and read comics. I would get on the bed, stretch out on my stomach and read. I don't know when it started, but Irv would come in and watch me read the comics. He must've started touching me, patting me. I don't think it started sexual in the beginning. I'm picturing myself, and I think I'm about six or seven. He has a very low, soft, quiet voice. Like a secretive voice. Little girls wore dresses. I wore dresses; I didn't wear pants. He would start to show me pictures. First he had pictures of guns. Then he asked me if I ever saw a naked lady. He showed me a picture of a woman standing next to a tree, with her hand out, touching the tree. It was a black and white photo, and all I could see was this big, black *bush*. It was shocking. I don't think I ever saw my mother naked, and *I* certainly didn't have a bush.

He just started caressing, and eventually his hands were in my panties and he was diddling me and diddling me. All I can remember, the whole entire time, is he was saying, "Shhhh. Don't make any noise." In that low voice. I was terrified and tense. Their house had a smell. Anytime I've been in a place that smells like that, I go back there. While he's doing what he's doing, I am tense like I'm going to spring, *listening* for somebody coming down the hall. I knew it was wrong; my whole body told me it was wrong, and I just let him do it. It happened for *years*. (*Pause.*) Did I like it? I don't think so. I was too tense. There may have been some pleasure, because I remember being wet, but I certainly haven't had any pleasure since. I could've said to my parents, "I don't want to go to Aunt Helen's," but I didn't because I was "good." I also wanted the comic books.

The memory is so visual, so vivid. I can close my eyes and see the bed, smell the room, see the closet next to the bed with old comic books on the floor. It went on for about three years. Somehow when it stopped, we wound up in Aunt Helen's bedroom. I think they had a double bed that was practically caved in. That smell again – it was dark and moldering in that room, like being in a coffin. And he took his penis out. I don't know whether he wanted me to touch it, or put it near my vagina. But the sight of this *penis* – it was erect and had hair around it – it was so repulsive to me. I don't know exactly what

I did, but I know I left the room. It never went any further than that. That was the *end* of it; I wouldn't go near him anymore.

I never told my parents. I wouldn't have known what to say. First of all, it was a secret. I knew it was wrong. I didn't know what any repercussions would have been, except in my adult life, I know if my father had found out, he would have killed him.

Many, many years later I did tell my mother, and she didn't believe me. We were down the shore, and I said to her, "You know Mommy, I thought you weren't there for me a lot of times growing up." She said, "What do you mean?" I said, "There was a time when I really needed you to save me, for you to be there, and you weren't there for me." She says, "What are you talking about?" And I said, "Remember when we used to go to Aunt Helen's?" She says, "Sure, we went all the time and everybody had a good time." I said, "Let me tell you what happened to *me* at Aunt Helen's all the time." I started to tell her, not explicitly, 'cause it was my mom. I used the euphemism, "played with me." She had this look on her face, and at first said she didn't believe me. (*Crying.*) I got angry and started crying and said, "Why would I make this up?" I said, "Mom, I was hoping for somebody to come and make it stop. I felt like you let me down."

Nobody rescued me. The whole thing with being tense when anything sexual was going on, not liking to be touched – this stayed with me through my whole life. Any relationship I've ever had with a man since then, they've been the operator. Even though I'm independent, I always do what men want me to do. Not with women, but with men I'm subservient and back in the dark ages. Sexually, forget it. I've gotten no pleasure out of sex. Maybe four times I've had an orgasm with a man. I'm sixty-six years old and I absolutely attribute that back to Irv. I'm tense. I'm waiting for something to happen. I can't relax.

Irv married a girl from the neighborhood, Sharon, and they had three kids. After my dad died, they would invite my mom to their house. If I was in the area, I would take her over there and socialize with them. I never said anything. I never confronted him. One time, I told my brother I was going to. I said to him, "When we get to Irv and Sharon's, I know he's gonna probably be in the garage tinkering. I'm gonna take him over to the side and I just want to tell him that I never forgot what he did to me." My brother got there before me. When I get to the house, he comes running out and says, "Don't say anything. I already spoke to him. Don't say anything because he's afraid you're gonna make a scene." I said, "You did *what*?" I felt like I got gut-punched. Here I was ready, and wanted to finally unload and just say to this person, "You've done something to me that is irreparable. I'll never, ever forgive you for it. I *hate* you for it." And my brother cut me off at the knees. I was a mess. I wanted it to be *me*.

A few years ago, Sharon came by the store and said her daughter was coming into town with her little girl, Sharon and Irv's granddaughter. She said, "I'd love you to come and see her. She's *so* beautiful." She was probably four or five. And she says, "Her grandfather loves her and can't keep his hands off of her." When she said that I got so physically sick I started to tremble. I had to leave the store. All I was thinking was, "I didn't save this kid. What if he's doing the same thing to her?" So much guilt. Of course, I didn't go see them. Those words, that phrase that she used: "He can't keep his hands off her..." (*Groaning.*)

About a year and a half ago, Sharon calls and says, "I haven't seen you in a long time." Yeah, no kidding. She wanted to meet for lunch, so we get together. She's talking, "the kids this, the kids that." She started to talk about their childhood and I don't know why I said this, but I said, "Sharon, things aren't always what they seem. Every family has secrets." And I started to tell her about Irv. And I shouldn't have told *her*. I think I was trying to hurt him through her, but that was the wrong way to go. The look on her face... She just said, "I have to go," and she left. I can understand her reaction. It didn't feel right doing it like that. There was no catharsis; I didn't unload anything. Because *he's* the one. I haven't spoken to her since. I regret saying something to her; he's the one I wanted to kill, not her. I think I could have killed him.

My dad took lots of pictures when we were young, and I look at the photos and see myself at different stages. I look closely and wonder, "Is this when it happened? Is this when it started?" I look at my face. Like I said to my mom: "You should have known. Something must have changed in me." (*Crying.*) So I look in those pictures to see if I can see the Merle before and the Merle afterwards. There's one particular picture of me with my shoulders hunched forward and my arms folded. Maybe then.

If I could talk to that little girl I'd say it wasn't her fault. She didn't really *do* anything wrong. She was a victim, but she was also a participant. She could have said "no," although I wasn't a kid who said "no." I was always trying to please. There's some negative parts of my life that go right back to that. Being so obedient, always being a good girl, always doing what somebody wanted me to do. And paying a price for it growing up. It's always that I want to be accepted, I want them to like me. Stupid. I'm not a martyr or anything, but I always seem to want to please.

For the longest time, I thought my childhood was perfect, because I put this in a separate place where it couldn't hurt me. I feel a lot of anger toward myself for letting it happen. I do. I berate myself all the time. How would my life have been different had I not been involved with that? I feel like it's been emotionally and sexually crippling. I would've told that kid, "I really feel sorry for you for having to go through that and live with it."

Exploration – Merle

1. Merle recalled, "From a young age, I always felt safe, certainly when (Dad) was around." Did you feel safe growing up? Who or what contributed to your sense of safety?

2. The first time Merle saw a naked lady "it was shocking." Do you remember your first time seeing a naked adult? How did it make you feel about your own body? Were you raised in a private or open environment?

3. As a child, Merle did not tell her parents about Irv because she was afraid of the repercussions. Have you talked with your children about sexual safety? What have you done to encourage open communication? Did you feel safe discussing secrets with your parents?

4. When Merle was an adult, she shared her secret with her mother and was disbelieved. Have you ever confided something to another person, only to be accused of lying? Why didn't they believe you?

5. The day Merle planned to confront Irv did not go as expected. She was shocked when her brother said, "I already spoke to him. Don't say anything because he's afraid you're going to make a scene." Merle felt like she got "gut-punched." What do you think is going on in this dynamic between Merle and her brother?

6. Although Merle always had the autonomy to confront Irv, she never did, believing her brother had taken away her opportunity. Why do you think she held onto this belief?

Has there been a time in your life when you chose anger over action?

7. The secret was finally revealed – to Irv's wife Sharon. Merle said, "I think I was trying to hurt him through her... There was no catharsis...Because *he's* the one." Have you ever tried to hurt someone through another person? How was that different from times when you've used direct confrontation?

8. Merle was upset that her mother was unable to notice a change and rescue her. Do you believe Merle's mother was negligent in not protecting or detecting a change in her daughter? Did your parents ever discover a secret or serious problem because of a change in your mood or behaviors?

9. Merle felt that so much of what happened was about her "always being a good girl, always doing what somebody wanted me to do." Do you think the ways girls are socialized contributes to the high incidences of sexual abuse? Have you paid a price for being a "good girl"?

10. Because the experience was "emotionally and sexually crippling," Merle was angry and berated herself for "letting it happen." At the same time, she felt some compassion for her younger self when she said, "I would've told that kid, 'I really feel sorry for you for having to go through that and live with it.'" Do you feel Merle had any responsibility in what happened with Irv? What would you say to her so she could forgive herself? Is confronting Irv necessary?

Nina, 44

Two years ago, I'm sitting at my desk at work, minding my business, and I get an email from my husband that says, "I'm going into rehab on Monday." What the hell? Are you kidding me?

Everybody's a drinker – everybody drinks. Gary Gallagher was a lightweight. We'd be sitting around the table drinking our beers, drinking our mixed drinks, next thing you know he's passed out. I'm like, "What is wrong with you?" Little did I know that there's vodka hidden in the rafters of my basement. For years this has been going on – and I had no idea.

A month before he sent the e-mail he started seeing a psychiatrist because he was depressed. He had lost his mother, father and sister all within three years. His sister basically died from alcoholism, his father had Alzheimer's, and his mom had a massive heart attack. So he starts seeing this psychiatrist and when I would get home from work he'd literally be passed out on the recliner. I'm saying, "You've got to be kidding me. What is wrong with you? You've got to call the doctor. These meds aren't good for you!"

At that time, I was taking classes a couple nights a week; he was working late on different nights. It was a time when you're not focused on your life anymore. You're focused on everything else that has to be done. This guy was my best buddy in the world, and now we never even saw each other. At that point, my mom and dad were living in an addition on the back of my house. I would come home and say, "What's up with him?"

My mom was going through chemo, my dad would be cooking dinner, and Gary would be passed out. It was just complete chaos. The chaos ran our lives. At this point I told him, "You have to go to the doctor and tell him what's happening with your medicine."

So I'm sitting at my desk and I get this e-mail that he's going to rehab on Monday. It was my daughter Becky's birthday that weekend and we were having a party. He e-mailed me on Thursday and I was like, "What the *fuck?*" I called him and said, "*Hello?* What are you doing e-mailing me?" He said, "I didn't have the guts to talk to you about this, but my boss suggested I go to rehab. I've been drinking every day at work." I was like, "What?!" He's been picking my kids up from daycare and bringing them home, while he was drinking. Besides the fact that I wanted to throw up, I had to get myself situated around all this. I was shocked.

I used to tease him about his family, saying, "All those Gallaghers are alcoholics," but the reality is that they are. His brother died of liver disease. The way Gary grew up, there were pour-spouts on top of the vodka and gin bottles, on the counter next to the sugar canister. Gary's drinking was not something out of control until the past couple of years, when, truly, there was a lot of shit going on with him. I guess that's the way he was able to manage things.

We had a little birthday party for Becky over the weekend, and that Monday he drove to rehab. I was at work, and he called me from the parking lot and said, "I'm going in." I said, "I think this is really good that you're doing this." After I got past the point where I was, "I can't believe you're doing this," I turned into this very supportive person because I think that's what I should do. Okay, this is the person I am. The shock is done; we've gotten through these days. Am I disappointed in you? Yeah. But am I going to be supportive? Yeah.

So he goes to inpatient rehab for I have no idea how long. I would come to work, close the door and fall apart. I can't believe this is my life. He was there for about seventeen days. I had to go and visit on a Saturday because they wanted the family of the addict to come in and see how they were going to get through this, and how they were going to be supportive. Now I have to take time off to do this, on a Saturday, when I had a million other things to do. I was totally resentful of that. I thought, "How dare you. I have three kids at home. What do you care about them? And here you are and I have to figure out how to manage *you*, when you're not even there?"

So I go to this place, and we sit in this big room, and there's all these other people. Then they break us up in groups and they're saying, "Well, my son is a heroin addict, and he's been in here four times, and I don't know how I'm going to take any more of this..." And I'm thinking, "All right, I *truly* don't belong here because he's just going to go in here, he's going to get out, and it's going to be done." It felt ridiculous. More than anything, I felt sick to my stomach to think there are so many people out there who are addicts. And such young kids.

The following week I had to go and meet with his counselor. She was like, "You know, you have to be supportive, and you have to do this and that." And the whole time I'm sitting there saying to myself, "First of all, I don't have to *do anything* because *I'm* not the addict." I was totally resentful and miserable. I came around a little bit later in that session, and I knew I obviously had to be supportive of him. That's a very big word in rehab, for the people who are left behind: "Supportive." So I ended up taking that supportive road, and I'm going to be the champion of support, and when he gets home everything's going to be great.

I pick him up Thursday night, and we come home, and he's thrilled to be there, and he looks really good. Friday night we had dinner planned with our friends. He had to go to his outpatient session, which is right near the rehab place. So I said, "Why don't you go to outpatient from work and I'll meet you at Donna and Bruce's." He calls Bruce's house and says, "I'm lost. I can't figure out how to get to your house the back way." I know right off the bat that's a total lie, 'cause he knows that area like the back of his hand. So I say to Bruce, who is his best friend, "I'm telling you right now, he is drinking." Sure enough, not even twenty-four hours after he gets out, he is *whacked.* And he is driving. He comes in denying he's drinking. I'm like, "I can't believe you're doing this. What is happening?" Bruce wasn't even sure if Gary had been drinking. I said, "No! This is it. This is what life has been." Gary got in his car and drove home drunk that night. When I got home, he totally denied it, and the next morning said, "Oh, I just want to tell you the truth; I was drinking."

From that point on, he became a raging alcoholic, drinking all the time, all the time. So I would go to work, and I would say to my dad, "Dad, can you run over and see where he is." And my dad's like, "Oh, he's in bed." God bless my parents, they were totally in the mix of the whole thing. Gary wasn't at work, obviously; he was out from September 'til March.

When he got back from that rehab, it got crazy, totally out of control. There was no more hiding it. He was just blatantly drunk. I said, "This is not going to happen in my house. This is unacceptable behavior in my house. You're not going to live here. You're not going to be the father, you're not going to be the husband, and you're not going to be *anybody,* because we

can't have you here. So you're going to have to find your way."
He left and went to his niece's, and stayed with her for three
days. She kicked him out, and one Friday night at three-thirty
in the morning he came knocking at my door, and I said, "I'm
sorry, but I'm not letting you in." And he was freezing. It was
probably November. He said, "Please, just let me come in. I'll
sleep in the basement." And I let him in the house, put him in
the basement, and the next day he got up and gets in the shower
as if he's going to be living there. He showers and sits on the
recliner and I say, "You're not welcome on the recliner. You
better get up, call your little AA buddies, and get the hell out of
my house." I said, "We are not going to do this."

There was another time – I wouldn't let him in the house,
and the cops came and made me let him in. Oh my God, I
never thought the cops would come to my house. It was out
of control. The neighbors were out, he's screaming, "Let me
in! Let me in!" He climbed through the window and my son
literally pulled him out of the house. It's just amazing stuff. I
look back now and don't even know how it happened.

I said to my oldest son, "I don't want him here. I can't have
him here. I don't want to be part of his life. This is not the life
that I chose." And my son's like, "Here's the deal, Mom. We
need his paycheck." The reality was is he's absolutely right.
Gary wasn't working, but he was still getting paid. He had a
very supportive boss. And we needed his paycheck.

At Christmastime, he ended up going back into rehab.
He went in on December third. His AA friends picked him
up and had him in a rehab within hours. He came home a
couple days before Christmas. I did all the decorating, I got the
tree, all these things…that, guess what? No matter what, I'll
never forget I had to do all this stuff by myself. Through the
whole thing, I said to my Mom, "I don't know what's going to

happen." I was mad. I said, "I'm not going to give any more of my time to do stuff that has to do with his recovery." My mom said, "You don't have to forgive him, but there is a way to support him."

He's been sober about a year and a half. He's Mr. AA, and the whole fellowship thing has been incredible. Every single day, there are issues of trust around his sobriety. I say my prayers every night, and the first thing I ask is, "Please help him to be sober." It's not something I take for granted. I think I have faith in him, but I don't want to have so much faith in him that I don't know what can happen. It completely turned our lives upside-down. The kicker of it is that I love him and he's my best friend. So it wasn't just about this guy betraying me, what he did to me. But what would I do if he's not there? By any means, I did not need him. I just wanted him. There's a big difference.

You have to put your hurt and betrayal behind you. In order for you to support someone you can't lead with that. I mean, I was cracked, I was totally... He took me down. He took me to that place. To this day, in my heart, I'm never going to be whole, because of what he did. My mom was going through chemo; did we need to have this happen? There was enough going on.

He is *so* not the guy he was when he was drinking. It's just something that we always need to be aware of now. If it wasn't for my mom saying, "Separate the forgiveness from being supportive; they are two different things," I don't know where I'd be. I honest-to-God don't. Because the hurt was brutal.

Exploration – Nina

1. When Nina opened the story, she remembered how hectic their lives were: "I was taking classes a couple nights a week; he was working late on different nights...The chaos ran our lives." Can you empathize with Nina's frustration in losing connection with her husband? What role does chaos play in your life? How do you manage it?

2. Gary grew up in a house with "pour-spouts on top of the vodka and gin bottles, on the counter next to the sugar canister." What was your family's approach to alcohol? Do you feel it was healthy?

3. After Gary decided to enter rehab and Nina's shock had worn off, she said, "I turned into this very supportive person because I think that's what I should do." When she was later asked to come to a family counseling on a Saturday, she felt "totally resentful." How do you think her first sentiment impacted the second? Have you tried to embrace a stance that just did not work?

4. At the first rehab group meeting, Nina believed Gary was "going to get out, and it's going to be done." Have you gone through the experience of supporting someone in recovery? Can you empathize with Nina's early reaction?

5. Nina continued to struggle with the concept of "support," but committed to the idea and believed when Gary got home "everything's going to be great." Unfortunately, he began drinking heavily immediately after leaving the facility. Do you think it's possible to stay committed to

supporting a loved one during relapse? What would that look like?

6. Nina set her boundaries and initially told Gary he had to leave her house. How do you feel about her "tough love" approach? Have you ever had to employ a similar strategy with family members?

7. Despite her desire to have Gary out of the house, Nina's son reminded her they needed Gary's paycheck. How do you feel about Nina's choice to allow her husband to return home based on her son's assessment?

8. Nina said, "Every single day there are issues of trust around his sobriety," and she prayed for him to remain sober. Are there other things Nina and Gary could do to foster more trust in their relationship? Has addiction created trust issues in your life?

9. Nina said, "To this day, in my heart, I'm never going to be whole, because of what he did." Have you been wounded to the point where you felt your heart would never be "whole" again? Is it possible to go through something like this and have it deepen you or the relationship?

10. Nina was able to move forward in supporting Gary after hearing her mom's counsel: "Separate the forgiveness from being supportive; they are two different things." What role do you think forgiveness could play in Nina and Gary's relationship?

Sue, 50

My darling little Taylor – she was eleven years old and diagnosed with pediatric cancer in May 2003. She fought her battle for almost five years, never giving up for a second, never believing she was going to die. What carried her through was love. That's all she ever wanted. One of her favorite songs was *All You Need Is Love*.

Three weeks before she died, she was hooked up to oxygen at home, seeming okay with everything, and I said, "Tails, why aren't you angry? You can't go to school, you can't go out with your friends. Again, you're not angry that you're hooked up to another machine." She said, "Mommy, what do I have to be angry about? Everybody loves me." She repeatedly said to me during those five years that if she hadn't gotten sick she would have never known how much people love her.

People say with the grieving process, you're supposed to get angry, but the only person I've been angry with is God. I'm angry because of Taylor's suffering. But I never turned the sadness and grief into anger. The reason I asked her that question was to find out where she was in thinking if she was dying. We still had all our hopes at that point; we knew she had taken a turn for the worse, but took her to Germany six days before she died for a potentially beneficial treatment.

We never gave up hope; she never gave up hope. The doctor in Germany told her that her cells were doing well in the petri dish. She was so excited the night before she died, she said to my husband, "When are my next set of scans? Daddy, I'm going to do so well." Incredibly upbeat. She never, ever talked about death. But she did say repeatedly, "Mommy and Daddy, I know I'm here because of you." Because my husband would go to work by day – by night he'd make a pot of coffee and research and call the entire world, trying to find a cure for this rare cancer that strikes one in fifty million people.

Taylor went to so many different hospitals and saw all her friends dying. She knew full well she was alive because we kept on going from treatment to treatment. And she just thought one hundred percent that we were going to take care of her; and we really did, too. We didn't expect her to die that week; she clearly wasn't doing well, but she had been worse other times. She rallied the day before she died – totally rallied. She was on regular oxygen, up talking, chatty.

We were really shocked that she died. (*Whispering.*) Her lungs failed in the middle of the night. She was in ICU and we were sleeping nearby. She woke up my husband to use the bathroom, and he could see on the monitors that her lungs were failing. (*Pause.*) It took her thirteen hours to die; I laid on the bed with her for thirteen hours. At the beginning she was taking four breaths and the machine was taking one. Then, after time, she was taking one breath and the machine was doing it five times. We could see the decline; as soon as her lungs failed we knew she was dying. I didn't know what to do. The doctors in Germany were so intent on us talking to her, saying that in some sense she's aware. I laid in bed with her and told her for thirteen hours how much I loved her and how everybody loved her. Her boyfriend and sister were in Germany; her oxygen spiked when they walked in the room; she knew. She was completely knocked out on morphine because we didn't want her to know she was dying, but she knew. She died within five minutes of them coming in the room.

But that's not the story I want to tell. I want to tell you about something that happened early on. About six months into her diagnosis, the initial chemotherapy was destroying her. She was obviously bald, and had undergone major surgery; they took out a tumor in her ribs and left an empty space, so she was getting severe scoliosis. Her head was crooked. The pallor of her skin had turned somewhat green, and she had two rubber tubes coming out of her chest so the chemo could be sent directly to her heart and dispersed through her system. She was thin as a rail, green, with her head on her shoulder, and the tubes coming out of her body.

Every night, in order for her to take a shower, I had to wrap her torso in saran wrap so the tubes wouldn't get wet. But this particular night, she got into the bathroom before me. When I came in with the saran wrap, she was standing in front of the full-length mirror, staring at herself. Twelve years old – bald, green, tubes, her head crooked. She looked like a ghost, a monster. Because of where the tumor had been in her ribs, one of her tiny breasts actually drooped. From a beautiful, athletic kid before. And she could see in my expression how upset I was. It was ghastly. She wasn't crying; she was just looking at herself, but she could see *my* face. Obviously I had seen her naked before, because I had to put her in the shower every night. But I hadn't seen her see her own reflection. It was pure sadness in her eyes.

She turned right away from the mirror – didn't want me to get upset. I wrapped her in saran wrap, and she got in – the shower was already on, the steam was going – and I couldn't help it; I sat on the edge of the Jacuzzi, put my head down and turned away so she couldn't see me. But she clearly knew I was crying. Even when she started losing her hair, she had my husband shave her head; everything was a game. But this was beyond heartbreaking for both of us. She had literally started looking like a monster. After a minute or so, I brought my head up to see how she was doing. She was waiting for me to raise my head and had written on the steamy glass, I ♥ you. (*Crying.*) She didn't want me to be sad. She put a big, beautiful smile on her face in the shower. It was beyond unbelievable. The most generous act of love from a twelve-year-old. She didn't want *me* to be sad.

That's one of the reasons why my husband and I tried desperately not to be victims. She never, ever once said, "Why me?" She would never act like she was a victim. Of course she missed going to school and all that stuff, but she had a boyfriend and tons of friends. She'd vomit into a bucket on one side of her bed, and on the other was her cell phone and in the next breath she'd ask, "Where are we going tonight?" (*Laughing.*)

One of the biggest gifts she gave me is a living legacy. One of the reasons I can even get up every morning is to run her foundation. She started a foundation for pediatric cancer research, and initially her goal was to raise a million dollars. We raised in excess of that pretty quickly. A solid tumor research lab was just dedicated to her in May. (*Whispering.*) The ribbon-cutting ceremony was wicked without her there. She started the foundation when she was eleven, and we all learned quickly that a million dollars is absolutely nothing. She said, "I just want to save one person's life. That's all I want to do, Mommy." She ran the foundation on and off through being sick; we had a zillion fundraisers. She wanted the foundation to be kids helping kids, which it still is, except now we have a board of directors. My goal is to keep her dreams, hopes, and wishes eternal. She wants me to save lives and continue what she was doing. It really, really is what I want to do. We saw so many kids die. After three years of treatment she said, "Mommy, we can't make friends with anybody anymore because everybody dies." If I could spare one child, one family, it would be miraculous.

She also gave me the gift of understanding that everything is all about everybody else. The only way you can be happy is by helping other people; being selfless. The other thing I do, that I know would make her so happy, is that I'm a hospice volunteer. I work with adults. I don't know if I'll ever be able to go on a kid's oncology floor, or work with dying children. Ultimately, I think I'd like to.

Selflessness – that's what she was all about. She would forge ahead through life – whatever it took. She just wanted to be surrounded by love and help other people. Sometimes, when I'm really down, I'll visit the cemetery and say, "You know Tails, you gotta help me keep that strength. I need your love, determination and courage."

I feel her spirit near me, hugging me – she has come through in so many ways. The first time, before we even left Germany, her body was being prepared to leave the country. We were waiting for a flight in Frankfurt; it's February, freezing cold, and we're walking around. We came to an open square where a folk band was playing music and singing in German. Kind of strange since it was so cold out. We were falling apart; that's an understatement. And all of a sudden, the band changes their words and starts singing in English, "Mother Mary come to me, speaking words of wisdom. Let it be. Let it be." Unbelievable. Before we even left the country.

A couple weeks after she passed, one of my other daughters was being confirmed. I didn't want to see anybody, so I went to some random store because I had to get invitations and give her a tiny family party. Both my daughters were with me and we're flipping through invitations. My one daughter goes, "Oh my God, Mommy. Look at this." There was a sample birth announcement, but it didn't say it was a baby girl. It said, "Our angel was born, Taylor Anne, on February twenty-second." Taylor Anne's name spelled exactly the same – February twenty-second was the day she died.

You know how there are books about kids' psychic abilities with the parents who pooh-poohed them? I did that without realizing it. September tenth, 2001, she kept me up the entire night. "Something is gonna happen, something terrible!" I was like, "Taylor, everybody is fine. Everything's okay. What's going on with you?" She came home from school the next day: "Didn't I tell you?" She was fascinated her whole life with September eleventh. Her last school project was a huge power point on it. The only reason why I'm bringing it up is because on that birth announcement the baby was nine pounds, eleven ounces.

She told me so many times, "Mommy, I'm so lucky. I would have never spent this time with you. I love you so much. Even though I'm sick, please don't be upset." The only place I could cry was in the shower. Last week, I was in the shower, thinking about the story I was going to tell, and I drew a heart on the door. A big drop of water ran down the center of it. The truth is, I am brokenhearted every day.

Exploration – Sue

1. Sue opened her story remembering Taylor's loving nature: "She repeatedly said to me during those five years that if she hadn't gotten sick she would have never known how much people love her." Have you been surprised by insights and love that have arisen during a critical situation?

2. Thinking about her emotional response to Taylor's illness, Sue said, "I never turned the sadness and grief into anger." What role has anger played when you've struggled with sadness or grief? Who took the brunt of your emotions?

3. Throughout her ordeal, Taylor remained upbeat and "never, ever talked about death." If you were Taylor's parent, would you have wanted to broach the subject of death with her? How might you have opened that conversation?

4. Taylor's father stayed up all night researching and calling around the world, trying to find a cure for her rare cancer. To what lengths have you gone in order to help a loved one? Have others gone to great lengths on your behalf?

5. Sue watched Taylor change from an athletic girl into someone who was "thin as a rail, green, with her head on her shoulder, and tubes coming out of her body...a ghost, a monster." Have you witnessed a loved one's radical transformation due to disease? What was the most challenging aspect for you?

6. Taylor drew a heart for her mom in the steam of the shower, and beamed a smile to pull Sue from her sadness. What is the most generous act of love someone has shared with you?

7. Because Taylor never asked, "Why me?" Sue and her husband "tried desperately not to be victims." Have you faced a challenge where you could have felt victimized but made a different choice? What was the ripple effect of that?

8. Taylor's foundation gave Sue a new purpose, and reason to "get up every morning." In the wake of a tragedy you may have experienced, were you able to find new meaning in life?

9. Another gift Taylor gave to Sue was her understanding that "the only way you can be happy is by helping other people; being selfless." Do you agree? In what context has happiness arrived in your life?

10. Sue recalled, "I feel her spirit near me, hugging me – she has come through in so many ways." The birth announcement was a dramatic sign for Sue and her daughters that Taylor's spirit lived on. Have you had communication from deceased loved ones? What are your beliefs regarding an afterlife? What helps you feel connected to those who have passed?

Margaret, 87

Uncle Adam was a lot of fun. He was my mother's younger brother and he was very, very good to her. Ad was a good-lookin', sophisticated kinda guy. Very soft. My earliest memory is anything she'd ask him to do, he'd always do it. He was that type of person.

We lived in Maine and he used to take me to dances all over – Solon, Madison, Skowhegan. And he'd take any friends I had, too. The dances were held in summer resort type places. They used to have real good big bands come in from different areas. He'd always dance with me or my girlfriends. I was probably seventeen and he was maybe twenty-one or twenty-two. He'd always make sure we got home safe and sound.

My mom loved him because he was quiet and thoughtful; that's the type of person he was. But he didn't go out with girls much; he was sorta shy. He used to play the guitar and sing, and he played in a little band sometimes. He didn't go out very much. I guess he just enjoyed being with the family, more or less.

Things were fine and dandy, then finally he met this girl whose uncle was the postmaster in Anson. Ad started to go out with this girl and when we went to dances or anything, he'd always bring... Irene, that was her name. She seemed very nice. And she was pretty, too. But for some reason or other, she didn't fit into the family; she just didn't. She was sort of a selfish person; she wanted all the attention. So it got to the point where he would take us to the dance and then he and

Irene would go somewhere to eat or find something else to do, but they didn't hang around with the kids anymore and dance. But he'd still come and get us and take us home. I could see that she was a little jealous.

So what happened then was, he started to go out with her, and they went together for quite a while, then first thing we know, they were getting married. He married Irene and they moved into the house where my grandmother lived, into the upstairs apartment. Grammy let 'em use upstairs. So they bought a stove and a piano, and all kinds of stuff; the place was really decorated nice. Ad had a good job at the paper mill in Anson. He was like a foreman; he worked there for quite a while.

He and Irene seemed to be getting along fine; they didn't have any children though. She didn't want any children. You could tell she just didn't like little kids too much. Then we started to notice that Ad started to drink, and he never drank in his life. And we thought, "Gee, that was strange." And they'd go out once in a while, but they didn't go out as often as they used to. She was workin' at the post office as a clerk, with her uncle.

He started to have a drink every once in a while, and that's not like him. He'd be just very quiet and always be playin' his guitar. But then all of a sudden, he started to go *out*, and then he was drinkin' more – without Irene, because Irene wasn't home. She used to take off. She was probably goin' out with somebody else by that time. My mother would find out things from my grandmother, and then my mother would talk about it to me. It upset us to think he wouldn't take us anywhere anymore because he wouldn't drive with us in the car if he had been drinkin'. That's the way he was. We thought, "Gee, that's funny. How come they're mad at each other?" 'Cause I was too dumb yet, I think; I wasn't old enough to know that she was runnin' around. I used to think it was his fault 'cause he was drinkin'. I thought she was goin' out, down to her relatives or somethin', because they lived in another town.

Then my mom says to us one day, she says, "You know, I *think* that Irene is gone away. Because," she says, "we haven't seen her for a few days." My grandmother hadn't seen her. I just figured Irene probably wanted to get away because he was drinkin'. So I didn't pay any attention; I was still young.

The next thing we heard, my mother says to us, "Don't be surprised if you notice Irene isn't here." So I said to Mom, I says, "Oh, what'd she do, go down to her uncle's house?" She says, "Probably." My mother didn't want to say anything because my *grandmother* was upset.

This one day when we came home for lunch, Mom says to us, "Irene is not here." And I says, "She isn't?" She says, "No. A big truck came today and Irene moved everything except the stove out of the house." So I says, "Well, where did she go?" She says, "We don't know. All we know is that she came home from work at noon, while Ad was at work, and she just moved everything out." I felt somethin' must be wrong. I knew he wasn't drinkin' because he was workin', and he didn't drink when he worked.

Towards evening, Mom was goin' upstairs and I guess she was talkin' with Ad and she found out from him that Irene had taken off, because he says she had a boyfriend. He says she was usin' the fact that he was drinkin' as an excuse, but he says she had been goin' out long before that, that's why he started drinking. She shared that with us. I thought, "Oh my God." So naturally, she was upset. There was no more talk about him after that. Just with my grandmother; she'd talk with my grandmother.

Ad didn't come around much after that. He used to stay upstairs in his apartment. Or he'd come downstairs to my grandmother's. He used to use one of the bedrooms, and he'd sit there, and *all evening* he'd play the guitar and sing, real *sad* songs. And we used to think that's really strange that he's doin' it. But we figured, well evidently he feels bad that she's gone. When we would see him, it was as if we didn't know anything about it; we'd just play dumb, that's all. And he never said anything to us kids. But he used to be very quiet. And then he didn't drink anymore. And the next thing you knew, he wasn't even goin' to work. When he wasn't goin' to work, my mother started to get worried.

We stayed down my grandmother's during the summer to make her feel better because Grammy was very, very upset. When Ad got married and fixed up the house Grammy thought, "Well, that's really wonderful." But it really wasn't wonderful because all the while they were having problems. And we didn't know it; nobody knew it.

When we were stayin' with my grandmother, I was beginnin' to see there's somethin' wrong with him, because he's very different and my grandmother always looked sad. She was afraid to go to bed at night because she says he wouldn't sleep all night; he'd walk around the house. So she was afraid somethin' was wrong with him. I guess maybe he felt bad. He probably used to think about his wife. I don't know where Irene went, but she took off. We'd hear my mother and grandmother talkin'. We weren't eavesdroppin' but you couldn't help but hear it, 'cause Grammy didn't even think about the fact that we'd be in the room. She used to talk in Slovak and we understood what she was sayin'. She'd say, "I'm afraid to go to bed at night. I don't know what he's gonna do; he just doesn't sleep." She didn't know why he was doin' that and beginnin' to think there was somethin' wrong with him. But she never said anything to him. She'd just say, "Why don't you go to bed?" And he'd say he's not sleepy and that would be it.

He didn't do much talkin' with her or my grandfather either. My grandfather used to get mad 'cause he had quite a temper and he'd want to know, "What's his problem? Why don't he go to bed?" Ad would just smile and that would get Grampy all the more upset – because Ad wouldn't argue with him or anything. So that went on for quite a while. Then my grandmother says she can't stand to live like that. She said, "I can't sleep; I can't do anything." He was only working once in a while and started drinkin' in the daytime. He was strange. She thinks somethin' is mentally wrong. Grammy was afraid.

So then what happened, she called my mom again, and she wanted my mom to do somethin'. Gotta call the doctor or somethin' 'cause she can't live like that. So my mom called the doctor and he said to bring Ad to the psychiatric ward in Augusta. Take him there, have him looked at, have him checked to see if there's somethin' wrong with him. The local doctor said, "It could be somethin' wrong, or it could be he's just brooding over the fact that he lost his wife."

So my mom asked Ad to go to with her to Augusta. He didn't want to go at first, but then he says, "All right, Kath, if you want me to go, I'll go with you." So he went with her, and the doctor said to my mother, "I think he should be here." He says, "Because he should not be walkin' the streets. He's startin' to get very melancholy and he drinks." Ad needed to be in the institution and talk with someone to see if he could get that out of his system. Because he was *thinking* too much about Irene. He just couldn't get over the fact that she left. 'Cause he didn't know where she was; she just took off.

My mom didn't want to have to put him in the mental institution because she says that wouldn't look very good for her, his sister, to do that. The doctor says, "Well, somebody's gonna have to do it; it's either you or your mom." She says, "Mom will have to do that then. I just couldn't do that to him."

They went back to the house and they told Ad, "You're going to the hospital for a little while, to get better." He was just gonna stay there a little while so to get his mental capacities to the point where he'd be able to do it himself, instead of thinkin' about her so much. But then they wanted to give him electroshock treatments, and see, my grandmother wouldn't sign the paper for them to do that. The doctors said in case they had to or wanted to, they would be able to do it. Grammy would *not* sign. She said no, she didn't want to do that. She says to try get him back to normal the best way they could.

So then that's what they did; they had him put in the institution. They had to rent a car and have a driver take him there, because my mother didn't have a car. Ad had a car but she didn't think it was right to drive him to the hospital in his car. My mom just told us, "He's gonna have to go to the hospital and stay there for a little while." I found out later it was a mental hospital and was very upset about it.

Grammy went back home after he went to the hospital and would write my mother letters. I had a hard time figuring out some of the letters 'cause they were in Slovak, but I could figure out enough so that I could tell what was goin' on. The doctor said they'd put him in for a few weeks, but it ended up they were gonna keep him longer than a few weeks 'cause he wasn't gettin' any better. Ad was angry; the fact they were puttin' him in that kind of a hospital. So then he was givin' them a hard time 'bout the fact he wanted to go home because he didn't think he should be there; there's nothin' wrong with him.

Whenever Grammy wanted to go to the hospital, she'd write and tell my mother to get a car to take them. My mother didn't like the fact that she was the one involved all the time. Everything was on her, *everything*. Mom started to tell me little things but she didn't say too much. She'd just say, "Don't worry about it; everything'll be all right. But Grammy's gonna have to take care of him." But what happened, I think, he started to get *worse* after he went to the hospital. When my grandmother was stayin' at our house we'd overhear them. Mom didn't tell us, 'cause she felt we might get upset or scared because we really did think the world of him.

About six months went by and they weren't lettin' him go home anymore. He'd ask to go home and they would say, "Well, you can't go right now." And they would keep him. Then what they did, they gave him one shock treatment. And that was *horrible*...horrible. When they give you that shock treatment they give you these electrodes, and it makes your body *convulse*. So he was very, very upset after he had that. He just wanted to go home. He said he didn't want to stay there. But he wasn't any different; he was always very sad. He started to be *very* sad.

My mother just hated that she had to do all of it, because my grandmother couldn't; she couldn't speak the language. My mom had to interpret and then she'd have to go there too, and have to see him. And then she was at home and had to listen to my other grandmother. She didn't like the fact that the kids knew about it. My poor mother was like a nervous wreck 'cause she's trying to pacify her own mother and trying to pacify her mother-in-law.

I was afraid. At first, I didn't want to go to Augusta 'cause I didn't know how he would react. I was scared; I thought, "Gee, what if he's funny or somethin'." After he got the electroshock treatment we started to get scared. We didn't know why did it have to happen to him like that? Was it from the drinkin'? There must've been somethin' wrong or he wouldn't have gotten that bad. It was a sad situation.

When my mom would get a letter from my grandmother she'd be very upset. My mom was a very easygoing person; things didn't bother her, but she was embarrassed because then people began to know. Friends of hers. My grandmother and my mom didn't want anybody to know because they said it would be a *shame*. 'Cause people might think *we're* like that. Maybe there's somethin' wrong with us. I mean, why did this happen?

I never talked about it with anyone. We just didn't. My mother used to say it's better not to say anything. I didn't want to talk about it with anybody, because I didn't really know how it was gonna end or why he was like that. Is it because the family's like that, or what? The doctor said, "No." Ad made his own bed by drinkin' and actin' the way he did. By puttin' himself alone so much. The doctor said that wasn't because of anything the family did.

Ad wasn't insane; his came on from what he was doin'. So the doctor says, "Don't worry about it." I used to think, "What if it happens to my kids or happens to me?" But the doctor says not to worry because that's not the kind of problem he had. He says, "Ad never had any problems until he started to drink and his wife left him." He says, "How would you feel if you came home and found everything was gone outta your house?" There was nobody in the family that was ever like that. I mean,

I didn't feel bad about it then. When I found that out I thought, "Well, it isn't our fault he's like that." I just didn't think about it.

He'd write to us. He wrote very legible and very nice letters. So I used to think, "I wonder if there is somethin' really wrong with him, or if it's just them, or what is it?" Because he used to say some horrible things about what the doctors used to do to him. But we didn't know if he was telling the truth. He'd tell my mom all the things that were goin' on, like about them givin' him the shock treatments. He says, "I know they're not gettin' permission every time they're doin' it." And they *weren't*. Because you know, in them days, they did it when they thought it was right to do. He said the doctors used to abuse them; a lot of the women would get beat up. But then you didn't know, is he tellin' the truth or isn't he? Since then, we found out, that yes, he was tellin' the truth because they did have some horrible things that used to happen.

He was released for short periods of time over the years, but always ended up back there. At one point, he moved out of my grandmother's house and lived in a lady's boarding home. He'd pay the taxi cab driver like a hundred dollars just to go up to the cemetery to see if the family plot was bein' taken care of. He could've gone up there for a quarter or fifty cents. That's when we found out that, well, somethin's not right. He's workin' in the mill, and he used to put crosses on all the time cards because he started to get religious. He never was as a young man. Someone got in touch with my father, 'cause my father was the sheriff. Then Daddy had to take Ad back to Augusta. But he went with my father and didn't give him a hard time.

My dad had to take him 'cause before that my mom had got killed. That really broke Ad up, when my mom got killed. My dad was teaching my mom how to drive and we had a convertible. She was comin' down this country road and instead of steppin' on the brake, she stepped on the gas and her car shot across the road and hit a big tree. She was practically dead when they took her to the hospital. She died shortly thereafter... That was a shock because she was only *thirty-nine*. She was just a young person. Oh my God, it was horrible. At that time, Ad had been living with a cousin in Washington State and he was really happy, but when he found out about my mother gettin' killed, (*whispers*) he wanted to come home.

After he got home it started all over again; he just started to get real strange because he just didn't want to bother with anybody. And when he did go out, he was spendin' money like crazy. He'd pay hundreds of dollars just to go up to the cemetery, where my mom was buried. It should've cost a quarter.

Before Daddy took him back, when Ad was livin' at this lady's boarding house, I went to see him. I'll never forget, when I went there I got *scared*. He had never done this, but when I went in his room, he locked the door. And I got scared. I thought, "Oh my God, I wonder why he did that?" Then I started to think about all these things I used to hear my grandmother say and I thought, "Jeez, maybe I should get outta here." I was pregnant, and all I could think of was that I better get out. But he says, "You stay here 'til I get back," and he locked me into the room from the outside. So I sat there like a couple hours by myself in that room. Then when he came back he says, "I'm gonna go down and have something to eat. I know you can get home okay." Actin' as if everything was just fine, I says, "Okay." I wanted *out*.

After my son was born, I went down there another time to see him because I felt bad. He was all excited 'cause I had a baby. I says to him, "Come see my baby." And when Ad saw my son he started to preach over him. (*Intake of breath.*) And

I got scared 'cause he started to *preach*, sayin' "You're gonna grow up to be as big as a bull, and stronger than this..." I was shakin' and then I started to scream. I wanted him to leave but didn't know how to tell him. My father came in and he says, "I think you better go because she's upset." Ad left and stayed away for a while, then my father took him up to Augusta again.

After that I didn't see him for a long time. When we were living in Louisiana, he wrote to me one time and asked if he could come live with us. And I said I didn't have any room because I would never take him with the children. I had two boys and they were little. He says, "Well there might be some people I know there, Slovak people." I says, "Ad, there are none here, and furthermore, the place is too small. We don't have a big enough place." I always felt bad about that, that I lied.

When the boys were a little older and we had come home, we used to go to Augusta and see him. It was about an hour and a half drive from where we lived in Lisbon Falls. He had nobody. My grandmother was dead, my grandfather was dead, my mom was gone. He had nobody but us, and he loved the children. He really did. We'd have a picnic, and if I wanted to, I could take him for a ride, as long as I brought him back at a certain time. The kids enjoyed it 'cause he'd play ball and they had beautiful grounds there. I did feel content and very safe. We'd go down and see the capital and I'd drive all around. He'd say, "Let's go down to Lisbon Falls and see your dad." I'd say, "Well, I can't today." I was a little bit concerned that if I took him he may not want to go back, and what was I gonna do if he refused and I had the kids? I'd make up some excuse that I couldn't go and I'd tell the kids to be quiet 'cause I was afraid that one of them would blab.

He was in there for a long time. When we weren't living in Maine we would write letters, and the kids would draw pictures. I think he died after one of his shock treatments. They called my father and told him what happened. I was at my dad's when they called, and I was very sad. But in a way, I was glad, because I felt his suffering was over. My dad bought the coffin and Ad was buried back in Lisbon Falls with his parents. I felt relieved, but I didn't. Because then I started to feel bad about all the times that I shoulda taken him, I coulda taken him. But a person don't know what's right in a situation like that. It's scary.

It was just a horrible mess. I just feel sad for the fact that he never got a chance to live like he wanted to; he wanted a wife and children so bad. You know, when you'd hear things about people, you'd say, "Oh, they're nuts." After Ad died I thought to myself, "God Almighty, you just don't say that." Because you don't know, it could happen anywhere. Look at what was happening in our family, and we weren't even aware of it. It was a sad situation. Probably it was a good thing my mother didn't live long; I think it would've been awful for her.

Exploration – Margaret

1. Ad was a loving presence in Margaret's childhood and adolescence, driving her to town dances, chaperoning, and making sure she and her friends got home safely. Did you have a real or surrogate big brother growing up? How were you treated?

2. A lot of the early information Margaret learned about Ad was from listening to her mom and grandmother discuss the situation. When there was trouble in your family, how did you learn about it? Were you aware of things your parents tried to keep from you?

3. Margaret's mother and grandmother didn't want anyone to know about Ad because they said it would be a "shame." They were concerned that "people might think *we're* like that." Has shame been part of your family dynamic? Do you think that fears and biases around mental illness have changed since Margaret's childhood?

4. Margaret worried that whatever was wrong with Ad might one day afflict her or her children, but took comfort in the doctor's reassurance that Ad's problems were due to the circumstances of his life. What do you think of the doctor's pronouncement? Do you have personal concerns about the hereditary aspects of mental illness?

5. There was an ongoing question in Margaret's mind about whether or not Ad was sick enough to be in the state hospital, especially after he received electroshock treatments. After reading her story, what is your opinion?

6. After losing her mother, Margaret had some experiences with Ad that really scared her. How do you think her mother's death impacted Margaret's relationship with Ad? Have you had interactions with mentally ill people that were frightening or unsettling?

7. When Ad asked to live with Margaret and her family in Louisiana, she lied about the size of their house. She also fibbed when Ad asked her to drive to Lisbon Falls on a day pass. If you were in Margaret's shoes, how would you have handled Ad's requests?

8. After Ad died, Margaret felt guilty for "all the times that I shoulda taken him, I coulda taken him. But a person don't know what's right in a situation like that." Have you made decisions that were a source of guilt or ambivalence? How did you come to terms with those difficult choices?

9. Has someone close to you gone through a trauma that changed who they were? How did that alter your relationship?

10. The culture of Margaret's family was such that nobody talked about Ad's problems with him. How do you think this impacted the way he processed what was happening? How does your family communicate when there is a serious problem with one member?

Gloria, 46

I had a mother who abused me physically and emotionally. I think she was diagnosed with bipolar, and I guess was supposed to take pills, but didn't take them all the time. The first thing that really sticks in my mind is when we were little girls, she used to dress up my older sister and me in cute little outfits. We were going to get our professional photos taken. I had to be about three years old, my sister was six, because I see the photos now, and that polka-dotted dress I hated so much. I remember her smacking me and hitting me. I get so sad when I see that photo because it reminds me. That was my earliest memory.

Then one time when I was about seven or eight, she got really mad at me. My grandmother lived in Maryland and we were driving to visit her. My mother made me get down on the passenger side of the floor in the front seat, and put my head down and curl up, because she didn't want to look at me. We went to Maryland, and back then it wasn't as developed, and she said she didn't want me anymore. She drove down this little road and dumped me off in the woods, in the middle of this desolate place. I was terrified. I see her drive off a ways, stop the car, and let my sister out. I'd seen lots of Disney movies, so I was like, "Okay, Diane, let's build a fort." So went looking around for logs and branches, and I remember being so excited because I didn't have to have this woman in my life, treating me like this anymore. I'm like, "We'll live in the woods; we'll forage for berries..." Ten minutes later, my mother drives back and makes Diane get in the car. (*Long pause*.) The terror I felt as they drove away was just horrible. It started to get dark and it started to rain; I curled up underneath the branches. It got pretty dark before I saw the headlights come back. I'm forty-six-years-old, and to this day when I drive by those woods, a flash of terror hits me.

There were times when I would go to school and have bruises all over me from being hit so hard. I remember one time, in elementary school, one of the nurses noticed it. She called my mother and we had a meeting the next day with her. This was back in the day when you could get away with all kinds of crazy stuff. Before we went in, my mother grabbed me by the arm and she said (*clenched teeth*), "You tell them you fell off the swings." And I remember thinking that this was my last hope, this was my last chance to get an adult to listen to me, to let them know what was going on. It didn't work. "I fell off the swing." "Are you sure honey?" "I fell off the swing." I was terrified of her. I thought if I told anybody and it didn't work, (*whispered*) I'd get the shit beat out of me; it would be even worse. So I thought it was best to keep quiet. I didn't think that anybody would believe me; I didn't think anybody would do anything for me.

I never shared it with anyone. I was embarrassed. I had girlfriends come over and would hide it. You know, you hide things. Mom had two faces. Everybody thought she was the most wonderful, loving mom. "Oh, your mom's so great, she's so great!" She always had that face in front of people. Then as soon as they'd leave, "You shut up you little brat, don't you say anything." It's that kind of behavior that continues in her to this day.

When I got to be a teenager it got worse because I was becoming more independent. Of course, teenagers want to dress provocatively. I wasn't allowed to wear pantyhose until I was sixteen. I wasn't allowed to use tampons because she said they would take away my virginity. She wouldn't let me wear makeup; I'd sneak it. Even in high school she tried to make me wear pretty dresses, and I would wear jeans rolled up underneath those dorky dresses. She wanted me to be this little Nineteen-Fifties doll.

One time, she told me I was too vain. And she had an iron in her hand; she was ironing. She said she was going to teach me that God did not appreciate vanity. She tried to take that hot iron and burn my face. Oh, I fought back. That was the first time I *really* fought back. That's the first time I really started to kick and fight and punch back. Of course, I took a lot of shit for it after that. She would get a rolling pin, whatever, and just start *smacking*, with whatever she had in her hand, and break a lot of stuff. But at least I didn't get that hot iron on my face. I still remember laying on the floor and it's coming at me and coming at me. She ended up burning the bottom of my leg – but not my face.

I started to fight back more and more, but it seemed to make the situation worse. She would become so enraged, and even more violent. She's short but very stocky and strong. That was her M.O., to just jump on you, get you to the floor and pin your arms down.

Diane and I shared a bedroom, and there were times when my mother would wake us up about three or four in the morning, and we'd have to get up for school at six or seven. She'd turn all the lights on – be on one of her tirades about the Bible. She'd stand us there for an hour or two and we'd listen to her quote Bible verses and lecture us. She'd ramble, and if we blinked she'd start screaming or hit us.

At sixteen, I finally decided I was going to run away. I left in the dead of night. Just kept walking and walking and walking. I remember passing my elementary school and seeing the swing set. It was the middle of the night and I was just swinging and swinging. I thought, "I gotta get further away; I gotta get further away." I didn't have a plan. I just kept moving. I don't even know where I thought I was going; I just had to get away. I had a small little duffel bag. I just grabbed stuff and ran. In the morning I ran into a friend near my high school and asked if I could stay with her, but she said, "My mom won't let you stay 'cause she knows you ran away." I didn't get very far. The cops picked me up and brought me back.

I never confided in anyone about my mom. I told my friends that my home life "wasn't good." I think that's all my friends knew. Maybe some of my friends kind of suspected, but they didn't know. I had a really good friend, Missy, who I found out recently was going through some bad shit too, and we talk about it now and say, "God, we never told each other." We both knew something was going on, but couldn't talk about it. We had tried talking about it once, but it was so shameful and embarrassing. I thought everybody else had a normal life and normal parents and weren't getting the shit beat out of them, or being woken up in the middle of the night to stand there for hours while your mother reads Bible verses at you. It was *insane*. You just don't tell people this; it's mortifying – it's shameful.

There didn't really have to be any kind of trigger to set her off. It could happen like that (*finger snap*). I would come home from school and I would have to read her: "Is she in a good mood or a bad mood today?" Because what's really weird with bipolar is that when you're happy, you're really happy. She would be really happy for a week or so, and really nice, and do things. Then all of a sudden she'd fly off the handle for no reason at all. You could almost see it come over her face – it was like something in her eyes, and she'd just snap. And sometimes she'd be in bed for a day or two or three. She wouldn't shower; she wouldn't change. She'd scream at me to go bring her food.

My mother never really housecleaned. My sister and I were the housecleaners. She wouldn't let us use a mop; we had to get on our hands and knees and scrub the floor. Everything had to be done the old fashioned way. I never knew what would set her off. I could have looked at her the wrong way. "Why are you looking at me like that?" Smack, boom, bang. She was a big, heavy woman. She would get me down on the floor and pin my arms down and take my head and smash it, smash it. I remember one time, she was smashing me against the wall so much that I felt my whole body go numb, and I remember this feeling, thinking, "Just kill me already." I still remember that. And it's so funny, because when you're being so beat up like that, all of a sudden your body doesn't feel pain anymore. It's something really weird.

My older sister Diane was not like me. She was very quiet and demure and did everything Mom wanted. Diane would yell at me all the time, "Just shut up, just do what Mom wants, just shut up." I'd be like, "I can't! The woman's crazy. She's *fucking* crazy, Diane, she's crazy!" "Gloria, just shut up, just leave it alone." My mother was the kind of person who, if she said the sky has pink polka dots and purple elephants in it, you better agree with her, or else you're getting your head knocked in. So Diane was a real good girl, a real sweet girl, a real *Christian* girl. She cooked and cleaned for Mommy and did everything Mommy wanted, so she did everything right. And I don't know what the hell my problem was that I had to constantly provoke and egg her on. At a certain point in my teens, I couldn't shut my mouth. I just couldn't; (*laughing*) I don't know why. But there were times I had to because at this point I had a little sister and a baby brother. My little brother was born when I was sixteen. My little sister was six years younger. And for a while my mom was okay 'cause she had a new baby, a baby *boy* now. But I was diapering and changing and feeding him.

I do remember at a certain point, I started to date, and Mother didn't like that. And she would just start yelling at my father about me. My dad would always leave the house. He was a workaholic, and of course he didn't want to be around the house, but he was totally henpecked. Dad knew what was happening. I remember one day my father came to me with tears in his eyes and said, "Gloria, why can't you just shut up? Why can't you just stop making *trouble*?" Like it was my problem, my fault. He would try to confront her and she'd just freak out. I remember one particular freak-out when she went after him with an *axe*. I don't even know where she found an axe, but I ended up taking Diane, who I always had to protect, along with my little sister Ruthie, and my baby brother Tom, and locking them in the bedroom. It's hard to explain what it's like when she's in that kind of psychotic state. Her eyes would just roll around. They would get big and you'd see the whites. They're brown but it's like they would become *black* and *glassy*. And her whole face would tighten.

I heard my father screaming down there. She was taking the axe and chopping the furniture. He was an organ player and he loved the organ, and she chopped at that with the axe. And he was screaming for help. So I went down there, and he was trying to fend her off with an ironing board and I remember trying to help him. Then I screamed to Diane, "Diane, call the police!" She did. She called the police. They sent out about five or six squad cars (*laughing*). I remember the squad cars; I remember the lights; I remember my father being mad that we called the police. (*Whispering.*) "Look what you've done, Gloria, you've made this worse." But I think she would have taken his head off with that axe. My dad was always so mad at me; Diane was always so mad at me. Why couldn't I have just shut up?

Even now, she's seventy, and I still see that look in her sometimes. It's *frightening*. It's *frightening*. But now she's a grandma, she's a sweetie pie (*Sarcastic sigh*). Telling you this, you're probably thinking, "How could you even talk to her now?" I don't even know how that happened.

When I was about twenty-seven, my little brother was about twelve and she started beating him up really bad. She was taking diet pills at the time. She'd take like five or six of them and either sleep for five days or become really whacky. And I'd always gone by the house to check up on my little brother, make sure he was fine. Prior to that, I had moved out when I was eighteen, hell yeah, gone! So I used to have to go back and check on him. It got really bad. I was seeing a therapist at the time and I took my brother to see her because I knew he was having problems. He didn't have parental consent to see the therapist, but afterwards she told me, "Gloria, you have to do something about this." I called Social Services. (*Long pause.*) I believe I did the right thing, but I've taken *so* much shit for this over the years from all the relatives and all my parents' friends. I blew the whistle on the big ugly family secret. I think the therapist got in major trouble or something because she wouldn't see me or take my phone calls after that.

I was able to keep my brother at my house for about a week. Of course my parents called screaming. My dad was like, "Come on, what are you doing? You can't do this." I remember going to him once, I met him in private and I'm like, "Dad, you know Mom has had these problems throughout your life, with all your kids." (*Whispering.*) "I know. I know." He agreed with me. He knew all this stuff. But then he's like, "You can't do this." He didn't want Social Services involved. It wasn't that they were going to take Tom away. I said, "Dad, how about if we just get Mom the help she needs. This is the help she needs. Social Services will meet with her and talk to her and we'll figure it out and we can get her into therapy or get her back on medication." He was like, "Yeah, yeah." And then the next day he's calling and screaming at me, "Bring Tom back and stop this! Stop this whole mess. Stop this fiasco!" So maybe he went home and my mom got on his case and beat him up, or whatever. She'd hit and smack him a lot, but with him it was more emotional. Her favorite thing to yell at him was, "You're a pantywaist just like your mother said you were."

I did not back off Social Services, hell no. I kept up, kept up. 'Cause that' me: "Rrrrr, this is messed up." At that point, I tried everything possible, and what's really messed up about our system is they said, "Listen, we have to have people go in and look into this. You can't keep him, you have to take him back." I'm like, "No, I can't!" But they said, "No you have to." (*Long pause.*) Do you understand? I had to give him back to my parents and I knew he would pay. I was terrified, but they said if I didn't do that I would be going to jail or get in a lot of trouble. So even though we told them what was happening, they said, "Well, we don't have proof positive, and it's your say against theirs." Poor Tom was terrified; he was twelve years old.

Anyway, I did send him back and I said, "Call if anything happens, please call if anything happens." Well, I didn't hear from him for a couple of days. My little sister Ruthie had been with me on this; I got her on board. My older sister Diane finally agreed; I had to drag her in. Well, we couldn't find him. Here he disappeared – he disappeared. My parents sent him away. (*Long pause.*) They didn't give us any information. Social Services couldn't do anything; we couldn't find out where he was. Where the hell did he go? Turns out they sent him to some religious compound down in Louisiana. It's where they kept these young, wayward kids, and they *beat* them into Christ's submission. And they made them *stronger* in Christ's image. It was one of those compounds.

My sister Diane and my friend Janine – I was older and had finally told someone about it – we did this stalking thing where we waited 'til my parents left, and then we snuck into the house and started going through all their papers. We found a phone bill and all this information, and quick got out of the house. And that's how we found out where he was. I ended up calling Louisiana and finding a private detective. And paying him a lot of money. It took us a couple months, and everything that the detective sent back, he's like, "Oh my God, this is a horrible place. We get runaways from here all the time. They beat the kids, they torture them. We've got to get your brother out of here."

We wanted Tom to know we knew where he was, that we had found him. We confiscated a letter he had sent to my parents saying they were doing physical labor and he needed work boots. We knew from the detective that the place inspected everything that came in; they check everything. So we got a pair of work boots, cut the inside of the toe out, and put a letter inside there saying, "Don't worry, we're coming for you." And we put a bunch of twenty dollar bills folded up in there and sealed it back up. We were hoping the horrible Christian nutbags wouldn't find it.

At that time, I was just beyond myself, crazy angry. (*Loud exhale.*) Angry at my parents, and at the system for not helping to do anything – for allowing this to happen. So I started to ring every phone I could, call everybody I could. Call this police station, this and that, everybody I knew. I ended up meeting a really nice police detective, Harry Dixon. I remember sitting down in the police station and just pouring my guts out. "You *have* to listen, we *have* to do something about this, we *have* to!" He ended up making some phone calls and we got in touch with the Assistant District Attorney at the courthouse. I went up to meet with her with tears streaming down my face, and anger: "Look at what's happening. We *have* to do something. This is my life."

It took a few months, but the cop from here and some other legal person went down and met the police in Louisiana, and they were able to go onto the compound with the right papers. It took five or six months, but we got him back. (*Crying.*) We were so happy when we met – oh! He saw me, and the first thing he did when he saw me was run towards me and give me this *big* hug and he picked me up and he hugged me, hugged me, hugged me. And he's like, "Thank you, thank you, thank you, thank you." He told us how horribly the kids were treated at the compound and said, "I got the boots. I put my foot in and I felt it, I felt it. I didn't know how or why, but I knew you guys were coming for me. I thought I was going to lose you, that I was going to become one of those zombies because I couldn't take it anymore. When I finally got some privacy I opened it up. I got that note and the money – it was the best thing ever. I *knew* you guys were coming for me, I *knew* it!" Diane and I were really proud of that.

He had to stay in foster care and then there was a *big*, *huge* court thing. I had to testify, depositions, everything. It's terrible sitting up there, in front of all these people asking details about your childhood and your life. My sisters had to do it too, and then my brother. It just came out: "Here it is people, this has been my whole *fucking* life. Here you go!" (*Vomit sounds.*) It was insane.

I ended up getting custody of Tom. I was in my late twenties at the time, had just gotten married, and had a nice house. It was a really hard time. The whole court thing had been really horrible. It was on the news; it had been in the paper several times, on the front page, with our names and a picture of my mom. When we were at the courthouse, we had the TV news crews chasing us around. My little brother was so traumatized by this whole thing, he was having night terrors. Slowly, his story about the abuse at home and the compound came out. He was so terrified, and the crazy religious people were stalking our house! My husband talked me into getting a gun, which I hated. Tom had almost no contact with my parents. I raised him from that point on, until he was nineteen and went to college. He ended up getting his own apartment and moving on in life.

I've been through a lot of therapy over this, over the years, on and off, on and off. One of the biggest problems I have with having a mother like this is that (*long pause*) I have problems with self-esteem. I really do. Self-esteem and intimacy issues. Sometimes I hear that voice in my head from when I was a little girl: "You're no good, you're just *rotten* inside, and God doesn't love you, and you have to be this, and you have to be that." Intimacy is another thing. For the longest time I had problems connecting with men. Really big problems. I used sex as my feel-good medicine, so I was really slutty through my teens, needing that as a drug to make me feel better about myself, and it just ended up making me feel worse. So I think I made a lot of really bad choices in my life.

But it made me stronger. I'm able to put up with a lot, and tolerate a lot. I just look at it as a part of who I am; it's made me stronger, it's made me more able to deal with all the crap that rolls down the pike.

I'm paying a really high price for standing up to my mom, right now in my life. I'm the outcast of the family. I'm the black sheep. I'm the crap hole. I'm the one that gets left out of family parties. I'm the one they forget about. And they all have kids. My sisters have kids, my little brother has a kid; they all have kids. So they're this big group now and they've all somehow managed to get back together, and I do talk to my mom and dad, but I'm just kind of on the outside. They even let my mother watch their kids. I don't understand that.

About a month ago, we had my parents' fiftieth wedding anniversary (*raspberry sound*) and there I was, faced with all these relatives I hadn't seen since this whole thing went down. I could see them whispering about me. My sister did this photomontage of the family and I wasn't even in a single, goddamn picture. I'm always held at a distance, like I was some kind of big monster, viper – that I created this whole stir. Diane said to me once or twice, "Maybe we shouldn't have done all that with Tom. Maybe it would've worked itself out." I did the right thing. Sometimes my sister makes me doubt, with all this closeness and "Oh, Grandma is so sweet." Sometimes I start to doubt. But mostly I feel I did the right thing. I did the right thing.

I still feel a pull to be connected to my family because I love them. I still love my crazy, fucked-up mother. I have compassion for her. When she was a little girl, Social Services found her and her two brothers locked in the attic of her mother's home. Their mother was an abusive drunk, and didn't want to take care of them, so she stuffed them up in the attic for three days. From that point on, my mother was sent from foster home to foster home, until finally ending up at her aunt's house. So when I heard that my mother had been really abused as a child, I just thought, "There you go; it cycles all the way down." I understand her pain.

Exploration – Gloria

1. Gloria's earliest memory was of being smacked in the polka-dot dress. What is your earliest memory? How do you think our first recollections influence our identity?

2. In elementary school, Gloria had an opportunity to tell someone about being abused, but was afraid of the repercussions and didn't think anybody would believe her. Who were you most afraid of as a child? Have you ever been too scared to seek help?

3. Gloria said, "Mom had two faces." The public persona led her friends to believe "she was the most wonderful, loving mom." Do you know people who wear completely different masks? How different are your public and private faces?

4. Gloria made the assumption that "everybody else had a normal life and normal parents," but later found out her friend Missy was going through something similar. Was there a time in your life when you wanted to confide in a friend but felt too ashamed? Have you made assumptions about other people's experiences that were ultimately unfounded?

5. Living with a mother who had a bipolar disorder, Gloria had to "read her" when she came home from school. Have you had tough experiences that contributed to your interpersonal sensitivity? Do you perceive this as a help or hindrance in your life?

6. Gloria was considered to be a troublemaker because she stood up to her mother and protected other family members. What do you think was the source of her courage? Is there a black sheep in your family? What makes them different from the other members?

7. Gloria continued to struggle with issues of self-esteem, hearing her mother's demeaning words from childhood. Do you believe a person can recover from that kind of abuse? How would you help her cope with lingering feelings of inadequacy?

8. When you are self-critical, whose voice is present? What tone and phrases do you hear?

9. In spite of the past, Gloria said, "I still feel a pull to be connected to my family because I love them." Does the human desire for belonging take precedence over everything else? Do you think you could love someone who treated you the way Gloria was treated?

10. Gloria had compassion for what her mother went through as a child and was able to say, "I understand her pain." How important do you think that was for Gloria in healing her emotional wounds? Has understanding another's pain helped you heal?

Veronica, 35

This is a love story about a relationship I had when I was just out of college. I was twenty-one and moved to Florida in the fall for a job opportunity. I was the dining room manager of a country club in a gated community. Early on, I met a man who worked with the property association. Dave would be in all the time for lunch and we got to be friendly. He was older than me; I was twenty-one and he was forty-eight when we first met. Right away, I was interested and attracted to him. I'd catch him looking at me. I never thought much would come of this because he was married. Maybe I was being naïve, but he was married and twenty-seven years older than me. I thought, "Holy crap, that's a significant amount of time." He was right in between my mom and my dad's ages.

After a couple months being friends and working together, Dave and I were talking one afternoon when the place was very quiet. It was right after New Year's and we discovered we both had January birthdays, just a week-and-a-half apart. I don't remember who said it, but one of us said, "Well, let's go out for a drink and celebrate our birthdays." I had been through a few broken hearts and breakups already, and I thought, "Why in the hell would this guy have any interest in me?" He was charming and sexy and gorgeous.

So we wound up going out for drinks. That was sort of "the moment" for me. We sit down to have drinks, we're off-site from our normal environment and there's nobody around we know, and we just start talking. It was pretty much so instantaneous that I totally got freaked out and thought, "Oh my God, I've met my soul mate." Then I thought, "Yeah, bullshit, that's not even possible. There's this huge age difference." But it was immediate and instant, and like nothing I'd ever experienced before – nothing I've experienced since. It was far beyond the physical attraction because that was already there. It happened as soon as we started to talk; I felt like we had this connection that was transcendent of space and time and our age. I think he was pretty freaked out about it as well, and surprised. At that point, neither of us had verbalized any feelings, but we sat there for probably three or four hours and then he said, "My wife's going away at the end of the month. I want to take you away for the weekend." I was very surprised he said that, but I think it was an obvious thing between us. I was excited – I thought, "Oh my God, he feels the same way." We walked to our cars and were kissing. It was just all so sudden and all so immediate and crazy. That started our affair.

We kept seeing each other. He would come into work on Saturday, which was my day off, and we would meet up and spend the day together. We'd do something almost every week together. On weekdays we'd try to get out during the day for an hour; go to a bar and just talk. The first few weeks into it, I was just living with it, just going with the flow and being elated, and wondering, "Is this real? Is this really happening?" We were just developing this connection, and getting into this crazy, soulful place with each other. We went away for our first weekend and it was the most incredible experience of my life. I mean, sexually and romantically I felt like whether we were making love or just hanging out that there was no clear boundary where he started and where I ended. It's kind of cliché; you finish each other's sentences and we just had the same beliefs and values about life and the world. I'm not talking about all the morals and everything. He didn't agree with what he was doing; I didn't agree with it as far as a moral standpoint and hurting people, but it was *so*... It just all happened so quickly and was so out of our control. I guess we should have known better, but I don't know that we were ready for, or even expecting this to happen.

We were together Valentine's Day and he was telling me he was really struggling with "his *decision*, his decision." I finally said, "What decision?" He said, "Well, if I'm gonna leave my wife." I was shocked because I hadn't brought it up, because I was *afraid* to, and I was just enjoying him so much, and loving our time together and what we were sharing that I didn't even want to entertain that thought. It was still hard because obviously I knew he was going home to his family every night. He had two kids; a thirteen-year-old daughter and a seventeen-year-old son who was about ready to go to college. So he put that out there, and *gradually* over the course of the next month or so, it really started to hit both of us – the reality of the situation, and what are we gonna do, and it's not something we can just turn off. That's when it started getting really hard. (*Crying.*)

We spent a lot of time holding each other and crying. I thought his hang-up was being married. When we talked about it, he said his hang-up wasn't so much that as the age difference. He felt that regardless of what people would say, and besides the fact that people would get hurt if he were to break up his family, he felt I was so young. "What are you gonna do in ten or twenty years? Push me around in a wheel chair?" He knew I was young. He didn't actually say this part, but I think he was afraid; hey, I'm twenty-two. What happens in three or four years when "I don't feel this way anymore"? I don't know if he really thought that... It got very painful, to the point where I finally decided to leave Florida because I couldn't imagine living there anymore and not seeing him. I just couldn't do it. And I knew that we didn't have a future. If I had stayed we would have just kept going the way we were going, and I don't know how it would've finally ended. I don't think either of us was strong enough to pull away from it, with me staying in Florida.

I've kept a journal since I was about thirteen and within the last week I've re-read our whole story. I'm reading the things he would say to me, and what we would talk about, and how we felt about each other, and I believed it was real. And I *do* believe it was real, and magical. When he started to pull away it was soul-crushing. I've been crying all the time for the last week, reading all this stuff and thinking about it, and plus I just learned a couple weeks ago that he died. (*Crying.*) Three years ago.

When I'm reading the journal, it's like I'm talking to myself, even though I'm so much younger. Some of the things I wrote about it, as far as what would happen in my future, and why I needed to leave – that I was afraid I would never be able to stop loving him, (*crying*) or missing him, or believing that we had such a soulful connection. And I don't know if I believe that there's *one* soul mate with zillions of people on this earth, but he was definitely the closest thing I ever had to somebody who was part of who I am. He said, "As close as I've ever tried to be to anyone, I've never been able to be as close as I am to you." Oh my God. And I know it was coming from a very real place.

I'm a little bit sad reading it because I realize some of my fears have come true: I've never really been able to let go of Dave; I'm afraid I'm never going to have love or happiness like this again; I'm afraid I'm never going to be as close and connected to this degree and with this intensity. And that's real. And that makes me sad 'cause I've been married for eight years and it hasn't come close.

I met my husband while I was living in Florida. I was on vacation and came up to Vermont in July. For me, it was like, "Okay, I'm going away for a week to see my friends. Hopefully I'll meet someone else so I can get over Dave." That was my idea. I needed someone else, so I feel badly in retrospect; my husband was the *ultimate* rebound. And he was great. He was only a year older, super sweet and adorable, kind and really giving. He was great and I adored him. I was really excited and I thought, "Wow, we can have a future. Now I can leave Florida." Not that I was counting on this. I wasn't sure what would happen. I met him and spent a week with him on vacation with my friends.

I came back from vacation, and had pretty much told Dave I didn't want to continue our relationship because it was just too painful and I couldn't handle it anymore. Once I realized there was no future, it was absolutely unbearable; it just tormented me. And then I finally decided I was gonna leave.

My journal from January to June is me ranting about how much pain I was in, how sad I was, how much I yearned to live my life with this man. And how brokenhearted I was every time I would get cancelled on, or blown off because he had other obligations and priorities in his life. I felt even then: I don't deserve this; I deserve more than this. And if he can't be available to me I need to be with someone who is available to me. I just didn't know if I would ever be part of something with that level of passion and intense connection. I don't really know how to describe it. I'd been in relationships before, and been in love, but this was something different.

Even after I left, we stayed in touch for a little while, off and on, for a few years. I can't remember the last time we spoke on the phone, which kills me. I always knew, (*crying*) always knew we would talk again, be in touch again, maybe see each other again. I tried so hard, and for so long to... I didn't even want to reach out to this man. It wasn't like he was just an ex-boyfriend to me. I didn't want to disrespect my husband or threaten our relationship, and that was even before we were married. Not that he would've necessarily known, but I would've felt guilty and I didn't want to do that to him. If he had a clue that I've been crying incessantly about this for the last few weeks, he'd be heartbroken. And I love him and I care about him, but I'm just really sad that I don't *feel* what I believe I should feel for a husband.

It's thirteen years later, and I've been with my husband almost that long, since we met anyway. I know I'm *married*, I know I have two little kids. I know that a marriage and the love you share with someone is not always fireworks and magic. I get that it matures, develops and is tested. And I even hate to admit this, but when I married my husband I knew better. I was really afraid and I was *young*. But I didn't realize I was young. I was like, "Oh my God, I'm almost thirty; I'm never gonna meet someone; I want to have a family..." *That's* what I was thinking. I really wanted to make my happiness.

In my marriage there's just a lot of peace-keeping and managing. (*Pause.*) I remember Dave telling me how his thirteen-year-old daughter said to him, "Daddy, promise you'll never leave me," and how it just broke his heart. You know, I get it now. I've got two little kids and I couldn't imagine rocking their world, breaking up their family and being *alone*. I don't know.

I remember talking to my mom about this, too. You have a baby and that becomes your whole life. I didn't care about not having romantic love or that soulful connection because I had my babies. But now they're three and five, and for the first time I feel like, "I want something. I want something that fills me up besides my kids." And I love my kids, and would not trade them for the world. But I realize that life is short, and here's one of the big things I've gotten out of this: I always thought he would be there. Dave. I always thought I would be able to reach back out to him and talk to him again. And every time we would talk, months would go by, and he would say, "Miss Pretty…" He always called me "Miss Pretty," and I could tell we were still in the same place. As much as we tried, we could never stop feeling what we felt.

I had been searching for him on line for about four years. I found a number and it looked like they had moved. Every time I called I got voicemail and didn't leave a message. But it had been digging at me for a while, so I finally left a message and said that I was a former colleague trying to get in touch about using Dave as a professional reference. A day or two later I got a call back from his son. As soon as he said who he was, my heart sank. He said, "I'm really sorry to be the one to tell you this, but my dad died a few years ago." He told me Dave had had a blood clot of some sort, and died within three minutes. Oh God. It was just such a tremendous loss. (*Crying.*) I really did believe we would connect again in some way.

I don't know that I want to be in my marriage. I've felt that way for a long time. I feel really guilty and really bad because I don't think it's fair. It's not fair for me not to feel about him the way I believe he feels about me. I know he picks up on it, and I know he can tell. We've definitely had a lot of issues, especially since having the kids. In our best moments, we're only good. We've been married almost eight years and in the time we've been married, I feel like we've had a run of about six good months. I just don't feel that we are well connected. Now I am thinking I can't live wishing and hoping and wanting for something else. I've said a couple times to my mom and a couple of my closest friends, "I can sign on for this marriage, and just be in it and make the best of it." But now I just don't know. I just don't know if I can do it. I want to be more fulfilled, more soulfully and spiritually understood. And not understood because I've *explained* it, but understood because it's felt.

Exploration – Veronica

1. Because Veronica saw Dave as "charming and sexy and gorgeous," she didn't believe he would have any interest in her. How did your self-image impact your romantic choices? Did you feel worthy of someone with Dave's attributes?

2. Veronica felt an immediate attraction to Dave. After they began talking, she felt "a connection that was transcendent of space and time." Have you ever been swept into a romance so forcefully? Has the passing of time impacted your perception of what happened?

3. Remembering the beginning of the extra-marital affair, Veronica said, "…it just happened so quickly and was so out of our control." How do you feel hearing Veronica's rationale? Do you hold Veronica and Dave equally accountable?

4. Veronica recalled the times with Dave when she was "blown off because he had other obligations and priorities in his life." She felt she deserved more than that. Have you been in a relationship where you were not a priority? Did you come to feel that you deserved more than what you were getting?

5. As she thought back to when Dave pulled away from her, Veronica called it "soul-crushing." How would you describe your most difficult breakup? What helped you move forward?

6. Veronica felt sad that her marriage "hasn't come close" to what she had in her affair. What do you think of her comparison? What kinds of comparisons have you made among your romantic relationships?

7. When she went on vacation, Veronica thought, "Hopefully I'll meet someone so I can get over Dave." How do you feel about her strategy? Have you ever depended on someone to help you "get over" something?

8. After meeting her soon-to-be husband, Veronica was excited that she could "have a future," and remembered thinking, "Now I can leave Florida." Why do you think Veronica needed to be in a relationship before leaving the state? When you were in your twenties, what did a "future" mean to you?

9. Veronica admitted that as she was approaching thirty, she was "really afraid" she wouldn't meet someone with whom she could have a family. She married her husband and later said, "…I knew better." Has fear played a role in the bigger decisions of your life? Do you generally navigate life with courage or fear as your compass?

10. Having babies took the place of "romantic love or that soulful connection" for Veronica. But when her children turned three and five, she thought, "I want something that fills me up besides my kids." Do you empathize with Veronica's desire to seek fulfillment from others? What are some of the different ways you've tried to fill emotional voids? What has brought you the most happiness?

11. Rather than having to explain herself, Veronica wanted to be "more soulfully and spiritually understood" in her marriage. What does "soulfully and spiritually understood" mean to you? Is there a person in your life who knows you in this way? What forged that connection?

Beth, 48

I was a college freshman and lived in a dorm. I had been out with my friends roller-skating. I was waiting for a ride home, so I didn't get back to the dorm until pretty late. And the dorm was mostly empty because it was around some break and everyone had left to go home. But I was tired and didn't want to go out with people after skating. My boyfriend decided to go out, but he said he might come back to my room later. My roommates were gone, so I left the door unlocked. I listened to music for a little while, then went to sleep.

I was awakened, the dorm room was completely dark, I was groggy and thought it was my boyfriend. And then the person, the people... I'm having some trouble remembering this... At some point I realized they weren't talking, and then they were doing something somewhat violent. This stuff probably took seconds, but it was weird confusion for a little while, thinking it was my boyfriend and then realizing it wasn't. It was terror – it was fear. It was pretty much like an awful, scary dream. I couldn't talk; I didn't fight. They probably said, "Don't talk..." I do remember thinking if I yelled no one would hear because nobody was around. There actually was a girl a couple doors down who was handicapped, so I just felt there was no help.

It was two guys and I didn't have any idea what they looked like. It was only after the police asked me questions that I remembered glasses, and their hair. They held my throat, and later, they ripped my necklace. He didn't hit me; he just raped me, with his hand around my throat. Then there was transferring, and the other guy, I don't think he could get hard, and he mumbled some apology. I said something like, "Go away," and there was some kind of pushback meanness after that, so I just shut up.

While it was happening, I think I just kind of went to a different place. I just endured. I was shut down. It's not like I had a psychotic break or anything, but I just said to myself, "You can do it. It'll be over." I thought if I lived, I could get through it. In the beginning, it was established I was in danger, especially with two. I guess if I thought there was a chance of escape I would have done something. But I just couldn't.

Afterwards, this is kind of weird, but I think I waited; I waited 'til later, or waited 'til morning. My boyfriend was on the boys' side of the building and I went to him, hung out for a while, and told him I was attacked. I didn't say anything about being raped, just that I had been "attacked." Then I called the police. I must've told my boyfriend not to come with me. I was still concerned about people not knowing, including him. I was keeping it a secret.

The police came to my dorm. It was a policewoman who came and talked to me, and I had not cried or anything, until she came and maybe put her arms around me. But I just stopped it after two sobs. She asked me a lot of questions. She asked me how the guys smelled. I had a smell on me, like sweat. So I went to the hospital and did the rape kit thing. They cut your nails off and they kept my necklace for evidence. The hospital was fine, but it was weird because they cut my nails. I mean, there were no outward signs of what happened, but when I went home, I could look at my clipped-off nails and know.

It doesn't make any sense, because I didn't do anything wrong except unlock my door, but I must have felt ashamed because I obviously didn't want anybody to know.

I kept up the charade with my boyfriend for I don't know how long. I think I was protecting myself from his reaction, that he might be repulsed. That was my first boyfriend, and we hadn't been together that long. I wasn't a virgin, but still. I remember thinking I was glad that what happened to me wasn't the first sexual experience I had – that what happened was mechanical and I just kind of separated it from the real stuff I did. I remember, that boyfriend, wasn't big in stature. Since that time, I was never attracted to someone who had an intimidating manner. I was always drawn to gentle men – no one who could ever overpower me.

I didn't tell anybody. I think maybe I told one girl in the dorm because they put up flyers after. I told her. Then I finally shared it with my boyfriend. He was important because I immediately had comfort, and a friend, and knew he still wanted me. I didn't feel damaged.

Sometime this year, I told my seventeen-year-old daughter about it. I think it had to do with how you present yourself in public, and being safe. She listened. I told her I was raped in my dorm room; that I had let my guard down. I'm more protective than my mom was. The world's a different place. I tried, until recently, to know where my daughters are every second. I still know who they're with. I really do.

I never have told my mom. I remember part of my thinking on that was, "I don't want to hear what she has to say." (*Laughing.*) I didn't want to hear her worry and anxiety. I anticipated that's what I would hear; who knows what she would've said because I didn't give her a chance. She might've been better than I thought. I just didn't want to deal with any of her emotions. I also didn't want to be perceived as a person who needed to be taken care of. I had just gotten out of town; I was on my own and moving toward independence.

I pretty much went on with my life, and kind of squashed it down, but it came up once in a while in weird ways. I used to imagine I could rip off their faces – that they would suffer as much as I had. Once, my sister came to visit, wherever I was living. She was getting ready to walk home by herself and I just freaked out on her. I remember another time, I was with a guy and I guess he wanted to do something sexually I wasn't ready to do, and I got upset about that. Nobody would've thought he was being aggressive, but I just felt I wasn't being listened to. And sometimes it would show up in dreams; even now, when I have bad dreams, I can't talk – I have no voice.

Exploration – Beth

1. Beth "went to a different place" while being raped. Have you ever had to mentally leave a situation in order to endure it?

2. Her clipped fingernails were a reminder of Beth's recent trauma, which she was still keeping secret. Have you experienced pain invisible to others? What private reminders were associated with that?

3. Beth felt a sense of shame in being raped, even though the only thing she thought she did "wrong" was not lock her door. Why do you think she felt ashamed? How would you help her come to terms with that feeling?

4. When Beth finally shared the ordeal with her boyfriend, he responded with love and acceptance. She said, "I didn't feel damaged." How important do you think his response was to her recovery? Has there been a time in your life when someone helped you from feeling "damaged"?

5. Why do you think Beth has never shared the story of her rape with her mom? Have you ever withheld a traumatic or important personal event from your parents? Why did you make that choice?

6. Beth told her seventeen-year-old daughter about being raped in hopes of protecting her. If this had been your ordeal, what would you tell your daughter?

7. Do you agree with Beth that "the world is a more dangerous place" than when we were young?

8.   Beth was sexually assaulted while the rapist squeezed her throat. In her worst dreams, she has no voice. Does Beth's dream hold metaphoric meaning for you as a woman?

9.   For many, being a victim of rape becomes a defining event – that can sometimes incapacitate. Beth was able to go forward in her life. She said, "I was just moving toward independence." Why do you think she was able to prevent this trauma from paralyzing her?

Donna, 53

I have three daughters. My middle child, Megan, has always been different. We just haven't able to communicate as well. She's three years younger than my oldest, and was competitive, really saw things differently, had a great mind, was very interesting and delightful, but just hard. She didn't want to play the game about grades; really, really bright but was more interested in learning about the things that interested her rather than grades. That was really hard for me when high school came and the grades counted. We just had a history of not communicating well, as much as I think both of us tried.

When Megan graduated from college, we made a big deal about it. First we had a big family dinner with lots of people, and then went to the graduation weekend. Oh my gosh – it was an incredibly emotional weekend. I was so proud and happy. But my husband Ronald picked up on something that completely escaped me – he noticed some glances between Megan and her friend Kelly, and said he definitely felt a tension.

Megan came home afterwards before going out to Portland for an internship. She sat down to talk to me before she left. Megan told me she was having a relationship with a woman. She didn't say she was gay, just that she was in relationship with a woman. I remember we were at the kitchen counter, just the two of us, and I think if you were there you could have pushed me over and I would've collapsed. Out of left field, just completely. Totally out of left field. We talked about the girl,

Kelly, and we talked about the situation. She said, "Obviously you're a little surprised." I said, "I couldn't be more surprised." And she said, "Well, how do you feel?" And I said, "I don't even know." I really, really didn't know.

A couple of hours later she came up and talked to Ronald and me in our room. And he said all the right things. All the wonderful things: "How supportive we'll be of you, how wonderful you are..." I swear, I couldn't talk. Ronald was relieved because he knew during graduation weekend something was going on. He knew from looks and stuff that something was up, and he felt betrayed that she was keeping something from him. He wasn't all that surprised. What Megan said to me was, "I wanted to tell you last weekend at graduation." All I could think was, "Thank God you didn't." To this day, I can't put into words how I felt.

We really had a good week together; it was really okay. She did a nice job when we talked because she said, "Your generation just looks at things differently than mine." I think it's just a lot more common than people know. And not that it needs to be known, and not that it needs to be judged. What really made me anxious was that she couldn't say she was gay. I wanted her to say, "I'm gay." Because I'm sitting here on the fence. Ronald and I went out and bought all the books. How do you support your gay child? What do you do? I said to him, "Hey, look at it this way: we'll have the perfect American family now. One of this, one of that..." (*Laughing.*) I think humor did help a lot. And knowing that Megan had someone special in her life was really, really nice.

My older daughter Amy said to me at one point, "Mom, are you doin' okay?" And I said, "No, I'm really not. But I don't know how I'm doing." Amy is three years older and I said, "Why can't *you* find a fella?" She had dated a couple people, but no one really seriously. So I'm going, "What's the matter with *my* kids? Everybody else can do this. What's the matter with my kids?" Amy is twenty-eight now, and she's finally found one, although her career may get in the way. The girls were too strong, too independent and too intelligent. But is that a bad thing? No, I knew it wasn't a bad thing. There were always guys who were in love with them. With Megan, as recently as four months ago, there was a boy I really had my hopes out for.

After Megan told us about her relationship with this woman, I said to Amy, "I just want her to tell me, 'I'm gay,' and she couldn't do that." That was my ambivalence. I don't think she is. But she had this relationship with this woman for almost a year and a half. It was all very odd, to tell you the truth. Megan was the strong one. Kelly played on the softball team and was a tiny little girl who was very needy. Although she appeared strong sometimes, she just got too overwhelming for Megan.

So Megan moves to Portland. And Kelly doesn't have a job so she goes home to Arizona and all of a sudden I hear she's in Portland to stay. And then Megan calls to tell me she's moving into a house, and she and Kelly are going to be living there together with a couple other people. I can't tell you how bad the timing was. Our call was interrupted by another, and I learned that a dear friend of ours – their twenty-four-year-old son had just been killed. Yeah, so I am like, "What's going on today?" In some ways maybe that helped me, because I was able to say, "Megan, we'll get through this. It's all okay; it's not *bad*."

This is what bothered me the most: Here's this girl who's following Megan around the country. I didn't like that. I didn't like that *at all*. Megan is just leaving college, going out on her own, forging a brand new life full of excitement, and this girl who has no job, no anything, is tagging along. Give Megan an opportunity to make a life for herself first, and if after a year it comes back, that's okay. But give her time. I could see this girl's dependence on Megan and that made me uncomfortable. But complicated with all the other issues, I do think if Megan had been able to say, "I'm gay," I could've dealt with it better. I could've embraced it. She was totally ambivalent and it was *very* confusing for me. As I think it was confusing for her.

It was strange, because I was the only one who thought it was a little odd. I'm wondering if she can't be honest with herself. But I embraced Kelly. I embraced Megan. At one point, we talked about how to tell my youngest daughter, who was an eighth-grader at the time. We were a little uncomfortable with that. I mean, you don't say you're gay, but you have this relationship. And the relationship was significant. I thought it was important that Megan talk to her little sister about it. To me, that was a huge milestone. My youngest was just great. It all was really quite lovely.

Megan and Kelly go on a trip to South America for six months and then they both make these big, separate plans for graduate school. And once again, I'm just so confused. Megan did tell me on several occasions that she needed some distance. She was the one who set everything; she took the GREs and made plans to move away. Megan was leading the charge, and Kelly was following it about three months behind.

They went down to Kelly's house for her mother's sixtieth birthday, and I don't know what happened there, but I think by then everything was completely over for Megan. It had been about a year. Kelly's mom was so worried about Kelly that she asked Megan to go to therapy, so the three of them went to therapy together. It's the oddest thing. So I would chat with her before, and sometimes after; we'd talk about it. I said, "It doesn't have to be a relationship therapy session. It *can* be, but you just get whatever you can out of it." So I think we had a really great communication.

And then Megan moved to New York City and started graduate school. One day, just real lightly, she told me she'd dated a couple people. At first she wasn't clear about their gender. The one name was kind of ambiguous, like Randy or Casey, but then she clarified that she had a couple dates with men. I said, "I'm really confused." And she said, "Oh Mom, I'm not gay." And I'm like, "Okay." (*Laughing.*) Even she doesn't think she is.

She lived in Manhattan for a year with two gay guys. She told me she should be in a sitcom or reality TV show. One was black, one was white, but they weren't a couple. I wondered if she would start seeing women, surrounded by that culture. But she had a couple dates last year, and she told me the dating situation in New York is really bad. She said she's seen so many unhealthy relationships in New York that she's not going to bother. I think it's smart. I think it's emotionally healthy.

Now Megan lives in Brooklyn with three heterosexual people, a man and two women. Their schedules are all so diverse they don't really see each other. It's really good for her. She's in a community and it's wonderful. I think she's made some healthy, emotional decisions.

She does have some masculine traits. She's five foot eight with kind of broad shoulders. She's a tough soccer player, a tough athlete and competitor. She never babysat; not much girly stuff there. Now that she's twenty-five, for extra money she's babysitting a fifteen-month old. Which I find hysterical. (*Laughing.*) It just cracks me up. Megan told me she said to her friend the other day, "I'm going to have to have children sometime because I have such good genes and I need to pass them on." I think it's a marvelous compliment.

My wish for her would be to find a partner. In this group of people from her college crowd, this one young man fell head over heels for her. He's charming and wonderful, and loves her for who she is. And she said, "He's my best friend, but that's all there is." I don't think she's put a label on herself at all. I don't even think anyone in her generation would put a label on her. I think there's something about my girls; they're so independent that they scare men. They could have had their choice of so many. And they have a great relationship with their dad, which seems like it would make it easier, not harder.

My immediate family knows, and my brother found out, but we haven't talked about it. I would never tell my sister because her husband is so judgmental; I don't want him to know. I haven't shared it with my other sister because it's not the kind of thing you can tell in bites. You have to sit down.

I think going through this has softened me. Sometimes in the back of mind I go, (*laughing*) "What did I do to raise these young women who are so strong, independent and intellectual?" They have high standards for the men in their lives, and I don't want them to compromise that, but at the same time, I desperately want each of them to find *someone*.

I'd like to think that this has opened my eyes. I also think it's helped our relationship with Megan. I think it stretched all of us, but it probably stretched me the most. I feel like I'm more in tune with what I need and what my family needs. And that's another reason why I don't feel compelled to share this with people. I made a comment to two of my friends about the guy Megan was dating in New York, and I could tell by the look they exchanged they were thinking, "Doesn't she know?" If they wanted to talk to me about it, I would be open, but they don't understand it's not as black and white as they think it is. I guess because they're making these assumptions, I'm just not interested in volunteering much. I'm *so* proud of all my daughters, and that's about as much as other people need to know.

Exploration – Donna

1. After hearing that Megan was in relationship with a woman, Donna said, "…I think if you were there you could have pushed me over and I would've collapsed." Have you been stunned by someone's disclosure?

2. Some experiences are so complex that we struggle for a long time to process them. Donna remarked, "To this day I can't put into words how I felt." Are there events in your life that still leave you confused? What are the persistent questions?

3. When eldest daughter Amy asked Donna how she's doing, Donna responded, "Why can't *you* find a fella?" Have you ever taken the heat for a sibling's actions? If you were Amy, what would your response have been?

4. A number of times in her story, Donna expressed how hard it was for her to not know if Megan was gay. Donna said, "She was totally ambivalent and it was *very* confusing for me. As I think it was confusing for her." Why do you think it was important for Donna to have Megan label herself? If this was your child, could you find peace in the ambivalence?

5. When Megan was living in New York City, she said she had seen so many unhealthy relationships, she wasn't going to bother dating. Donna felt that was smart and emotionally healthy. Do you agree? Why do you think Donna felt that way?

6. Donna didn't want her daughters to compromise their personal attributes, but said, "...at the same time, I desperately want them to find *someone*." Is it important to you that your children are in long-term relationships? Did your mother hold similar expectations for you as a young adult?

7. The experience "stretched" Donna, helping her feel more "in tune" with her own needs, as well as those of her family. Have you had a family experience that has "stretched" you? What did you gain from it?

8. People outside the immediate family didn't know much about Donna's personal life, and she felt friends were making assumptions about her daughter's sexuality. Can you empathize with Donna's strong desire for privacy? Do you think she could benefit by opening up to friends or extended family?

Phyllis, 81

My husband died in November. We were married for nearly fifty-nine years. He died just before our fifty-ninth anniversary. The place in life I'm in now is very, very unique. It's unique to me; it's not unique to the millions of widows in this world. I'm at a place I have never been before.

My husband was a very strong person, emotionally, physically. Ed took care of everything; he did everything. I was the proverbial princess. He did it all for me. I did the things I had to do; he took care of our lives in general. He did the finances, he did anything that had to be done around the house. He was the rock for me and the children. I have two children.

Ed was always physically well. He really was a person who never got sick. Five years ago, he became ill and developed congestive heart failure, which wasn't a major problem. He was treated and on medication. At first I was very upset, but in finding out more about it and knowing it was being taken care of, I was okay. However, he started developing other illnesses from that. And each illness led to a period of hospitalization, which was completely new to me. And all of a sudden, I was the one in charge. First, it was very confusing. Then it was very scary. I didn't know if I was capable of doing this.

Ultimately, he developed something called osteomyelitis. And that's an important part of the story. It's a staph infection in the spine, which is very difficult to treat, and he was in terrible pain. It can be a fatal disease. He was in and out of hospitals and rehab; this went on and on. I kept telling myself he's going to get better. I was in denial, a total state of denial. Our quality of life had completely changed; there was no quality of life anymore. It was rehab, hospital, doctors appointments, and it was all me.

You had to know the type of person my husband was. He was stoic. He never complained. He could sense my moods and would always tell me, "It's going to get better." (*Crying.*) He was the rock. And he was making it easier for me. I went along with this; I wanted to believe it was going to get better and would say, "We will continue to do things; next year we'll go here on vacation." One of the things we enjoyed doing so much was to just get in the car and go off for the day. Now all that changed. I was in denial for many months.

I did everything I had to do. I got tremendous support from my children. They're not right here, but they can get in the car and come. If we had a doctor's appointment and it was going to be a tough one, and I might not understand what they were saying, I would call one of them: "Can you come with me?" They were there for me every step of the way. Dealing with the household finances was a whole different challenge. I didn't even know where the money came from. (*Laughing.*) But nevertheless, it had to be done. Ed was able to tell me what to do, but I didn't know where anything was. It was a new planet I had landed on, completely new territory.

I *never* had to deal with these things. Not only did I have to deal with the finances and the running of the house, I had to deal with his medical condition. I had to make all the doctors appointments; I had to follow up. And as his illness progressed I had to take care of all the medication. I would explode every now and then. I would start screaming.

We used to do a lot of things together. He would come to the supermarket with me and help with all the bundles. Now,

I would come home from the supermarket and he would be sitting in the recliner. I would be exhausted and I would just get so angry at him. And it was not right, and I felt guilty doing it, but I would think, "I mean, you're sitting there doing *nothing*, and I'm doing all this carrying, and dragging, and running and going." There was a lot of anger there.

I was one of these people who was always taken care of. Whenever I had doubts about anything, Ed would always say to me, "You can do it. You can do whatever you set your mind to – you're strong." He *always* instilled confidence in me, whenever I was hesitant about anything. I think that's what I grew on, because I found I was able to do the things I had to do.

But one day I was on the phone with my daughter and I had reached the breaking point. And she said something about "Daddy not getting better." That just was the final straw. I was hysterical and screaming at her on the phone: "He *will* get better, he will get better! We'll pick up our lives." (*Pause.*) I had to believe that. I truly think I had to believe because he was sick for five years. I couldn't go forward thinking each episode is going to be the end. I had to feel our life would get better, and he gave me the encouragement to feel that things would improve… Until I realized they wouldn't.

After that conversation with my daughter I hung up and two minutes later the phone rang again. It was my son. She had called him and said, "Mommy's having a nervous breakdown." (*Laughing.*) He said to me, "Well, you have to see somebody; you have to take something." I said, "With all the doctors we're involved with, I cannot look for anybody for myself." It was an emotional outburst I got through, and I just went on to the next step. I did everything I had to do. The children kept saying to me, "You're stronger than you think. You're doing a wonderful job." That's what kept me going, I think. They were giving me the confidence that I didn't have myself. And if I looked at it dispassionately, I could tell myself, "I'm doing very well. I'm doing very well for Ed."

And then it reached the point where he had to stop driving. When that happened, well, I knew. Things went on, and he was back and forth, in and out of the hospital. And it was exhausting for me. I was going to see him every day, wherever he was. And if he was home, every now and then we'd have to call the first aid squad (*crying*) to take him back in. It was very, very emotional. Very trying. But I *did* it all. I did it.

I complained to my children but I *never* complained to my friends. I never let anybody know. I have one very good friend; we go back to fifth grade. She's like family. She and I went through this together; her husband was also ill. So I would complain to her and my children, but to the world, I was in charge; I'm fine. I didn't want anybody to feel sorry for me. I didn't want them to think that this defined me or in any way diminished me. Right or wrong? I don't know. I wanted the world to know that I'm capable and I can take care of this. And I didn't want to diminish my husband in any way. He was ill, but he was still an important person. I didn't want the world to think he was dragging me down.

It was almost two separate lives I led. My outside life where I was in control: "I'm *fine*. I don't need help." But in the house it was different. I would go into the shower and cry. You have to fall apart. (*Stifled crying.*) You have to fall apart now and then; it just takes you over.

Things went from bad to worse, and ultimately Ed did go back into the hospital. He was there about a week and they asked, "Can we put him on a respirator? Can we put him on a feeding tube?" And I said to the doctors, "If you put him on a respirator and you put him on a feeding tube does that mean he's going to jump out of bed and be fine?" (*Pause.*) Ed had a living will and didn't want any artificial intervention.

So they finally said he was ready for hospice. That... That destroyed me. The thing that had kept me going was done. I was done. I knew that we had come to the end of the line. I said to the kids, "Daddy has to know. But I can't tell him." Ed was still alert and aware. I *could* not tell him. So my daughter told him. And hearing him say, "Well, I guess this is it." (*Crying.*) He knew; he was well aware at that point. He was a very smart man and knew everything that was going on. And I agreed; they had my approval and I signed all the papers. But that to me was just the culmination, knowing he was going into hospice. He went in on a Monday afternoon; my daughter was with me then. On Tuesday, my son and I were sitting in Ed's room quietly chatting, and I looked over at my husband and said to my son, "Daddy's not breathing." We called the nurse, (*crying, whispering*) and that was it.

We went through all the whatever that came afterward, but then the realization set in: I don't have a husband anymore. I am now in a new category. I am now a widow. This is my category, and I'm with all those other women. And then you go through all these mind changes: Well how do you approach life now? What do you do? And you know the stories that other people have told you: "Well, your married friends don't want you anymore. Your persona non-grata; you almost have a contagious disease. The married people don't want to be associated with widows." And I didn't understand *why*, if I'm friendly with somebody before, I would not be friendly with them after. With the friends that I have, I have not found those stories to be true; they've included me in everything.

The major thing was you were moving in a *whole* different reality. It's totally a different world that you've gone into. You just don't have anyone to lean on. You *have* to do everything yourself, and it becomes overwhelming. Every single detail of life that has to be taken care of, you have to do. In addition to which, there was all the clerical work as far as the estate and finances that had to be done, which was *totally* overwhelming. So many details. But once I got through the maze of all that, then I had my own life to consider; what will my life be like now?

Grieving is sort of a constant. I was given all sorts of material on support groups and grieving groups, and I truly didn't feel I needed any of that. I felt I was in control and could deal with it. I didn't want go anyplace to hear someone else complain. I didn't want to hear about their problems; I had my own life to deal with. I shared a little with a few friends, but didn't want them to think I'm going to be one of these professional widows. Those are the people who all they do is play the part of the widow; they can't get back into life. They're constantly dwelling on the fact that they're grieving widows. I didn't want to fall into that. So again, the face I kept to the world was the same: I'm *fine*. And I was fine. But every now and then you have a meltdown. It would be the tiniest little thing that would come out of nowhere.

I have a friend whose husband died. They were our very best friends. I was talking to her one day, and she said what she did was, she took her husband's picture when he was at his peak, and she put it in the kitchen, and whenever she wants to talk to him, he's right there for her. I said, "Oh, what a good idea. I'm going to do the same thing." So I found a picture of the two of us. It was a wonderful picture; I think we were vacationing in San Francisco. I put it on the refrigerator, and whenever I went to the refrigerator I'd start crying. (*Laughing hard.*) I told my friend what was happening and she said, "You're not ready yet. It takes time." The tears can come on so fast. It can take nothing; the simplest glance at a picture, thinking of something, watching something. I try not to dwell. And my children have been incredible.

I keep busy, I'm involved, I do things, I have my friends. The bottom line, the major thing that I have to deal with: When I walk into that house at night and close that door, I'm alone. And that awareness of the sense of being alone doesn't leave you. This is the way it's going to be; you will always be alone – forever. It doesn't matter what you do during the day. It doesn't matter how close you are to everyone. You're *alone* in the house. There's no one to turn to if you need something.

This past Saturday, my daughter had a big holiday dinner and invited the whole family and some friends. Ed's greatest joy was his family and the grandchildren. We have wonderful grandchildren. It was a lovely time, but it wasn't a particularly happy time for me. I was sad. Grieving is not a constant; I don't get up in the morning and go through the whole day saying, "Woe is me." I don't do that. That's the professional widow. I'm involved and do everything I can do. But I do have times where my grief overwhelms me. Sitting at that party I thought, "Daddy would've loved this."

But yet, with all that, I still have a certain sense of logic, and I know this could not have ended any other way. It had to end. In fact, we waited for it to end; we wanted it to end already. It was too painful for everyone. And it wasn't going to change. That's the whole point; nothing was going to change. It wasn't going to get better. So realistically, I know this is how it had to be. However, it's still a broken life. I still had a marriage,

I had a husband, we had a quality of life. Well, that's all done. That's all gone. (*Pause.*) I'm doing well. I'm doing well.

Thinking about my own mortality… It's scary. You try not to think of that, however, it's there. It goes back to this feeling of being alone. When you go through the emotions of being alone, from there, I'll also start thinking, "Well, how is this going to play out down the line? What am I going to do?" I try not to think about it; I truly do. It scares me. Being dependent on someone; my children will have the ultimate burden. And then thinking if I'll be able to keep living in my home. I don't want to think about it. I'm in denial. I don't want to plan ahead. Maybe I should be. It's all part of this new life I'm in. Well, Ed was always here to take care of everything.

One of the things that bothers me, and I haven't come to terms with this, and I don't know how you do: Ed was sick for five years. My memories of him are as an invalid, of him being sick. And I'm angry about that. Because up until the time he got sick, he was a wonderful, whole, strong, productive person. This is the person I want to remember, but I don't. I remember someone who was in pain, could not walk, and was stuck in the rehab. It was very traumatic. I have to *dig* into my head to bring those healthy pictures up, and that gets me angry. Because the pictures I have in my mind: Helping Ed go to the doctor, Ed walking with the walker, Ed in the recliner… He needed a lot of help. It wasn't who he was for most of our life together. I haven't been able to get over that hump yet, and I don't know if that comes.

I have like fifty-five albums of photographs, but I look at the pictures and start crying. It's almost a feeling of, "Why didn't I treasure this time more? Why didn't I realize how wonderful it was?" (*Crying.*) But you don't, because you're living it. It was just the days we went through. But in looking back, compared to what the past few years were, well, it was wonderful. Not only that, I'll look at the pictures and see that we were young, we were strong, we were good-looking, and everything was great. But you don't realize that it's great at the time.

Now, you have to deal with this death, but then there's this new problem of making a life for yourself. You're recreating your life, molding it from nothing, starting with nothing. The weekdays are okay; the hardest part is the weekends. The weekends are when you truly feel alone. If you don't have things planned. That's when you to try to tie up with these other single women. My friendships have deepened because of that. The handful of close friends I have, have handled this whole situation perfectly. They're just there. They're not going to be fawning over me, but I know they care.

This is the hardest thing I have ever done in my entire life. This period of time, from the time he died into this new stage I'm entering. The transition into widowhood, trying to figure out what widowhood means, for me. You don't like to be labeled, but you have to adjust to the fact that you *are* a widow. You're regarded differently. It's almost a stigma, but it's what it is. The five years of Ed's sickness kept me busy. I mean, that was my *life*. My life was taking care of Ed. But this is something else. I had children, they left for school, got married, had children; we bought houses, sold houses... None of that compares to widowhood. I don't know if other women would say the same thing, but it's the hardest thing I've ever been through.

Here's what I've learned: I am great. I am a great person. I'm smart, I'm capable, I can do things, I follow through. I can take care of myself. That doesn't mean I don't have my meltdowns. I *do* have my meltdowns, and I do need someone to say to me, "It's going to be all right." I have people I can

336

turn to for that. But I don't want the world to feel sorry for me. It's a new perception I have of myself. I was *always* very dependent. My husband was very strong; he was a takeover person. So he probably subjugated me in many ways, and I didn't have to assert myself. But now, I do. Now it's all me. It's all up to me. If I want anything done, I have to get it done. And I'm able to do it.

I think I can reach down and find the strength to go on, but that doesn't mean I will feel that way all the time. That doesn't mean I'm not going to have setbacks; it doesn't mean I'm not going to feel sorry for myself. It doesn't mean I won't feel lonely. And it doesn't mean I won't get angry. I get very angry at times: "How *dare* he have died?" But then I rationalize and I know; there was no other solution to this. This is the way it had to be.

Exploration – Phyllis

1. After Ed became ill, Phyllis found herself "in charge" for the first time in their lives together. She remembered, "First it was confusing. Then it was very scary. I didn't know if I was capable..." Have you ever found yourself suddenly thrust into a new level of responsibility? What was your reaction?

2. Ed developed osteomyelitis and Phyllis went into a "total state of denial." She continued to believe her husband when he said things would get better. Have you gone through a serious illness with a loved one? What helped you cope when things became really difficult?

3. The stress and workload sometimes made Phyllis very angry with Ed for being sick. Can you empathize with her emotional reaction? Have you ever been angry with someone for something over which they had no control?

4. Her children's encouragement and support kept Phyllis going, instilling confidence that she could care for her husband and manage her life. In times of self-doubt, who or what inspired you to believe you were capable?

5. Phyllis shared her true feelings with just one friend and her children because she didn't want anyone to think that her challenges "defined" or "diminished" her. She was also concerned that speaking honestly might also diminish her husband. If someone you loved became seriously ill, whom would you let into your emotional world?

6. Widowhood was "a *whole* different reality" for Phyllis. Although her married friends continued to be welcoming, she faced the question: "What will my life be like now?" What phase of life have you found most challenging? How were you able to navigate it?

7. Phyllis's major challenge had to do with the notion of "being alone." She remembered, "...that awareness of the sense of being alone doesn't leave you. This is the way it's going to be; you will always be alone – forever." In your experience, is there a difference between "alone" and "lonely"? Are you comfortable spending time alone?

8. In thinking about her current situation, Phyllis said, "...it's still a broken life. I still had a marriage, I had a husband, we had a quality of life. Well, that's all done." Do you think it's possible that Phyllis might one day see her life as something of quality that is not broken? What would have to happen for that change to take place?

9. Phyllis would rather not think about her own death and has chosen not to plan ahead. Are you comfortable thinking about your mortality? How does your family culture address issues of aging and dying?

10. While looking back at the family photographs, Phyllis asked, "Why didn't I treasure this time more? Why didn't I realize how wonderful it was?" Have you had an experience that made you aware of life's fragile beauty and the fleeting nature of time? In what ways did that awareness impact you?

11. In the process of becoming a widow, Phyllis forged a new perception of herself as a "great...smart...capable" woman. Have you gone through an ordeal that completely transformed the way you saw yourself? What aspects of who you became most surprise you?

Epilogue

Whether counseling a client or collecting a story, it is a sincere privilege to be allowed into another person's inner world. I care deeply about emotional health, and have seen the healing that can occur when people speak from the heart and share their most personal experiences. My hope is that after reading this book, you feel less alone in your struggles and understand it is possible to navigate and find meaning in life's biggest challenges.

Resource Guide

Mental and Emotional Health: helpguide.org

National Alliance on Mental Illness: nami.org

Reproductive Health/Unplanned pregnancy:
plannedparenthood.org

Kids and Teen Health: kidshealth.org

National Family Caregivers Association:
thefamilycaregiver.org

Hospice Foundation of America: hospicefoundation.org

The National Center for Grieving Children & Families:
dougy.org

Grief support after the death of a child:
compassionatefriends.org

National Suicide Prevention Lifeline: 1-800-273-8255,
suicidepreventionlifeline.org

For survivors of suicide: American Association of
Suicidology: suicidology.org

Gay, Lesbian, Bisexual, Transgender support: lambda.org

Crisis Intervention and Suicide Prevention for LGBTQ
Youth: 1-866-488-7386, thetrevorproject.org

Parents, Families and Friends of Lesbians and Gays:
pflag.org

National Domestic Violence Hotline: 1-800-799-7233,
thehotline.org

Rape, Abuse and Incest National Network Hotline: 1-800-656-4673, rainn.org

For Friends and Families of Problem Drinkers:
al-anon.alateen.org

National Eating Disorders Association Helpline:
1-800-931-2237, nationaleatingdisorders.org

National Child Abuse Prevention Hotline: 1-800-422-4453,
preventchildabuse.org

J ill Biros, M.A. Clinical-Counseling Psychology, has a private
counseling practice in Lower Makefield, Pennsylvania. She
believes vitality and purpose are fueled by emotional, physical
and spiritual well-being. Jill and her husband Greg have two
grown sons, two old cats and one indulged dog.

CPSIA information can be obtained at www.ICGtesting.com
Printed in the USA
BVOW011640010212

281891BV00002B/1/P